# The Palgrave Lacan Series

**Series Editors**
Calum Neill
School of Psychology and Sociology
Edinburgh Napier University
Edinburgh, UK

Derek Hook
Duquesne University
Pittsburgh, USA

Jacques Lacan is one of the most important and influential thinkers of the 20th century. The reach of this influence continues to grow as we settle into the 21st century, the resonance of Lacan's thought arguably only beginning now to be properly felt, both in terms of its application to clinical matters and in its application to a range of human activities and interests. The Palgrave Lacan Series is a book series for the best new writing in the Lacanian field, giving voice to the leading writers of a new generation of Lacanian thought. The series will comprise original monographs and thematic, multi-authored collections. The books in the series will explore aspects of Lacan's theory from new perspectives and with original insights. There will be books focused on particular areas of or issues in clinical work. There will be books focused on applying Lacanian theory to areas and issues beyond the clinic, to matters of society, politics, the arts and culture. Each book, whatever its particular concern, will work to expand our understanding of Lacan's theory and its value in the 21st century.

More information about this series at
http://www.palgrave.com/gp/series/15116

Christos Tombras

# Discourse Ontology

Body and the Construction
of a World, from Heidegger
through Lacan

Christos Tombras
London, UK

The Palgrave Lacan Series
ISBN 978-3-030-13661-1          ISBN 978-3-030-13662-8    (eBook)
https://doi.org/10.1007/978-3-030-13662-8

Library of Congress Control Number: 2019932950

Cover illustration: Christos Tombras

This Palgrave Macmillan imprint is published by the registered company Springer Nature
Switzerland AG
The registered company address is: Gewerbestrasse 11, 6330 Cham, Switzerland

# Contents

# List of Figures

# 1

# Introduction

This is a book discussing the philosophical foundations of psychoanalysis, in an attempt to bring together and reconcile, if possible,
Heidegger's criticisms with Lacan's post-Freudian metapsychology. This
is a task that I assigned to myself, being a practising psychoanalyst who
cannot afford to ignore Heidegger's questioning regarding the fundamentals of psychoanalytic theory.

Allow me to start, however, by bringing in a small personal memory. In my family home, we had a big radio, our main means of enter-
tainment in those pre-Internet days. Radio was like magic to me as a
small child. This was an old valve radio, and looking through the ven-
tilation grilles, I was especially fascinated by the gently illuminating
components inside. It looked like a strange stage. The valves, with their
filaments emanating warm yellow light and the cathodes, grids and
other wirings, looked like miniature music stands—each with its own
stool and small reading light, or so I thought. When music played, I
was convinced that if I observed carefully enough, I would be able to
discern the musicians in the half-light. I really believed that. Practical

© The Author(s) 2019
C. Tombras, *Discourse Ontology*, The Palgrave Lacan Series,
https://doi.org/10.1007/978-3-030-13662-8_1

questions—for example, how was it possible for the musicians to squeeze in there, how did they become so small, where would they go after the music was over and the like—were of no concern to me. They were not relevant to the issue. The issue was that musicians were there, and my challenge was to squint hard enough to see them.

Later I found out that my disregard of these practical aspects of the phenomenon, perhaps naïve to my adult eyes, was not too dissimilar to the reasoning of medieval philosophers when they discussed questions pertaining to the nature of angels. They wondered, for example: Is it possible for several angels to be in the same place? How many angels can coexist at any given point in space—say the head of a pin? What is the nature of an angel's bodily existence? The philosophers' answers were not at all self-evident, and today appear a bit absurd. You read Thomas Aquinas, for example, who discussed this and other issues in his *Summa Theologica*. In principle, he said, it *is* permissible to have more than one angel in the same place, since they don't have a material body and restrictions of impenetrability do not apply.

Surprisingly by today's standards, Aquinas approached the problem in terms of causality. His understanding of the world was Aristotelian. He took causality to be fundamentally dependent on locality. For Aquinas, as for Aristotle, space cannot be empty, and action from a distance is not permissible (nor conceivable). This simply means that action at any given point in space can be a cause of a change at an adjacent—i.e. not distant—point. Granted, angels are immaterial, and this means that more than one *can* in principle be in the same place; but they also are *causes* of something. As such, Aquinas reasoned, they cannot be in the same place, because if they could, this would mean that you can have two or more causes for one effect—something which is conceptually impermissible. His conclusion: no more than one angel can be in the exact same place at a given time.

Aquinas' reasoning does not make much sense today because we have different conceptual starting points. Our understanding of space is different, and our thinking of causality, even though still dependent on locality, is more abstract—and, admittedly, more flexible than Aristotle's.

# Changing Causes

Interestingly, Aristotle's theory of causality was at the heart of other questions that have puzzled ancient thinkers for centuries. The study of movement, for example, seemed to present equally perplexing problems. For Aristotle, movement is a change, and change occurs only where there is something causing it. A stone rolls because it is kicked. Water flows downwards, under the incessant influence of gravity, striving to reach its natural place. An apple falls for similar reasons. A person moves because they want to reach a destination. There is *always* a cause.

All is nice and clear until the moment one considers the trajectory of a projectile, say an arrow. Why (or, rather, how) does the arrow move? Its movement begins when it is pushed forward by the bowstring; the bowstring itself has been pulled by the archer. So, the initial cause of the arrow's motion is the archer. But what happens then? How does the arrow's motion continue? As soon as it leaves the bowstring, it seems to be moving on its own. How is it possible? What is the cause of this motion?

It was evident to all ancient thinkers that Aristotle's theory could not fully explain the phenomenon of projectile motion. The question remained open until some centuries after Aristotle, when in the sixth century AD John Philoponus introduced new explanatory concepts. According to Philoponus, as soon as the bowstring pushes the arrow forward, the arrow internalises the string's action in the form of what he called *impetus*. The cause of the continuing motion of the arrow is this internalised action; its flight would continue on a straight line until such moment when the impetus is exhausted. Then, and only then, the arrow will fall on the ground.

The whole question sounds unnecessary today and the answers given then appear now a bit naïve. For example, everybody knows today that the actual question is not regarding the continuation of the arrow's flight, but rather its fall. After Galileo, we know that a motion can, and will, continue forever, as long as it is not disturbed. The trajectory of the arrow will indeed be a straight line to infinity were it not for the force of gravity that pulls it downwards and the resistance of atmosphere that slowly decelerates the arrow's velocity.

Similarly, we are no longer bothered by the question of angels in space. Aquinas's question and attempt at an answer do not make much sense anymore, regardless of whether we believe in angels or not. What has really changed is our understanding of "space" and also our understanding of the world. After Descartes, we conceive of the material world as radically different from the spiritual world; even if we do accept the existence of angels, we think of them as inhabiting their own spiritual world. It follows readily that the question of whether one or more angels can be in the same place is nonsensical. "Place" as a concept is not applicable to spiritual entities.

But, more importantly, what has *really* changed is our understanding of causation. In ancient times, all change was understood as originating from a cause. This applied to all kinds of change, change in location, in form, in consistency, etc. Change is a response to imperfection, incompleteness; because of imperfection, it was needed as an attempt to reach perfection. Perfection, on the other hand, was thought to be equivalent to serenity, stillness, eternity. In contrast, in the modern understanding, change is not incompatible with perfection; in fact, perfection as such no longer has connotations of completeness but rather of excellence. The concept of cause has now been replaced by a new concept: *law*. Importantly, a law is not meant to be the cause for change. A law is merely the formal description of change. Instead of reflecting about causes of changes, it is now the world that is approached as an object of study. The modern world is scientific: the sometimes arbitrary agent of change of the past has been replaced by the impartial and objective rationality of the law. In the new, scientific world, the world itself—seen now in its totality as nature or cosmos—as well as the processes in it are rational and can be studied and understood rationally. Our scientific understanding is objective, that is, independent of the subjective particularities and qualities of the observer.

## A Science for the Psyche and a Challenge

It is in this world of scientific achievement and optimism that a young neurologist from Vienna decides to study the human psyche. Deeply impressed by the phenomenon of hypnotism and perplexed by the clinical picture of hysteria, Sigmund Freud approaches the human mind as a kind of rational device, a "mental apparatus" that is supposed to be operating according to specific psychic laws. In his understanding, there is little that is arbitrary in our psychic life. A slip of the tongue, a hysterical symptom or a dream are not chance phenomena, nor are they meaningless errors, nor messages from gods or other supernatural entities. For Freud, psychic life is in principle comprehensible and psychic phenomena deterministic. The only catch is that the inner workings of this determinism are taking place away from the searchlights of our conscious mind. Many things happen in the backstage, in "another scene", the scene of the *unconscious*, as he called it.

Being a scientist, Freud envisaged psychoanalysis as a proper science. In Freud's work, psychoanalytic hypotheses and theories—its metapsychology, as he called it—are constructed, tested, revised, extended and even abandoned in much the same way as any other scientific theories: through observations, hypotheses and testing. Psychoanalytic theorising advances carefully, hesitantly and slowly—quite unlike philosophy, which, in Freud's view, always needs to have the answer to every question. Psychoanalysis is a science and as such it is very tolerant of temporary ignorance and contradiction, and is equipped with all the tools of rational scientific enquiry that it needs in order to develop further.

At about the same time, Martin Heidegger, a young German professor of philosophy who had abandoned earlier aspirations to become a priest, unimpressed by this new scientific era, decides to turn his attention to its basic conceptual premises. A pupil of Husserl, Heidegger uses phenomenology to turn "to the things themselves". But Heidegger does not stop at the things, or at other kinds of beings; his questioning brings him to the more general question of being itself, that is, to the question about the source of the intelligibility of the world. The main feature of the human being's engagement with the world is that they are concerned with the entities they encounter. The human being, or *Dasein*, is concerned with the world they inhabit. Heidegger recognised that you cannot embark on this questioning journey unless you have an initial, naïve perhaps, opening to a space—or *clearing*, as he called it—where a human being's concernful comportment towards the beings it encounters is possible. This *circle of understanding* is where the key to grasping the essence of the human being in its "being-human" lies. For Heidegger, epistemology is preceded by ontology; but still, ontology is mediated by language. The circle is virtuous and there is no escaping it. It is unavoidable for any serious enquiry. For Heidegger, the question about the meaning of being is at the same time a question about the world of beings, as well as a question about Dasein—namely that being for whom the world (and being) are of concern.

Heidegger's intention was not to reject the modern scientific world view as such, but rather to uncover and demonstrate what he saw as its failure, and to enquire after its concepts and tools. In his *Being and Time*, published in 1927, he argued that in order to demonstrate the origin of our basic ontological concepts, it is necessary to *destroy* the history of ontology, that is, to deconstruct the history of ideas. In his view, sciences of the human being fail to grasp the totality of the phenomena they study; they miss their essence and almost unavoidably distort them. This stems from a major limitation of modern science in general, which, according to Heidegger, not only confuses what is real with what can be measured and studied objectively, but also remains oblivious to this confusion. Modern science is conditioned by a conceptual framework resting on the picture of a scientist qua observer who focuses objectively on his or her field of study, and studies its *objects*.

In contrast, Heidegger held that the relation of the human being to the world is not one of subject to object, or observer to observed, as people (and scientists) are accustomed to believe. He argued that any such conceptualisation is an interpretative abstraction founded on a more primordial unity, which he designated with the combined term *being-in-the-world*: the world concerns us and becomes intelligible to us because we human beings-in-the-world are already opened up to, and comported towards, being. The inaugurating event of opening up to being is lost for each and every one of us, in the sense that we have lost awareness that it ever happened. This opening up is mediated through language and entails, as such, the acceptance of an implicit but all-pervasive world view, which, in itself, is taken for granted and is not questioned. The very method of science predetermines what it can speak about; science is not in a position to question itself or its field of study as such. Such a task is for philosophy.

Heidegger's work represented a major challenge to any other contemporary philosophical or scientific attempt to study the world in general and the human condition in particular, and it exerted an enormous influence on the course of twentieth-century philosophy. It gradually became clear that its repercussions were much more far-reaching than immediately thought, with its impact especially felt in other disciplines that were also taking the human being as their object of study—such as psychiatry, psychology and psychoanalysis. Heidegger called into question Freud's optimistic and straightforward conception of science. In his view, Freud was a thinker who was operating solidly within the limited and naïve conceptual framework of the nineteenth-century natural sciences. Psychoanalysis not only fails to study the human being in its being human; it actually distorts phenomena in its effort to make them fit within an incongruous and mechanistic framework. Approaching the psyche as a deterministic mental "apparatus", we are already tacitly endorsing a Cartesian world view, according to which everything that can be studied scientifically is regarded in terms of its spatiality and the measurability of its features. The assumption that the psyche is an "apparatus" functioning according to laws reduces it to a mechanism, to an automaton that leaves no room for human agency. For Heidegger, the approach is problematic. The Cartesian scientific method is not applicable to the problem at hand.

This is where Jacques Lacan enters the picture. He was one of the major post-Freudian psychoanalysts and theorists, and he explicitly acknowledged the influence Heidegger's ideas had had on his own work, at least in the early stages of his teaching. He also believed that the spirit and radical nature of Freud's discovery were being misconstrued by those who paid more attention to its deterministic outlook, and to Freud's own biologism. Freud's discovery, in Lacan's view, consisted in recognising the extent to which human suffering is dependent on, and subject to, language. Psychoanalysis reveals the human being as a subject alienated and tortured by language, a subject submitted to the law of the signifier *and* at the same time split by their own desire. A major implication of Freud's discovery was, for Lacan, the return of agency. Whereas scientific thought aspires to an ideal of unmediated objective knowledge, Freud's attempts at a scientific understanding of the human psyche inadvertently bring the subjective back to the fore and, in the same time, uncover the unavoidable incompleteness inherent in any attempt to formulate all this concretely. The Cartesian ideal of a solid foundation of truth or certainty cannot obtain—or, as Lacan puts it, there is no Other of the Other. Still, paradoxically, for Lacan the subject of psychoanalysis is the subject of science. This is because only the subject of science would be willing to reflect on their symptoms (where symptom is everything, a slip of the tongue, a manifestation of hysteria, a dream) and take it as something meaningful that can be understood. In a direct attempt to reintroduce Aristotelean conceptions of causality to Freud's scientific enterprise, Lacan described the subject as representing the disruptive effect of *tuché* on the *automaton* of the signifying chain. At the later stage of his teaching, Lacan took on mathematics in an attempt to present an ideal formalisation of psychoanalysis, which consists in what is written but can only *ex-sist* when one presents it in language. One could see this as parallel to Heidegger's circle of understanding, in the sense that you need to be subjected to language in order to be able to formulate how your world is only revealed from language. But what is revealed, this recursive set of entities, concepts, relations, properties and frames of reference, this ontology as I call it, is a semblance, an ontology of make-believe, an *ontology from discourse*. I choose to designate it as an "ontology" because of the term's import in the history of ideas, and its relevance: it comprises two terms that will be of major importance in our discussions, the Greek term "on" (gen: "onto-"), in the sense of *entity*, *thing*; and "logos", in the sense that Heidegger emphasises, that of the *collection* or *gathering* of entities.

So, this will be the task of this book: to present an attempt to lay the foundations for a discourse ontology taking the lead from the work of Heidegger and proceeding through the work of Lacan.

## Aims and Scope of the Book

I hold that Heidegger's philosophy allows for a deep understanding of the human condition, without resorting to tacit assumptions about what a subject is, what an object is, what truth is, what the real and the knowable are, and what knowledge is. Heidegger's work reveals the historicity and limitations of modern science and, as I see it, helps bring out its uncritically accepted presuppositions in general and of psychoanalytic theory in particular. Lacan's revisiting of Freud's texts and his recasting of fundamental Freudian concepts allow for a formulation of a post-Freudian metapsychology which offers a way through or around Heidegger's criticism. Lacan was very sceptical about metaphysics and ontology. But Heidegger turned to be just as sceptical. Indeed, it can be said that the later Heidegger subscribed to a certain "anti-philosophy" just as militantly as the later Lacan did. In addition, both thinkers had a similar understanding of the historicity of science and coincided in their contempt for conventional philosophy. But their aims were different. In many respects, Heidegger shows himself to be a moralist, while Lacan appears as an agnostic cynic. This makes futile any direct attempt at reconciling their differing opinions and at making their conclusions fully compatible at any costs.

In what follows, I will discuss the basic theoretical hypotheses and models of Lacanian psychoanalysis, taking into consideration Heidegger's philosophy of being, his critique of modernity and his arguments against (Freudian) psychoanalysis. It will be, in other words, an attempt to use Heidegger's questioning in order to secure a philosophical foundation for a Lacanian metapsychology.[1] But there are two important questions that need to be considered before the task is undertaken.

The first is regarding Heidegger's thought itself. A discussion about the importance of his philosophy would be incomplete without reference to those who have claimed that Heidegger's connections with Nazism would be enough to discredit his whole philosophy once and for all. The debate, a sort of a Heidegger *affair*, goes on and forms a

---

[1]On a cursory glance, French philosopher Alain Badiou's work—an oeuvre in which he explicitly refers to Heidegger's re-positing of the ontological question and to Lacan's post-Cartesian conceptualisation of the divided subject—seems to overlap with my project. Badiou purports to construct a fully-fledged philosophical system in an attempt to respond to the challenges of what he conceives as a new epoch of science, the subject and truth. Badiou's understanding and use of crucial terms such as "being", "event", "truth" and "subject" appear to be highly idiosyncratic and largely incompatible with the ways in which Heidegger and Lacan employ them. Badiou is not interested in Heidegger's critique of Freudian theory or in the intricacies of Lacan's understanding of the speaking being. These are precisely the issues that interest me.

major part of the field of Heidegger studies, having been rekin-
dled in the most decisive manner by the publication of his so-called
*Black Notebooks*. Even though some (but not all) of the many anti-
Heideggerian arguments in this context have been rebutted or exposed
as ad hominem, there is certainly a question regarding what Heidegger
did or said—or *failed* to do or say—in connection with Nazism, the
Nazi party, the crimes of Nazis and the Holocaust. Regardless of his
specific reasons for it, Heidegger's silence on the matter is extremely
problematic, if not shocking. It has been described unequivocally
as a "failure of thinking",[2] a failure of great import for a philosopher
who sought to bring thinking back to the centre of our questioning
the world and our position in it. Connected with this is the question
of Heidegger's public presence and personal choices during the Nazi
period. They also leave a lot to be desired.

Much more serious, however, is the question about whether Nazi ideals could be shown to be unambiguously discernible in Heidegger's philosophy *as such*. This question is straightforward: Is there anything at all
in Heidegger's phenomenology that would suffice to expose it as harbour-
ing Nazi assumptions and ideals? Would we be able to discern anything
problematic in his fundamental ontology if we were not made suspicious
by his silence regarding Nazi crimes? If we suspended for a moment all
judgement based on what we know about his silence and conduct, or,
if he had indeed decided to speak out and unreservedly condemn Nazi
crimes and the Holocaust, would there still be reasons to reject his fundamental ontology on the basis of its basic tenets and content?

In so far as we are considering Heidegger's thought in terms of a phenomenological enquiry regarding Dasein's comportment towards being,
I do not think this is the case.

What I am interested in is Heidegger's fundamental ontology. I
consider it to be a direct corollary of his taking the promise of phenomenology seriously: one has to return to the things themselves; on
doing just this, one can recognise that the act of observation is not

---

[2]See David Farrell Krell, *Daimon Life: Heidegger and Life-Philosophy* (Bloomington: Indiana
University Press, 1992), p. 138.

unmediated. One sees that our attention needs first to be focused on the question of how things are available to the concerned human being. This is a question about the meaning of being. From there follows the recognition that being is historical, which leads to a further recognition of the equiprimordiality of truth (qua *a-letheia*), time, being and the world. In my view, there is not much—or anything—in all this that can be thought as contaminated by Nazi thinking.[3] To claim otherwise would be tantamount to retroactively attributing intention, transforming an attack on Heidegger, the political person, into an attack on his ontology. That is fallacious and I choose not to follow this path. So, to make myself perfectly clear, Heidegger's political philosophy, his alleged or real antisemitism, and his political leanings are of no interest to me. In what follows, I intend to critically take from Heidegger's work all what might be directly relevant to my task, and decidedly leave out all that what is not relevant, or justifies, in any way, suspicions of Nazism.

The second question is methodological. Both Heidegger and Lacan, two of the most important thinkers of last century, have produced a multifaceted and extensive body of work that evolved with time. How is one to approach it?

In connection with Heidegger, for example, there is the question of the so-called turn in this thinking that became more apparent sometime in the 1930s. It consisted in a slight change in focus, a notable change in terminology and a clear change in priorities. There are those who think that this turn represents a rupture in Heidegger's thought, a radical discontinuity. I am not of this opinion. In my view, the turn is about a change in Heidegger's priorities, a shift of focus and a greater clarity in regard to the pathways opened up. I concur with Joan Stambaugh when she writes about the turn that "it did not represent some sudden change of mind, but in a significant sense, it was anticipated from the very beginning".[4] Accordingly, I will approach Heidegger's work in the same

---

[3]See, however, below, p. 194n12.

[4]Joan Stambaugh, 'The Turn', in Babette E. Babich (ed.), *From Phenomenology to Thought, Errancy, and Desire: Essays in Honor of William J. Richardson, S.J.* (Dordrecht: Kluwer Academic, 1995), 209–212, p. 209.

way that a considerable body of work can be approached: as a whole but with a clear sense of moving along a direction.

With Lacan things are a bit less straightforward. Lacan published relatively little during his lifetime. A collection of some of his talks and a few previously published papers appeared in a book form, Écrits, only in 1966—while a full translation of these texts in English had to wait until 2006.[5] Lacan's teaching consisted mainly of his seminar, held from the beginning of the 50s, without interruption apart from summer breaks and other holidays, for almost 30 years. Transcriptions of seminar sessions were circulating among his pupils for reference and discussion, and eventually started being published in an "established" form by his son-in-law, Jacques-Alain Miller. At the time of this writing, 2019, the process is still ongoing—which in practical terms means that many of Lacan's seminars remain unpublished or without an official translation. This understandably slow process presents the researcher with a number of problems. What is one to do with those of Lacan's seminars which are not yet officially available? How is one to approach those texts that are available in various versions, one differing slightly from the other? And how should one approach those concepts and terms which change gradually and sometimes heavily in the course of Lacan's teaching?

In what follows, I have made the choice to regard Lacan's work as if from a (future-like) retrospective vantage point. I shall attempt to benefit from an artificial hindsight, so to speak, and will approach Lacan's major concepts as if they had been available to us from the beginning, treating their different forms as attempts at their elucidation. Obviously, I am aware that strictly speaking this was not the case. Time and again Lacan himself warns against taking his thought as a completed system—especially when "completed" is understood as having the connotations of closed, dogmatic or dead. This, of course, makes very good sense from his own point of view: he was still in the process of developing

[5]See Jacques Lacan, Écrits [1966] (New York: W. W. Norton & Company, 2006). To facilitate cross-referencing, page references to texts from Écrits will also include the French original page number after a slash.

ideas, testing hypotheses, breaking new ground; to take his thought as a finished system would be tantamount to turning it into a dead body, a corpse rather than a corpus, if I can put it that way. "Lacan", wrote Jacques-Alain Miller,

> is not an author. His work is a teaching. We must take this into consideration; we must know that following his star requires that we do not synchronise and dogmatise his teaching, that we do not hide but rather stress its contradictions, its antinomies, its deadlocks, its difficulties. For a teaching on the analytic experience is like a *work in progress* and implies a back and forth motion between text and experience.[6]

Still, after Lacan's death, we need to acknowledge that his teaching is now completed, even if just in the literal sense that it is now what it is and nothing new can be added to it. When I am advocating to approach it now as a system, even against Lacan's explicit wishes while he was alive, is not different from attempting to identify the major themes that ran through it. Indeed, as I see it reading it retrospectively, it is as if Lacan himself was doing some tidying up as he pushed forward. Some of his older concepts, hypotheses and models were abandoned or replaced, while others—the ones that prove to be important or fruitful—were fine-tuned or further elaborated, or completely transformed. At any given moment, Lacan delivered his teaching as if it was a product of a fully functioning and self-consistent theory. At least this is how it appears to an observer. Lacan presented himself as having the whole picture at his disposal, choosing to deliver to his audience as much as was needed in order to build an argument or make a point. "I have never considered myself as a researcher", he stressed. "As Picasso once said, to the shocked surprise of those around him—*I do not seek, I find*".[7]

---

[6]Jacques-Alain Miller, 'Extimité' [1985–86], in Mark Bracher et al. (eds.), *Lacanian Theory of Discourse: Subject, Structure, and Society* (New York: New York University Press, 1994), 74–87, p. 75.

[7]Jacques Lacan, *The Seminar of Jacques Lacan, Book XI: The Four Fundamental Concepts of Psychoanalysis* [1964–65], ed. Jacques-Alain Miller (New York: W. W. Norton & Company, 1998), p. 7.

Accordingly. he would leave out all explicit theoretical justification or references for the steps he was taking, opting instead for an aphoristic exposition full of hints, allusions and suggestions. He continued like this until the end of his teaching, with the exception, perhaps, of the last few years, when he was struggling with his Borromean knots and other mathematical formalisations. This contributed a lot to the notorious opacity of his style, but also gave him some theoretical flexibility to explore ideas and develop (or abandon) conceptual models and hypotheses as he saw fit. Lacan's choice provides us with a further justification to consider his work as if it were a complete, self-consistent system; at any given moment, he presented it as such. Identifying these persistent threads from our retrospective vantage point allows for the outlining of a remarkably consistent body of work. In this sense, I will be following Lacan's own suggestion: "My discourse proceeds, in the following way: each term is sustained only in its topological relation with the others".[8] In other words, I shall approach the Lacanian opus accepting that it is exactly this, an opus, a complete, self-consistent body of *work*—the term "work" used here in the sense utilised by Jean-Claude Milner in his *Considerations of a Work*.[9] Just as with Heidegger, in what follows I will critically take from Lacan's work all that might be directly relevant to my task, and will decidedly leave out all what is not.

## Chapter Outline

I will begin by focusing on the basic aspects of Heidegger's philosophy of being. I take *being* to stand for the fact that *the world is intelligible* to the human being. I will outline the basic aspects of Heidegger's ontology, underlining the rejection of the Cartesian subject–object dichotomy and his phenomenological description of the human being or Dasein. I will introduce Heidegger's method—phenomenology—and

---

[8] *Seminar XI*, p. 89.

[9] See Jean-Claude Milner, 'Considerations of a Work' [1995], trans. James Penney, *Journal for Lacanian Studies*, 4/1 (2006), 141–158, p. 142.

set out the framework of his *analytic of Dasein* with its unavoidable circle of understanding. I will discuss the crucial ontological difference, i.e. the difference between beings (as entities of this world) and being as such, and introduce concepts such as being-in-the-world, temporality, signs and equipment, language, authenticity, event of appropriation and death. Special attention will be paid to Heidegger's understanding of truth. As he claims, truth is not a correspondence between a language and a world, but rather an unconcealment and appropriation of being, that is, a world disclosure. It is this conceptualisation that allows Heidegger to discern the historical character of being, and leads him to abandon metaphysics and his original attempt at a fundamental ontology.

I will proceed then with presenting, in the following chapter, Heidegger's critique of science, as well as his specific arguments against psychoanalysis. Heidegger claimed that there is a rupture between the ancient and the modern world view. Entities are no longer understood as conforming to what their nature dictates, but rather as conforming to laws. The world of modernity is a scientific world of quantifiable entities, processes and phenomena, and rests on a subject–object distinction. For Heidegger, this distinction is problematic. The world, beings in the world, space and time are all opened up in an event (of appropriation) through Dasein's bodiliness and being-in-the-world in ways more complex and rich than the modern scientific regional ontology can take account of. Still, phenomena are approached with arrogance and are forced to conform to unnecessary or unexamined assumptions. Psychology and psychiatry, for example, can only monitor and assess complex psychological phenomena by having them reduced to measurements with the help of various experimental designs and technologies.

In the eyes of Heidegger, Freud, too, was trapped in a naïve subject–object understanding of the human being: his view of the psyche as a deterministic "mental apparatus" comprising subsystems that process stimuli and coordinate plans of action is a very problematic one and reflects, as Heidegger points out, a failure to question its implicit assumptions. This failure requires him (Freud) to resort to unnecessary hypotheses and introduce questionable concepts such as the unconscious, libido, cathexis or repression. Later developments of Freudian theory (e.g. the second structural model of ego, super-ego and id) are built upon similar, equally unstable foundations and fall apart as soon as they are rigorously questioned.

In the next chapter, the fourth of this book, I will have the opportunity to focus on Lacan's famous "return to Freud", namely the attention he drew, in the first period of his teaching, to what he thought was the "true" spirit of Freud's discovery. For Lacan, Freud's theoretical constructions were his provisional solutions to problems he encountered in the clinic. Freud was much more open to the phenomena he studied than generally thought; he never shied away from updating, transforming or abandoning altogether concepts and terms that proved to be inadequate. For Lacan, what Freud discovered was not entities or structures like the "unconscious", "libido" or the "drives", as such; what he discovered is that a lot of human suffering is dependent on, and subject to, language, indeed to the actual words comprising a language, that is, to words in their *material* aspect.

In this chapter, I will also give an outline of some of Lacan's original contributions to psychoanalysis, such as the mirror stage, the three registers of experience (real, symbolic and imaginary), jouissance and object *a*. I will present Lacan's conceptualisation of the human being as a being subjected to the law of the signifier and show that for Lacan the subject of psychoanalysis is not the Cartesian subject which encounters objects, but rather a subject of language, that is, a being "captured and tortured by language".[10] For Lacan, the Freudian "unconscious" is not an entity that was found hiding deep in the shadows of the psyche. Its status does not need to be asserted "ontically"; such an assertion would indeed be "fragile", as Lacan points out in his *Seminar XI*.[11] The unconscious is: a gap in the logic of the signifying chain; a claim for the speaking being; a manifestation of an unknown something that, when recognised by the subject, invites—or necessitates—a choice. For Lacan, the status of the unconscious is "ethical".

---

[10]Jacques Lacan, *The Seminar of Jacques Lacan, Book III: The Psychoses* [1955–56], ed. Jacques-Allain Miller (New York: W. W. Norton & Company, 1993), p. 243.
[11]*Seminar XI*, p. 33.

Lacan's reading of Freud renders many of Heidegger's dismissive comments irrelevant, but does not invalidate the core of his argument. Having laid the ground thus, I will then turn to what could be described as a Lacanian metapsychology—even though Lacan himself largely avoided using this term in connection with his work. Metapsychology can be understood as addressing questions such as *What does it mean to be a subject of language? What is the source of signifierness?* Or, *What is the structure of a discourse?* Lacanian metapsychology will be the subject matter of Chapter 5. I will present language as a symbolic system that human beings are subjected to and speak about the law of the signifier. From the corporeality of language ("lalangue") and Lacan's views on the emergence of signifierness, I will turn to recursivity and the retroactive attribution of meaning (the Freudian *Nachträglichkeit*), and the functions of metaphor and metonymy. I will also outline Lacan's theory of discourses and discuss the Lacanian conceptions of truth, time and historicity, all of which, as I show, are thought as emerging recursively in discourse.

I will use most of the chapter to explore the intricacies of such concepts and of their interrelations: questions of metapsychology will lead me to the more general issue of the status of metaphysics and philosophy in Lacan's thought. One of his repeated statements, from very early in his teaching, was that *there is no metalanguage.* This can be understood to mean that there is no vantage point from which one can study such phenomena, that is, there can be no philosophy of being. What philosophers call being is for Lacan "just a fact of what is said". Indeed, during this later period of Lacan's anti-philosophy, the only possible formalisation he accepts is the formalisation of mathematics, and specifically of set theory and topology. Mathematics is an "ideal metalanguage", he claims, and yet, it is only made possible by the very act of speaking.

Lacan appears to be very far away from Heidegger at this point, but he is not. For Lacan, being is a corollary of discourse; formalisation of discourse is only recursively possible through mathematics; and, interestingly, mathematics too is a discourse. This circle of understanding is similar, if not directly homologous, to Heidegger's circle of understanding. It is this observation that leads me to recognise the need for a conceptual bridging, the focus of my Chapter 6.

The name I give to this synthesis is *discourse ontology*. As I see it, it *is* an *ontology*—in so far as it concerns being, i.e. the open space where a world can present itself as intelligible to the human being—with the designation "*discourse*" denoting the source of this intelligibility. Its five basic themes are: the speaking being and the emergence of signifierness; truth as a rule-governed discursive activity; the discursive constitution of time; the body, jouissance and sexuation; world. The chapter is informed by the terminology, insights, concepts, hypotheses and conclusions of both Heidegger and Lacan, and entails discussions about the human being as a being which is *being there* in language; about the world into which the human being finds itself thrown and about the ways of its comportment towards this world; about the ontological recursive construction of a shared ontic world; and about the limits and the historicity of this world. I will conclude with a discussion of the body/mind split as recast by Lacan's conceptualisation of the speaking being; a return to the so-called "hard" problem of consciousness; and with some thoughts regarding the question of truth in our post-truth era.

**Acknowledgements and Thanks**  I have struggled with the texts of Freud and Lacan for more than thirty years. A fleeting first contact became the sparkle for an intense interest that has not left me since. Regarding Heidegger, I first became acquainted with his thought some years later. Heidegger taught me how to ask questions and gave me the tools to see how much goes on behind any simple and "self-evident" accepted truth. The encounter with Heidegger's questioning shook my dogmatic slumber, so to speak. As a practitioner of psychoanalysis, I have found it imperative, in an increasingly urgent manner, to be able to respond to his criticisms against psychoanalysis—or at least to have some idea of how a response was to be formulated.

This book is the product of more than ten years of intense thinking and questioning, having grown out of a doctoral thesis I defended at Middlesex University. It has benefitted and was enriched considerably from discussions and disagreements, both with colleagues and trainees at CFAR (London), and with people who did not have any professional or other reason to be well disposed towards psychoanalysis in its Lacanian or other forms. I wouldn't expect them to agree with all my arguments and support my conclusions, but I thank them all.

I am especially indebted to Prof. Bernard Burgoyne for our discussions and illuminating debates, and, crucially, for his support and encouragement all these years, even when he disagreed with me. I am grateful to Ross McElwain for generously offering to read the manuscript and helping me with his corrections, useful comments and thoughts. I would also like to thank Derek Hook and Calum Neill, editors of Palgrave Lacan Series, for their kind advice, encouragement and valuable feedback. Of course, this book would not be possible without the patience, help and support from Jo O'Neill and Grace Jackson of Palgrave. They made the process of preparing and delivering this manuscript as smooth and pleasant as possible. Finally, a great thank you would need to go to Aneta Stamenova, who has endured me throughout these years of struggling while challenging me with insightful questions and suggestions, and also to my parents, Spyros and Chara, who showed me a world where music is played to be shared, inspiring me to look through the grilles of our old valve radio and squint hard enough to see the musicians sharing their music in the half-light of that strange stage.

◇　◇　◇

# Bibliography

KRELL, DAVID FARRELL, *Daimon Life: Heidegger and Life-Philosophy* (Bloomington: Indiana University Press, 1992).

LACAN, JACQUES, *Écrits* [1966], trans. Bruce Fink, Héloïse Fink, and Russell Grigg (New York: W. W. Norton & Company, 2006).

———, *The Seminar of Jacques Lacan, Book III: The Psychoses* [1955–56], ed. Jacques-Allain Miller, trans. Russel Grigg (New York: W. W. Norton & Company, 1993).

———, *The Seminar of Jacques Lacan, Book XI: The Four Fundamental Concepts of Psychoanalysis* [1964–65], ed. Jacques-Allain Miller, trans. Alan Sheridan (New York: W. W. Norton & Company, 1998).

MILLER, JACQUES-ALLAIN, 'Extimité' [1985–86], trans. Françoise Massardier-Kenney, in Mark Bracher, et al. (eds.), *Lacanian Theory of Discourse: Subject, Structure, and Society* (New York: New York University Press, 1994), 74–87.

MILNER, JEAN-CLAUDE, 'Considerations of a Work' [1995], trans. James Penney, *Journal for Lacanian Studies*, 4/1 (2006), 141–158.

STAMBAUGH, JOAN, 'The Turn' in Babette E. Babich (ed.), *From Phenomenology to Thought, Errancy, and Desire: Essays in Honor of William J. Richardson, S.J.* (Phenomenologica, 133; Dordrecht: Kluwer Academic, 1995), 209–212.

# 2

# The Question of Being

Heidegger's *Being and Time* begins with a quote from Plato's dialogue *Sophist*. A character called Stranger is speaking with two other characters, Theaetetus and Theodorus, and attempts to show them how people (philosophers and non-philosophers alike) talk about being without really knowing what that means. We should invite them to explain, Stranger says to his interlocutors. We need to tell them that we do not understand and that we are in a difficulty. Please do explain, we should tell them, "for manifestly you have long been aware of what you mean when you use the expression 'being'. We, however, who used to think we understood it, have now become perplexed".[1]

For Heidegger, this very question—still difficult and perplexing—has long been pushed aside and forgotten and needs to be raised anew. We, human beings, conceive of ourselves as observing subjects present in a "here and now", each one of us in our individuality, facing a world that lies "objectively" out there. When we wonder about the

---

[1] Plato, quoted in Martin Heidegger, *Being and Time* [1927] (Malden, MA: Blackwell Publishers, 1962), p. 17/1. To facilitate cross-referencing, references to *Being and Time* will also include the German original page number after a slash.

© The Author(s) 2019
C. Tombras, *Discourse Ontology*, The Palgrave Lacan Series,
https://doi.org/10.1007/978-3-030-13662-8_2

**21**

world and the beings we encounter in it, we are readily able to refer to an explanation—or to an explanatory attempt—about how they found themselves in front of us. Now and again we allow ourselves to marvel at the miracle of existence, but we do this only temporarily, only in so far as we contemplate life, the past, the future, creation, and so on and so forth. Soon enough we resume our ordinary comportment—that of taking things for granted, engaging with a world which is open to us, available to our inspection.

Heidegger rejects this picture as limited and misleading. It is limited because it tends to overlook many aspects of our being human, and it is misleading because it obscures *this very fact* of overlooking. This is the task he sets himself: "Our aim in the following treatise is to work out the question of the meaning of being and do so concretely".[2]

## Heidegger's Phenomenology

At the end of the nineteenth century, the German philosopher Franz Brentano spoke about the mind's inherent *intentionality*. Taking his lead from the Scholastics of the Middle Ages, Brentano observed that in any psychical phenomenon the mind is always directed towards its objects; he argued that psychology's focus of study should not be the mind's contents but rather its acts. One of Brentano's students, Edmund Husserl, took the idea of intentionality and made it the starting point for a philosophy of consciousness that would be structured with scientific rigorousness. According to Husserl's maxim, we must go *back to the things themselves*; by this, he meant that any philosophy of consciousness cannot but focus on the objects that this consciousness is intending towards and to its ways of operation. For Husserl, the objects that appear to consciousness (a thing, a memory, a feeling, a desire) are "phenomena"; accordingly, their study should be called phenomenology, a term that had been used previously by philosophers like Kant or Hegel. The method of Husserl's phenomenology was to *arrest* consciousness in

---

[2] *Being and Time*, p. 17/1.

its intentional acts, that is, to suspend both the intentional acts as such and the intended objects, by putting them in "brackets", as he described it. This was adopting the *phenomenological attitude*.

Heidegger was one of Husserl's students and was, for a period, thought of as his successor. Heidegger had come to Husserl through Brentano. Heidegger's thought was oriented to questions of ontology and, more specifically, to the question of being. As he explained, he was introduced to the question by reading Brentano's 1862 dissertation, *On the Manifold Sense of Being in Aristotle*.[3]

Heidegger's insight was that Husserl's concept of a consciousness which tends itself towards objects by way of its intentional acts, is constructed on the basis of a more elementary structure of comporting towards entities which is taken for granted; that elementary structure already involves the unexamined assumption of a distinction between consciousness and its objects. One might choose to subscribe to an "objective" or *neutral* point of view, according to which the world can be thought of as an environment of objects that a human being approaches as an observing subject; but as soon as one tries to question these concepts a bit further, it becomes clear that terms such as "subject", "object", "consciousness" and "observation" already include a primordial understanding of what is at stake. Heidegger saw that such a distinction cannot withstand serious scrutiny and, taking Husserl's maxim to the letter, argued that consciousness is but one aspect of the human being's engagement with the world: a world of subjects, and objects, and observations has already been revealed before one can even conceive of or subscribe to a neutral point of view. Accordingly, Heidegger's approach to Husserlian phenomenology was to take the two terms that comprise the term, "phenomenon" and "logos", and trace them back to their ancient Greek origins. Phenomenon (in Greek: φαινόμενον) is that which shows itself, the manifest. And far from being just what we cursorily call "discourse", "ratio", "reason", etc., logos comes from the verb *legein* (in Greek: λόγος < λέγειν) which, in

---

[3]See 'Preface (Letter to W. Richardson)' in William J. Richardson, *Heidegger: Through Phenomenology to Thought* (New York: Fordham University Press, 2003), viii–xxiii, p. x.

its original sense means to let appear, to make manifest, to collect, to gather. Thus, for him, the term "phenomenology", rather than being simply the name of one school of philosophy amongst many, was taken to mean "to let that which shows itself be seen from itself in the very way in which it shows itself from itself".[4]

In his study, his "analytic", as he called it, Heidegger employed two crucial concepts. The first was *Dasein*, a term he used to denote the human being employing some degree of abstraction—i.e. not as this or that human being, but a human being as an entity "which each of us is himself, and which includes inquiring as one of the possibilities of its being".[5] Heidegger did not invent the word *Dasein* which comes from the German adverb "*da*", *there* (or *here*), and the infinitive "*Sein*", *to be*, or being. In the seventeenth century, the word was used in the sense of *presence* while in the eighteenth century it was used by philosophers as synonym to *Existenz*, and generally in the sense of *life*. In (at least pre-Heideggerian) everyday speech, Dasein was used for the being or life of persons.[6]

The second concept was *being-in-the-world*. For Heidegger, the notion of a world conceived somehow as a container of entities—the earth, the sky, rocks and rivers, plants and animals, human beings—is nonsensical. The world does not contain things; the world *is* all these things and all these things *are* the world, in a fundamental sense. The human being qua Dasein cannot but be-in-the-world. As Heidegger explains, "The compound expression 'Being-in-the-world' indicates, in the very way we have coined it, that it stands for a unitary phenomenon. This primary datum must be seen as a whole".[7] Dasein cannot but be conceived in its being-in-the-world. We *are* in the world in the most complete sense of the verb "to be". We are in the world and this cannot

---

[4]*Being and Time*, p. 58/34.

[5]*Being and Time*, p. 27/7.

[6]The term *Dasein* is commonly left untranslated and is written either as a single word or hyphenated, *Da-sein*, to stress its original, spatial sense. For reasons of uniformity and clarity, I will be using the non-hyphenated form. Quoted passages of Heidegger or others will also be modified as needed, in order to conform to this convention.

[7]Heidegger, *Being and Time*, p. 78/53.

but be so. The world is revealed to us in our purposeful engagement with it, not as something that we choose to occupy or inhabit, nor as something that we may choose to observe: "Subject and Object do not coincide with Dasein and the world".[8]

Dasein and being-in-the-world are equiprimordial. Both reveal themselves to be relevant to our investigation when we attempt to consider our engagement with the world as it is. The structure described as being-in-the-world is understood as more primordial to "world" or to "beings" of this world.

## Beings, and the Question of Being

Humans are concerned and do things with entities we come across in our world: other human beings, animals, plants, natural phenomena, objects, tools, artefacts and so on. All these we call "beings" that we may be observing, talking about, talking to, talking with, remembering, forgetting, handling, studying, manipulating, creating, destroying and modifying. Human beings comport towards beings in myriads of ways and tend to think that this state of affairs is self-evident and transparent. As Heidegger writes,

> There are many things which we designate as 'being', and we do so in various senses. Everything we talk about, everything we have in view, everything towards which we comport ourselves in any way, is being; what we are is being, and so is how we are. Being lies in the fact that something is, and in its being as it is.[9]

Questioning being then is tantamount to attempting to reflect on this state of affairs—attempting, that is, to see beyond the transparency of our relatedness to the world, and to entities in the world. That is a task for humans. The question itself only makes sense to humans, i.e.

---

[8] *Being and Time*, p. 87/60.
[9] *Being and Time*, pp. 26/6–7.

it is a specifically *human* question. Being is that on the basis—and because—of which entities are present before us and can become the focus of our concern. Strictly speaking, there would be no such thing as being if there were no humans concerned with it: being is the *product* and the *prerequisite* of the concerned comportment of humans towards what they encounter, i.e. beings. We humans cannot even arrive at the question of being unless we already have an understanding of entities as beings. In order to be able to observe, conceive, understand, describe or contemplate our dealings with the world and its entities—with beings in general—we, human beings, already employ a tacit understanding of what being is. It is not meant by this that we have an understanding of each and every entity or being we encounter, but rather that we are open, in some fundamental way, to beings as such. Being is "that which determines entities as entities, that *on the basis of which* entities are already understood".[10] Or, as Thomas Sheehan suggests: "Human being is the 'open space' or clearing within which the meaningful presence of things can occur".[11]

It would appear that for Heidegger the question of being is deeper than the question of knowing. Richard Polt, for example, writes that for Heidegger "ontology precedes epistemology".[12] This, strictly speaking, is not the case: both concepts, epistemology *and* ontology, belong in, and obtain their content from, a tradition of metaphysics that Heidegger wants to "destroy". Traditional ontology—which can be defined as the study of being—studies beings in the various domains they are encountered, rather than in the fundamental manner that Heidegger demands. Neither ontology nor epistemology would be possible without a primordial relatedness to being and the tacit understanding of being that this relatedness entails. As Heidegger asserts, "Phenomenology is our way of access to what is to be the theme of ontology, and it is our way of giving it demonstrative precision. *Only as phenomenology, is ontology possible*".[13]

[10]*Being and Time*, pp. 25–26/6 (emphasis added).
[11]Thomas Sheehan, *Making Sense of Heidegger: A Paradigm Shift* (London: Rowman & Littlefield, 2015), p. xv.
[12]Richard Polt, *Heidegger: An Introduction* (London: Routledge, 1999), p. 47.
[13]Heidegger, *Being and Time*, p. 60/35.

2 The Question of Being 27

This task, to enquire about our tacit understanding of being, is a necessary one insofar as we are reflecting on what it is to be human, what
the horizon of human engagement with, and understanding of, the
world is, and what the domain of human knowledge is.

> Only as long as Dasein *is* (that is, only as long as an understanding of
> being is ontically possible), 'is there' being. When Dasein does not exist
> … even entities within-the-world can neither be discovered nor lie hid-
> den. *In such a case* it cannot be said that entities are, nor can it be said
> that they are not.[14]

At the heart of Heidegger's enquiry, we find a verb used to denote
being in its various senses—namely the verb "to be". When I use it,
I make it possible for a specific state of affairs to become part of my
world. My utterances allow the world, beings inside this world, and
being in general, to reveal themselves to me, and to become an issue
for me. As Heidegger puts it, "Language is the house of being".[15] This,
of course, does not mean that I, as a speaking human being, *create* the
world—or the whole of reality, for that matter—in any factical or tangi-
ble sense, merely by using language. A sunset on an exo-planet around
Alpha Centauri cannot seriously be said to have been "created" by
human beings. Yet, it can only *be* something (e.g.: intriguing, beauti-
ful, spectacular, frightening, boring) in the eyes of human beings—that
is, those beings who comport themselves towards being, and for whom
being is an issue.

Heidegger used the term *existence* to denote "that kind of being
towards which Dasein can comport itself in one way or another, and
always does comport itself somehow".[16] The term reflected the phenomenon that for Dasein entities in the world appear both in what they are,

---

[14]*Being and Time*, p. 255/212.
[15]'Letter on Humanism' [1947], in William Mcneill (ed.), *Pathmarks* (Cambridge: Cambridge
University Press, 1978), 239–276, p. 239.
[16]*Being and Time*, p. 32/12.

as well as in how they fit (or may fit) in Dasein's world as a whole.[17] Just
as the tree is not just a tree but also something that fits into a greater
whole with trees and plants, and fields, and branches, and leaves, and
birds, or just as a gap in the bookshelf is not just an empty space but
also an indication of a volume missing, entities present themselves to
Dasein as "standing out" so to speak, from their mere presence. For
Dasein, they do no simply exist, but they ek-sist as Heidegger sometimes writes it.[18]

## Ontological Difference

Being is not *a* being, it's not an entity; it is that which makes our comportment to entities, to other beings—human or not—possible. It is
*because* we are open to being that entities and other beings in the world
present themselves to us as such. Openness to being is that what allows
us to look across the room and see a tree. We might take a camera and
take a picture of this tree through the window; still the camera is not
able to "see" the tree in any but a metaphorical sense of the word "see".
To the camera, a "tree" is merely that what the light rays trace on the
camera's sensor. As far as the sensor is concerned the tree is no different from a building crane or a park bench. For a human observer, however, a tree is a tree. In fact, a tree is never just a tree; it comes together
with other trees and plants, and fields, and branches, and leaves, and
birds, and so on and so forth. In other words, there is a fundamental
difference between the ways a human being—Dasein—and a camera sees a thing. For human beings', things are entities that fit into a
greater whole, a *world*. This awareness is described by Heidegger as an

---

[17]It should be stressed that "existence" here is understood in a far narrower sense than in traditional metaphysics, where the existence of an entity is contrasted to its essence. The Heideggerian
term applies only to Dasein: "The term 'existence', as a designation of being, will be allotted
solely to Dasein. *The essence of Dasein lies in its existence*" (*Being and Time*, p. 67/42).

[18]This spelling, ek-sist (and its equivalent, ex-sist), is meant to draw attention to the fact that
when referring to *existence* (or ex-sistence) there is always the connotation of stepping besides
oneself; you are not just standing there, you are ex-standing, so to speak. A related concept is that
of ek-stasis (or ex-stasis) that is used in connection to temporality. See below, p. 40.

understanding of, or openness to being, and this is a feature that only human beings possess: "The question of the meaning of being becomes possible at all only if there *is* something like an understanding of being. Understanding of being belongs to the kind of being which the entity called 'Dasein' possesses".[19]

There is a difference, in other words, between an awareness of entities as beings (we can call it "ontic" awareness) and an awareness of being that allows us, human beings, to bring together, to *gather* all entities in a comprehensive—and comprehensible—world (an "ontological" awareness). A camera can be set up in such a way that it exhibits ontic awareness of entities—for example, with the help of a motion detector/activator—but can never exhibit an ontological awareness of the world. In all respects, the camera does not have a world. This difference between ontic and ontological awareness, or, better, between beings in their *being* and the *being* of beings is termed *ontological difference*. It is the difference between being as such and the various beings that Dasein might encounter and is of crucial importance.

If we fail to take the ontological difference into account we fail to see what—at the level of the phenomena themselves—differentiates a human being's action of, say, looking at a tree from a camera's. Recognising the ontological difference allows us to see that Dasein's comportment towards the world cannot be adequately described as a subject–object relationship. Dasein's being-in-the-world can only be approached when understood in terms of an ontological awareness of the world. This awareness—or openness to being—is what Heidegger invites us to return to: the question about the meaning of being. To be sure, that is a confusing question, just as confusing as is the onto-logical difference itself—something that has allowed it to be regularly misunderstood.

The confusion might be accentuated by the fact that some entities or structures can be seen as both ontic and ontological. These are either entities which Dasein encounters as ontic entities, but which indicate

---

[19]Heidegger, *Being and Time*, p. 244/200.

the ontological structure in which they belong, forming part of a *circle of understanding*, as Heidegger puts it.

> The 'circle' in understanding belongs to the structure of meaning, and the latter phenomenon is rooted in the existential constitution of Dasein. ... An entity for which, as being-in-the-world, its being is itself an issue, has, ontologically, a circular structure.[20]

## The World, and Things in This World

In its everyday concernful dwelling in the world, Dasein encounters a multitude of entities. These entities are of different kinds. Dasein may encounter other human beings; it may encounter animals, plants or other living creatures; it may encounter entities of the physical world that can perhaps be touched, held and observed closely; it may also encounter other entities of the physical world that can only be observed from a distance, such as the sun, the moon and the stars; it may also encounter intangible entities, such as a sound or a smell; or entities of human origin, such as a tool, a piece of cloth; or intangible (or immaterial) entities, such as a feeling, a sentiment, an illusion or a memory. Dasein finds itself involved in a world that is *opened* to it by its comportment towards beings. For Dasein, to exist is to be-in-the-world; upon this primordial *concerned dwelling*, Dasein founds its knowledge and belief. But establishing knowledge and forming beliefs are not our primary attitudes towards the world. The primary one is our concernful comportment towards the beings we encounter. Heidegger uses the term "care" (in German: *Sorge*) to denote exactly this: "Care, as a primordial structural totality, lies 'before' every factical 'attitude' and 'situation' of Dasein, and it does so existentially a priori; this means that it always lies *in* them".[21] Factical Dasein can be *absorbed* in its engagement with whatever it is engaged with; it's only when something temporarily

---

[20]*Being and Time*, p. 195/153.
[21]*Being and Time*, p. 238/193.

interrupts this absorption, that Dasein is forced to adopt an attitude that Heidegger described as *circumspective* or *theoretical*.[22] You are only thinking consciously about something when there is an interruption of your absorbed involvement that forces you to change your attitude.

From the vast multitude of the beings that can be encountered by Dasein, it follows that beings qua entities do not share the same kind of being. With regard to Dasein, a stone has a different kind of being from a tree, and both are beings of a different kind in comparison with, say, a human being, a computer keyboard or a work of art.

In *Being and Time*, Heidegger considers two main categories of beings or entities: human beings (i.e. Dasein) and non-human beings. He chooses not to speak systematically about other kinds of entities (e.g. animals, cultural artefacts, works of art) because his objective is not to provide an exhaustive catalogue of all possible kinds of being, but rather to make explicit two crucial aspects of the question. The first is the difference between human beings and all other kinds of entities; the second is the difference between entities that Dasein can use, which Heidegger calls *available* or *ready-to-hand* (in German: *vorhanden*); and entities that Dasein encounters in its dwelling in the world, which he describes as *occurrent* or *present-at*-hand (in German: *zuhanden*).[23] Available entities are there, ready to be employed in some way—for example, a hammer, a piece of clothing, a house. This is in contrast to occurrent entities, which are just encountered in their presence—for example, a rock or the broken branch of a tree. Of all the entities that Dasein encounters as available, there are those that Dasein uses for something specific. For example, a pen is used for writing. To these entities, Heidegger gives the collective name of *equipment* (in German: *Zeug*). He clarifies: "Taken strictly, there 'is' no such thing as an equipment. To the being of any equipment, there always belongs a totality of equipment, in which it can be this equipment that it is. Equipment

---

[22]See *Being and Time*, p. 409/357.

[23]In Heideggerian literature the terms *vorhanden* and *zuhanden* are usually rendered as *ready-to-hand* and *present-at-hand*, respectively. I find H. Dreyfus's alternative rendering, *available* and *occurrent*, more transparent. See Hubert L. Dreyfus, *Being-in-the-World: A Commentary on Heidegger's Being and Time, Division I* (Cambridge, MA: The MIT Press, 1991), p. xi.

is essentially 'something in-order-to...'".[24] What this means is simply that all equipment stands in reference to other equipment, in reference to a network of interconnections and dependencies that allows each and every entity that is equipment to be what it is. For example, a pen, together with ink and paper and writing surfaces and chairs, etc., all belong to an equipmental *whole* in which writing is possible. In general, Dasein uses equipment for something; likewise, equipment always has an *in-order-to* and cannot be thought of without it.

These two categories, equipment and available entities on the one hand, and occurrent entities, on the other, comprise the world of the human being. "But then", Heidegger asks,

> what about the other beings which, like man, are also part of the world: the animals and plants, the material things like the stone, for example? Are they merely parts of the world, as distinct from man who in addition *has* world? Or does the animal too have world, and if so, in what way? In the same way as man, or in some other way? And how would we grasp this otherness? And what about the stone? However crudely, certain distinctions immediately manifest themselves here. We can formulate these distinctions in the following three theses: [1.] the stone (material object) is *worldless*; [2.] the animal is *poor in world*; [3.] man is *world-forming*.[25]

These distinctions allow us to focus on the "*specific relation* that stone, animal, and man in each case has toward *world*. The distinctions in respect of this relation, or in the absence of such a relation, will help to set in relief what we call *world*".[26] Dasein is in-the-world and cannot but be so—but, also, a world is formed by Dasein, in its concernful dealings with it. This is not a "meta"-world: it does not exist parallel to some other world that could be thought of as more "real", or as world *proper*. It's not a world of epiphenomena, or ideas, that hides (or covers) a material world presumably existing alongside it. Heidegger wishes to

---

[24]Heidegger, *Being and Time*, p. 97/68.
[25]*The Fundamental Concepts of Metaphysics: World, Finitude, Solitude* [1929–30] (Bloomington: Indiana University Press, 1995), p. 177.
[26]*Fundamental Concepts*, p. 185.

side with neither an idealist nor a realist position. Both presuppose a conception of the human being as an observing intellect and make the subject–object relation the basis of their relation.[27] Heidegger, in contrast, wants us to see the necessarily circular process of world-forming, and dismisses both the realist and the idealist positions as inadequate for the task at hand, namely explicating Dasein's being-in-the-world. In more than one sense, Dasein's world is the only world that Dasein *can* occupy, a world that is collectively formed and shared with all other human beings. It is the world that Dasein *has*.

# Signs and Language

From the general conception of equipment as something that has an in-order-to, one specific kind of equipment stands out: it is the equipment whose in-order-to is to act as a reference to other equipment. This he calls *sign*. A sign indicates that other entities are equipment too. It allows the *equipmentality* of equipment to announce itself. "A sign is something ontically ready-to-hand [or available] which functions both as this definite equipment and as something indicative of the ontological structure of readiness-to-hand [or availability], of referential totalities, and of worldhood".[28]

Since signs are, in fact, equipment, they all belong to an equipmental whole, which is also pointed to by the fact that there *are* signs, i.e. entities that point to other entities as available. Signs reveal a referential totality:

> The 'for-the-sake-of-which' signifies an 'in-order-to'; this in turn, a 'towards-this'; the latter, an 'in-which' of letting something be involved; and that, in turn, the 'with-which' of an involvement. These relationships are bound up with one another as a primordial totality; they are what they are as this signifying in which Dasein gives itself beforehand its

---

[27]On this point, see *The Metaphysical Foundations of Logic* [1928] (Bloomington: Indiana University Press, 1992), p. 131.
[28]*Being and Time*, p. 114/82 (emphasis removed).

Being-in-the-world as something to be understood. The relational totality of this signifying we call '*significance*'. This is what makes up the structure of the world—the structure of that wherein Dasein as such already is.[29]

So, in Heidegger's conception, signs are special entities, in that they are ontic *and* ontological at the same time. They are ontic in that they exist as specific entities in this world and ontological in that they point to significance as such—just like being, which is not itself an entity, *significance* is not itself a sign either but rather that which makes signs possible.[30]

Language is a system of signs too. Words are entities which are available; they share the ontological characteristics of signs, and as such they reveal the ontological structure of their referential totality, that is, of a symbolically articulated world in which Dasein finds itself immersed. It is important to remember that this world is related to but not identical with the world which Dasein finds itself being-in; however, the two worlds, the symbolically articulated one and the one in which Dasein is being-in, are almost always confused and taken as one. It is because of this confusion that modern human beings tend to conceive being-in-the-world as a relationship between a subject and objects: because they tend to see the symbolically articulated world (which consists of references to available entities) as identical to the "world" part of the structure "being-in-the-world". For Dasein, it's not clear what kind of relationship exists between them. This question is obscured, just as the originary meaning of being was.

At this point, one might notice again a certain circularity: language, after all, is created by humans for whom being was, presumably, *already* an issue. How can it be that language allows being to *become* an issue? It's not difficult, however, to see that this apparent circularity is a product of the confusion between two different axes of reference and disappears as soon as the confusion is clarified. The first axis of reference is

---

[29]*Being and Time*, p. 120/87.

[30]It is interesting, in this connection, to draw the parallels between what Heidegger calls "significance" and what Lacan calls "signifierness". See below, pp. 135–140.

that of the individual human being—we could call it the "synchronic axis": For each and every human being, each and every one of us, language is what discloses and reveals being. However, it's only after we are within language that we can see human beings in their historical dimension or historicity—an axis of reference which could be called "diachronic".[31] In other words, the historicity of the human being, and that of language, become an issue for an individual only after language has revealed being to this particular individual; language as a structured whole antedates the individual.

Heidegger is not interested in the origins of language as such, an important but *ontic* question. It is of course important that language be ontically available, because only then can being be thematised. But this is a sort of a virtuous circle, an upwards spiral: language allows being to be thematised and being makes thinking possible. In Heidegger's words: "*Language makes manifest.* ... It does not produce ... discoveredness. Rather, discoveredness and its enactment of being ... are conditions of possibility for something becoming manifest".[32]

## Truth as Unconcealment

The world, collectively formed and shared by all human beings, features Dasein as the "open space" or clearing within which things can gather and ex-sist. In this sense, consciousness, observer, intellect and the like are mere corollaries of a primordial understanding of, or openness to, being. This allows the question of truth to be thematised more concretely.

Common views concerning truth always involve: an observing intellect; one or more observable states of affairs; some kind of language in which statements can be pronounced; and a procedure for deciding the

---

[31]Heidegger does not employ the terms "synchronic" and "diachronic". I borrow them from the linguist F. de Saussure, and use them to underline an aspect of Heidegger's analysis, which, while not explicitly termed by him, is, however, always present.

[32]Martin Heidegger, *History of the Concept of Time: Prolegomena* [1925] (Bloomington: Indiana University Press, 1992), p. 262.

truth value of a valid statement in that language by assessing the degree of correspondence between the statement and a given state of affairs. So, to give an example, one might have a statement such as, for example, "the cat is on the mat", and one can decide its veracity by checking its correspondence to a state of affairs: Is the cat on the mat? Yes, it is: then, the statement is true. No, it is not: Then the statement is not true. In short: "'The cat is on the mat' is true if and only if the cat is on the mat".[33]

How can one judge whether a cat is on a mat? Or, more generally, how can one wonder about any state of affairs, if the state of affairs in question is not already open to one's observing powers? And who or what can reassure us that one's judgements about a state of affairs are faithful and *correct*? Focusing on the case of the cat on the mat, one would need to know beforehand what a *cat* is, what a *mat* is, and what it is for a cat *to be on* a mat. Moreover, one needs a meaningful language in which these observations can be expressed as statements. In other words, the veracity, or truth value, of statements would indeed be judged by probing their correspondence to states of affairs that these statements pertain to, but there must have been something in place already. For Heidegger, that "something" is a primordial openness to being. Heidegger asserts that the foundation of "truth" is not the correspondence of statements to a state of affairs, but the primordial disclosure (or uncovering) of being to Dasein:

> 'Truth' is not a feature of correct propositions that are asserted of an 'object' by a human 'subject' and then 'are valid' somewhere, in what sphere we know not; rather, truth is disclosure of beings through which an openness essentially unfolds.[34]

According to Heidegger the term "truth" (in Latin: *veritas*) is a misled attempt to translate the original ancient Greek concept of *aletheia*

---

[33]See also below, p. 145n31.

[34]Martin Heidegger, 'On the Essense of Truth' [1930], in William Mcneill (ed.), *Pathmarks* (Cambridge: Cambridge University Press, 1998), 136–154, p. 146.

(in Greek: αλήθεια). The ancient Greek philosophers, at least before Plato, were able to see that "truth" is founded on the removal (privative *a-*) of forgetfulness or *lethe* (in Greek: λήθη): *a-letheia*. It was only after Plato that the concept of a-letheia declined into correctness, and truth was conceptualised as agreement. As Plato's allegory of the cave indicates, access to entities was now understood as mediated by ideas, which took priority.

> This 'allegory' [of the cave] contains Plato's 'doctrine' of truth, for the 'allegory' is grounded on the unspoken event whereby ιδέα gains dominance over αλήθεια. ... Thus, the priority of ιδέα and ιδείν over αλήθεια results in a transformation in the essence of truth. Truth becomes ορθότης, the correctness of apprehending and asserting.[35]

Heidegger's return to truth as a-letheia captures more concretely the phenomenon of Dasein's openness of comportment towards being. Things present themselves to Dasein *as they are* insofar as Dasein has already had a primordial understanding of being. "If the correctness (truth) of statements becomes possible only through this openness of comportment, then what first makes correctness possible must with more original legitimacy be taken as the essence of truth".[36] A-letheia is much more basic (in the sense of *fundamental*) than truth thought of as correspondence.

> Dasein, as constituted by disclosedness, is essentially in the truth. Disclosedness is a kind of being which is essential to Dasein. 'There is' truth only in so far as Dasein *is* and so long as Dasein *is*. Entities are uncovered only when Dasein is; and only as long as Dasein is, are they disclosed.[37]

The question, however, is now this: if the essence of truth is that of unconcealment or revelation, and not of correspondence, what is the

---

[35]'On the Essense of Truth', *Pathmarks*, pp. 176–177.
[36]'On the Essense of Truth', *Pathmarks*, p. 142.
[37]*Being and Time*, p. 269/226.

origin of this revelation? For Heidegger, this is but another form of the question of being. Discussing truth (qua a-letheia) as revelation is tantamount to discussing Dasein's openness and comportment to being. "Being-true, as being-uncovering, is in turn ontologically possible only on the basis of being-in-the-world. This latter phenomenon, which we have known as a basic state of Dasein, is the *foundation* for the primordial phenomenon of truth".[38] It follows from this that "being (not entities) is something which 'there is' only in so far as truth is. And truth *is* only insofar as and as long as Dasein *is*. Being and truth 'are' equiprimordially".[39] Heidegger's question, then, takes this form: What can be said about the origin of Dasein's primordial openness to being? We will have to keep this question open for the moment.

## Being-with Others, Authenticity, the "They"

A totality of interconnected references and dependences is revealed qua world to Dasein through language. Everything that Dasein experiences in its world is shared with other human beings in this world, not only in the ontic sense that equipment or other entities can—and *will*—be shared, but also in the sense that the referential totality of the world, as revealed by language, as well as language itself, both ontically and ontologically, are also shared. When other people are encountered by Dasein, they are not encountered as objects, which would then need to be recognised by Dasein as beings similar to itself. Rather, they are encountered as being-there, together with Dasein, in the world in which they all dwell. As Heidegger writes, "the world of Dasein is a *with-world*. Being-in is *being-with* Others. Their being-in-themselves within-the-world is *Dasein-with* [in German: *Mitdasein*]".[40]

In its everyday being-with others, Dasein finds itself absorbed by them. The world that Dasein shares with them is a world that dictates

---

[38] *Being and Time*, p. 261/219.
[39] *Being and Time*, p. 272/230.
[40] *Being and Time*, pp. 154–155/118.

every aspect of Dasein's comportment towards the beings it reveals to it. The totality of these beings forms a kind of a public "environment" in which any and all non-human beings are shared, while any and all other human beings are averaged and indefinite.

For Heidegger, the distinction between self and others, between I and You, is not a primordial one; it does not belong structurally to Dasein's being-in-the-world and being-with others. The distinction is between Dasein and the "they" (in German: *das Man*), or, as we could say, between the individual and the collective. Now, Dasein is introduced as this kind of being which is always "mine". And yet Dasein's world, as disclosed to it by language, is always a shared world; ontologically, Dasein cannot but *be-with* others.

> This being-with-one-another dissolves one's own Dasein completely into the kind of being of 'the Others', in such a way, indeed, that the Others, as distinguishable and explicit, vanish more and more. In this inconspicuousness and unascertainability, the real dictatorship of the 'they' is unfolded. We take pleasure and enjoy ourselves as *they* take pleasure; we read, see, and judge about literature and art as *they* see and judge; likewise we shrink back from the 'great mass' as *they* shrink back; we find 'shocking' what *they* find shocking. The 'they', which is nothing definite, and which all are, though not as the sum, prescribes the kind of being of everydayness.[41]

If such is the case, what is the scope of Dasein's *mineness*? "Mine" as opposed to—what? Yours? Whose?

Heidegger explores the question by identifying a distinction between what is Dasein's own (i.e. "mine") and what is shared. He employs the term "authentic" (in German: *eigentlich*) to designate what is Dasein's own—i.e. not shared—and contrasts it to what is "inauthentic" (and shared).

> As modes of being, *authenticity* and *inauthenticity* (these expressions have been chosen terminologically in a strict sense) are both grounded in the

---

[41] *Being and Time*, pp. 164/126–127.

fact that any Dasein whatsoever is characterized by mineness. But the inauthenticity of Dasein does not signify any 'less' being or any 'lower' degree of being. Rather it is the case that even in its fullest concretion Dasein can be characterized by inauthenticity—when busy, when excited, when interested, when ready for enjoyment.[42]

The concept of authenticity reflects the different possibilities of Dasein's comportment towards being in reference to what is Dasein's own or shared.[43] As an ontological concept, authenticity reflects Dasein's position in the world vis-à-vis the "they"; and as an ontic concept, it refers to choice and freedom. Dasein comports itself towards the world at any given moment but is not restricted there; it is always in the world presently but pointing to a possibility of being that is *not yet*. In conventional terms, one could say that in its concernful comportment towards entities, Dasein always opens up *future* possibilities.

## Time, Historicity, and the "Event"

To be opened up to possibilities of being: this is Dasein's *historicity*. Dasein is historical, and with it the world itself is historical. Historicity, however, reveals time. In every in-order-to and for-the-sake-of-which, what is revealed is time. Time is that which makes the structure of equipmentality possible. Time is also closely related to temporality, i.e. that which allows beings to "step outside" themselves and become temporally meaningful in the three "*ek-stases*", *future*, *present* and *past*.

One of Dasein's possibilities is revealed as the one with the utmost authenticity, i.e. one "*which is one's ownmost, which is non-relational, and which is not to be outstripped*".[44] This possibility is *death*, "the possibility

---

[42] *Being and Time*, p. 68/43.

[43] "Authenticity" has certain positive connotations in English that do not exist in the German original and give the false impression that "authentic" is somehow better, or truer, than "inauthentic". In German the word *eigentlich* comes from the adjective *eigen* which means *own, separate, particular*, and could be rendered as something like *one's very own*.

[44] Heidegger, *Being and Time*, pp. 294/250–251 (emphasis in the original).

of the absolute impossibility of Dasein".[45] Death, in this conjecture, is not conceived ontically—i.e. as the unavoidable fact of one's demise—but ontologically. Dasein is fundamentally oriented in time as a *being-towards-death*. Death, as the possibility of an absolute impossibility, establishes ontologically Dasein's finitude and provides Dasein with a trajectory and an end.

The text of *Being and Time* ends with a question: "Does *time* itself manifest itself as the horizon of being?"[46] Heidegger does not provide an explicit answer; he returns to the question again and again. Several years later, he writes: "Being and time determine each other reciprocally, but in such a manner that neither can the former—being—be addressed as something temporal nor can the latter—time—be addressed as a being".[47] The ontic presence of beings before Dasein implies and *requires* temporality. Or, in other words, it is because there *is* time that being has a meaning. The meaning is given by Dasein. In this sense, time is also the horizon of Dasein. Historicity is only possible because of the world and death. In a way that is vaguely similar to the way in which signs point ontologically to signification as such, the certainty of one's own death gives a foundation to Dasein's historicity, a direction (or sense) to time, and points ontologically to Dasein's possibilities. To put it differently, it is because there is death that the ek-static, or historical, dimension of Dasein—as a being rooted in a past and headed towards a future—is revealed. The importance that Heidegger gives to death, then, does not reflect some morbid preoccupation with the non-living on his part. Quite the opposite. Death is what provides an ontological foundation for Dasein's authenticity and Dasein's possibilities, in terms of that for-the-sake-of-which Dasein is orienting itself. Indeed, one could say that for Heidegger the ontological certainty of death is that what opens up Dasein to set about doing its things—in the sense that it provides Dasein with a history and a

---

[45]*Being and Time*, p. 294/250.

[46]*Being and Time*, p. 488/437. The term "horizon" here needs to be understood as synonym to a term like *determinant*.

[47]'Time and Being' [1962], in *On Time and Being* (New York: Harper & Row, 1972), 1–24, p. 3.

trajectory. Death, history and trajectory are unique for each and every human being; the present, however, is always shared.

With *Being and Time*, Heidegger had reached the understanding that being is disclosed as presence within a framework of *primordial* time.

> But still more elemental than the circumstance that the 'time factor' is one that occurs in the sciences of history and Nature, is the fact that before Dasein does any thematical research, it 'reckons with time' and regulates itself according to it. And here again what remains decisive is Dasein's way of 'reckoning with its time'—a way of reckoning which precedes any use of measuring equipment by which time can be determined. The reckoning is prior to such equipment, and is what makes anything like the use of clocks possible at all.[48]

Still, speaking about time in this context it becomes clear that primordial temporality is revealed to Dasein together with being and the world.[49] If that's the case, what would be the horizon of time itself? In other words, if being is disclosed as presence, is there a way to attend to *this* phenomenon—disclosure of being—more closely? How can one escape this chicken-and-egg situation?

The breakthrough, for Heidegger, came when he recognised that the question *cannot* be answered, because being and time belong together. Time is the horizon of being, but also time is determined by being. Heidegger uses the term Ereignis to denote their belonging together. He writes: "What determines both, time and being, in their own, that is, in their belonging together, we shall call: Ereignis, the event of appropriation".[50] The term represents an attempt to capture the

---

[48]*Being and Time*, p. 456/404.

[49]M. Roubach has argued that in Heidegger's thought the framework of primordial temporality rests upon the concept of number and counting. As he writes "Number links the three strata of time: primordial temporality, world-time and ordinary time. That is, counting connects primordial temporality, which is essentially finite, to measured time, which is infinite. By virtue of this connection, infinite time is dependent on finite primordial time". (Michael Roubach, *Being and Number in Heidegger's Thought* (London: Continuum, 2008), pp. 59–60).

[50]Heidegger, "Time and Being", *On Time and Being*, p. 19. *Ereignis* in German means *event* and Heidegger had already used the term in *Being and Time* in this sense. Gradually, he allowed it to obtain other connotations, more notably the connotation of making something one's own. It is in

logical (rather than temporal) moment when Dasein opens itself up to the world (i.e. to being, time, entities, equipment, signs, language). In a way, Dasein becomes the topos (and agent) of the *event* (of appropriation) that renders being into truth through language (as logos, i.e. the collection or gathering of entities). Heidegger describes the world as always co-created and shared by all human beings. But the event of appropriation unfolds, so to speak, on a "synchronic" axis. But this axis can only be visible on a "diachronic" background.[51] Thus, being and truth are revealed as historical in a deep, ontological sense. To emphasise this novel understanding, Heidegger starts employing the archaic spelling *Seyn* (instead of Sein), which has been rendered as *beyng* (instead of being).

## "Turning" Away from Fundamental Ontology

Heidegger's approach to the question of being was originally conceived as an attempt at fundamental ontology, which began with *Being and Time*. His initial focus was on deconstructing or *destroying* the history of ontology. His insight was that the traditional distinction between subject and object obscures the modes of engagement of the human being, or Dasein, with the world. By pursuing a deep exploration of Dasein's most basic structure, which he denoted as *being-in-the-world*, Heidegger made visible the centrality of a circle of understanding whereby the agents comprising the structure in question, as well as all aspects and facets of the structure, need to be revealed and considered simultaneously. It became clear that traditional terminology of philosophy could not be up to the task. It was not a question of creating a "new" or "better" fundamental ontology. To talk about ontology as such would be like making it possible to succumb to the same old error—namely

---

this sense that he uses it here, and to reflect this, the term has been sometimes rendered by means of the neologism *enowning*, or as *appropriating* or *taking over something*. I choose here to render it as *appropriation* or *event of appropriation*.

[51]See above, p. 35n31.

mistaking the structure of being-in-the-world as a subject–object relationship whereby Dasein as an observer studies and discusses the being
of beings qua objects. Heidegger gradually came to understand that the
task he had originally set for himself—that of explicating the meaning
of being—was tantamount to going beyond fundamental ontology. He
abandoned the project of *Being and Time* and, during what has been
labelled as his *turn* (In German: *Kehre*), stopped using some of his earlier concepts and introduced others.

There is a significant debate regarding Heidegger's "turn", its radicality, and its import.[52] In my view, most of the basic questions integral to
Heidegger's thinking remain as present and pressing as ever, both before
and after this turn. For example, some thirty odd years after *Being and
Time*, one can see him in his Zollikon Seminars returning to the same
fundamental questions and using more or less the same terminology.
William Richardson has suggested designating the pre-turn Heidegger
as "Heidegger I", and the one after the turn as "Heidegger II".[53] But, as
Heidegger himself commented, "only by way of what Heidegger I has
thought does one gain access to what is to-be-thought by Heidegger II.
But Heidegger I becomes possible only if it is contained in Heidegger
II".[54]

"Heidegger II" ceased conceiving of the question of being as a question of an ahistorical fundamental ontology and saw it as a question of
world disclosure, historicity and language. Groping his way into the
question of being allowed him to recognise it as a question about the
ways in which being is historical and about the world epochs revealed
by it. This, in turn, opened a way for him to focus more clearly on the
specifics of the modern epoch, the epoch of science and technology.

---

[52]See, for example, Joan Stambaugh, 'The Turn', in Babette E. Babich (ed.), *From Phenomenology
to Thought, Errancy, and Desire: Essays in Honor of William J. Richardson, S.J.* (Dordrecht: Kluwer
Academic, 1995), 209–212.

[53]William J. Richardson, *Heidegger: Through Phenomenology to Thought* [1963] (New York:
Fordham University Press, 2003), p. 624.

[54]Heidegger, 'Preface (Letter to W. Richardson)', p. xxii.

This new epoch had begun with Descartes, who had conceived of the human being as an agent of knowledge, striving to find absolute certainty from a starting point of absolute doubt. This was the locus of Descartes's cogito, which Heidegger had targeted in *Being and Time*. There, he wrote about the phenomenological destruction of the "cogito sum" which was supposed to be completed in Part 2, Division 2 of *Being and Time*; however, he did not complete it. Instead, he turned his attention to the specifics of the new epoch. The modern, scientific world view is obscuring crucial aspects of Dasein's engagement with the world. Modern man seems to be uninterested in realising his or her authenticity, losing focus on what is his or her *own* (in the Heideggerian understanding). In the time of modernity, Dasein seems to be increasingly under the sway of the *they*. Dasein's comportment towards other human beings becomes increasingly similar to Dasein's comportment towards things: human beings are reduced to mere occurrent objects or available tools.

Heidegger's critique of technology, science, and the modern, mechanistic, world could be seen as a logical outcome of his attempt at elucidating the question of being. By tracing truth to a-letheia, and connecting being to truth as logos, Heidegger became more and more concerned with the forgetfulness of being. It was no longer an observation of a difficulty in the path of understanding, as he has it in *Being and Time*; it was not even just a question of identifying something that the ancients saw but the moderns have lost—i.e. an ontic manifestation of the historicity of being. It became a matter of great moral urgency, revealing a kind of *nostalgia*, as Jacques Derrida has put it—a "myth of a purely maternal or paternal language, a lost country of thought".[55]

For Heidegger, Dasein has a duty towards being, a task of *thinking* as he calls it. The task is to strive against its forgetfulness, exemplified, in his view, in the advent of modern technology, science, cybernetics etc. It is, in other words, a task to bring the question of being to the forefront. It is an urgent task:

---

[55]Jacques Derrida, 'Différance' [1968], in *Margins of Philosophy* (Brighton: The Harvester Press, 1982), 1–27, p. 27.

Does the name for the task of thinking then read instead of Being and Time: Opening and Presence? But where does the opening come from and how is it given? … The task of thinking would then be the surrender of previous thinking to the determination of the matter of thinking.[56]

In this sense, one can see the whole philosophical trajectory of Heidegger as a trajectory towards disappointment and moral despair. Adopting the modern world view involved disregarding fundamental aspects of Dasein's comportment towards being. Heidegger made it his task to bring this question back to the fore—to proceed as a moral, or, rather, as a *deontic* philosopher. Indeed, he gradually revealed himself as a thinker who was more attentive to deontic questions pertaining to authenticity, deficient understanding of being, and deficient modes of comportment towards the world. In a way, we can say that Heidegger's later thinking remained ontological but had now an eye to the ontic. He was increasingly concerned about the malaises of modernity and was no longer convinced that philosophy alone was enough to counteract what he saw as decline. In his posthumously published interview with *Der Spiegel*, he was clear:

Philosophy will be unable to effect any immediate change in the current state of the world. This is true not only of philosophy but of all purely human reflection and endeavour. Only a god can save us. The only possibility available to us is that by thinking and poetizing we prepare a readiness for the appearance of a god, or for the absence of a god in [our] decline, insofar as in view of the absent god we are in a state of decline.[57]

It might not be so easy for us to decide how to interpret Heidegger's position vis-à-vis this "state of decline". His silence regarding Nazi crimes has been described, as we saw, as a failure of thinking.[58] After the

---

[56]Heidegger, 'End of Philosophy', *On Time and Being*, p. 73.
[57]'"Only a God Can Save Us": The Spiegel Interview' [1976 (1966)], in Thomas Sheehan (ed.), *Heidegger: The Man and the Thinker* (New Brunswick: Transaction Publishers, 2010), 45–67, p. 57.
[58]See above, p. 10.

publication in 2014 of Heidegger's *Black Notebooks*, David Farrell Krell attempted a further interpretation:

> To say the least, there is something about Heidegger's silence even after the War that reflects an astonishing mindlessness. … The militancy of Heidegger's nationalism which seems to be responsible for much if not all of the oblivion, is truly disconcerting. … No reader of Heidegger can or should be able to make his or her peace with Heidegger's (or their own) nationalism, militancy, and decisionism.[59]

Krell notes that the "odd alternating current of piety and polemic" sometimes evident in Heidegger's work of the period needs to be understood in what he (Krell) calls:

> Heidegger's *paranoetic* thinking. Not *paranoid* thinking, inasmuch as here there is no being, no *Seiendes*, to be feared and hated. … Not paranoid thinking inasmuch as in Heidegger's case there is no being that can be sought out and blamed for the unspeakable catastrophe that is about to advene.[60]

This is a situation "worse than paranoia", Krell argues, in which "no one and no thing is to blame, but only beyng".[61] Whether Krell is onto something or not is beyond the scope of this book. The important thing, in my view, is to recognise that after the turn Heidegger became more and more distant from the phenomenological enquiries of his early work. Dominique Janicaud has commented that:

> the essential difference that seems to characterise the thinking of 'Heidegger II' is that this thinking slides toward apolitics by undergoing a seemingly negligible displacement, not by default, but by clear design. … This explicitly 'apolitical' attitude, which has nothing to do with a regular

---

[59]David Farrell Krell, *Ecstasy, Catastrophe: Heidegger from Being and Time to the Black Notebooks* (Albany: State University of New York Press, 2015), pp. 189–190.

[60]*Daimon Life: Heidegger and Life-Philosophy* (Bloomington: Indiana University Press, 1992), p. 199.

[61]*Ecstasy, Catastrophe*, pp. 6–7.

indifference toward politics or with the 'apolitical' stance of *Being and Time*, is based upon a re-interpretation of the world situation as a function of his reading of the history of metaphysics.[62]

Janicaud has proposed the name "destinal historicalism" for this thinking that sees metaphysics conceived as the history of being. The most concrete product of this destinal historicalism has been Heidegger's growing concern about the uncritical acceptance of what he called modern technological thinking and world view, and his critique of science.

◈    ◈    ◈

# Bibliography

DERRIDA, JACQUES, 'Différance' [1968], trans. Alan Bass, in *Margins of Philosophy* (Brighton: The Harvester Press, 1982), 1–27.

DREYFUS, HUBERT L., *Being-in-the-World: A Commentary on Heidegger's Being and Time, Division I* (Cambridge, MA: The MIT Press, 1991).

HEIDEGGER, MARTIN, *Being and Time* [1927], trans. John Macquarrie and Edward Robinson (Malden, MA: Blackwell Publishers, 1962).

———, 'The End of Philosophy and the Task of Thinking' [1964], trans. Joan Stambaugh, in *On Time and Being* (New York: Harper & Row, 1972), 55–73.

———, *The Fundamental Concepts of Metaphysics: World, Finitude, Solitude* [1929–30], trans. William McNeill and Nicholas Walker (Bloomington: Indiana University Press, 1995).

———, *History of the Concept of Time: Prolegomena* [1925], trans. Theodore Kisiel (Bloomington: Indiana University Press, 1992).

———, 'Letter on Humanism' [1947], trans. Frank A. Capuzzi, in William McNeill (ed.), *Pathmarks* (Cambridge: Cambridge University Press, 1978), 239–276.

———, *The Metaphysical Foundations of Logic* [1928], trans. Michael Heim (Bloomington: Indiana University Press, 1992).

---

[62]Dominique Janicaud, *The Shadow of That Thought* (Evanston, IL: Northwestern University Press, 1996), pp. 67–68.

————, 'On the Essense of Truth' [1930], trans. John Sallis, in William McNeill (ed.), *Pathmarks* (Cambridge: Cambridge University Press, 1998), 136–154.

————, '"Only a God Can Save Us"': The Spiegel Interview' [1976 (1966)], trans. William J. Richardson, in Thomas Sheehan (ed.), *Heidegger: The Man and the Thinker* (New Brunswick: Transaction Publishers, 2010), 45–67.

————, 'Preface (Letter to W. Richardson)' in William J. Richardson, *Heidegger: Through Phenomenology to Thought* (New York: Fordham University Press, 2003), viii–xxiii.

————, 'Time and Being' [1962], trans. Joan Stambaugh, in *On Time and Being* (New York: Harper & Row, 1972), 1–24.

Janicaud, Dominique, *The Shadow of That Thought*, trans. Michael Gendre (Evanston, IL: Northwestern University Press, 1996).

Krell, David Farrell, *Daimon Life: Heidegger and Life-Philosophy* (Bloomington: Indiana University Press, 1992).

————, *Ecstasy, Catastrophe: Heidegger from Being and Time to the Black Notebooks* (Albany: State University of New York Press, 2015).

Polt, Richard, *Heidegger: An Introduction* (London: Routledge, 1999).

Richardson, William J., *Heidegger: Through Phenomenology to Thought* [1963] (New York: Fordham University Press, 2003).

Roubach, Michael, *Being and Number in Heidegger's Thought*, trans. Nessa Olshansky-Ashtar (London: Continuum, 2008).

Sheehan, Thomas, *Making Sense of Heidegger: A Paradigm Shift* (London: Rowman & Littlefield, 2015).

Stambaugh, Joan, 'The Turn' in Babette E. Babich (ed.), *From Phenomenology to Thought, Errancy, and Desire: Essays in Honor of William J. Richardson, S.J.* (Phenomenologica, 133; Dordrecht: Kluwer Academic, 1995), 209–212.

# 3

# A Critique of Science and Psychoanalysis

In our everyday engagement with our world, we human beings create inter-pretative and explanatory narratives of that world, as well as of our involve-ment with it. We are *curious* about this world. At different times and in different societies, the demands human beings make on their explanatory systems are dissimilar and depend upon their intended uses. At the basis of all engagement with the world, there is a similar basic assumption, or expec-tation, or hope, namely that the world is intelligible, that is, it makes (some) sense. Whether it is the whims of a deity, animal, or the weather, or a scien-tific understanding of the workings of nature, the underlying assumption is that things can be explained, that they are somehow knowable.

Strictly speaking, the question is not about what is *knowable* as such, but rather about including all encounterable entities in a referential totality where things can make *sense* and be employed in some way, *for-the-sake-of* or *in-order-to* something. Our efforts can differ in terms of their systematicity and scope. A civilisation might choose to rely on some set of loosely connected myths; or, on the contrary, it might decide to speak about the cosmos as a totality. In the most general sense, we could give the name "science" to the systematisation of the multitudes of cross-referenced concepts, statements and descriptions of

© The Author(s) 2019
C. Tombras, *Discourse Ontology*, The Palgrave Lacan Series,
https://doi.org/10.1007/978-3-030-13662-8_3

entities we can discern in the world we share. Understood in this sense, we can see that science and the scientific method has been central in Heidegger's questioning throughout his life. Heidegger followed the methodological distinction between natural and human sciences rigorously established by the German philosopher Wilhelm Dilthey in his *Introduction to the Human Sciences* of 1883. Dilthey had argued that there is a limit to the kind of theoretical regularities that can be established in human sciences. Psychology, in particular, as a science dealing with human beings, cannot, according to Dilthey, examine them apart from their interactions with society.

For a period of ten good years, sciences and more generally the scientific method became the focus of a series of seminars given by Heidegger at Zollikon, Switzerland, home of Medard Boss. Boss was a Swiss psychiatrist who had developed a long-lasting friendship with Heidegger since he first contacted him in 1947. The seminars started in 1959 and continued regularly—until Heidegger's physical powers started declining because of his age.[1]

A fundamental premise of modern science is its objectivity, rigorously guaranteed by its reliance on observations, evidence, theoretical models, hypotheses and experimental verification. At the heart of what scientists claim to do lies the assumption that there is in principle a correspondence between reality and the world on the one hand, and the scientific theories, models, and data that scientists work with. Modern science's main supposition is that processes of nature conform to laws. Conformity to a law means that objects of nature are measurable and that processes in nature can be precisely described, represented and calculated with the help of appropriate mathematical models. Heidegger asserted that scientists take this conformity for granted and fail to recognise that their assumptions and methods already entail a number of

---

[1] All the seminars' protocols, together with parts of conversations between Heidegger and Boss, as well as the fragments of their correspondence, have been published in book form, forming the most comprehensive, yet at times fragmentary, collection of Heidegger's thoughts about psychiatry, psychology and, especially, psychoanalysis. See Martin Heidegger, *Zollikon Seminars: Protocols, Conversations, Letters*, ed. Medard Boss (Evanston, IL: Northwestern University Press, 2001).

tacit, unexamined, presuppositions both of their subject matter as well as of their own scientific ways to approach it. Science fails to acknowledge its limitations, and tends, uncritically, to regard anything not conforming to its "scientific" view with arrogance. The implicit aim of the modern scientific method is, according to Heidegger, the control and use of nature.[2] But this was not always the case.

# From the Ancient to the Modern World

In an early systematisation of what could be called ancient science (and world view), Aristotle understood human knowledge within a rational framework of observations and general principles. As historian of science J. Losee explains, for Aristotle a scientist would induce "explanatory principles from the phenomena to be explained, and then deduce statements about the phenomena from premises which include these principles".[3] In terms of methodology, science in the times of Aristotle was not so very different from science as we understand it now. What *was* radically different, however, was the world view.

For Alexandre Koyré, a philosopher of science who was decidedly influenced by Husserl's phenomenology, the key aspects of the ancient world view were:

(a) the belief in the existence of specific 'natures' and (b) the belief in the existence of a Cosmos, i.e., the belief in the existence of principles of order by virtue of which the totality of real beings form a (naturally) well-ordered whole. … Everything in the Universe has its proper place in conformity with its nature.[4]

[2]*Zollikon Seminars*, p. 107.
[3]John Losee, *A Historical Introduction to the Philosophy of Science* (Oxford: Oxford University Press, 2001), p. 5.
[4]Alexandre Koyré, *Galileo Studies* [1939] (Hassocks, Sussex: The Harvester Press, 1978), p. 5. Koyré has written extensively about the passing from what he called the *closed world* or Cosmos of the ancients to the *infinite universe* of modern science. See *From the Closed World to the Infinite Universe* (Baltimore: The Johns Hopkins Press, 1957); and "The Origins of Modern Science: A New Interpretation" *Diogenes*, 4/16 (1956), 1–22.

The ancient Greeks explained the observed differences between the earthly and the heavenly world by referring to the natural order or *nature* of things.[5] Take, for example, motion. All motion on Earth seemed to be irregular and always unfolding in such a way that entities were either at rest or striving to return to a point of rest, an "end", or *telos* (in Greek: τέλος). This was their natural place. More generally, the earthly world in its totality was seen as an imperfect world, where things had not yet reached their *telos*. If not there already, it would make its way, so to speak, to reach it. All transformation and change would need an external cause, and the telos of all change would conform to the nature of the thing undergoing the change.

The antithesis between the earthly and heavenly worlds was first postulated by the Pythagoreans and systematised by Aristotle in his theory of causality.[6] Aristotle distinguished between four types of cause: material, formal, final, and efficient.[7] Let us, for example, consider a silversmith who has received an order to make a silver bowl and begins work to make it. According to Aristotle, the *final* cause (in Greek: τελικόν αίτιον) is the bowl for which the order was given; the *formal* cause (in Greek: ειδικόν αίτιον) is the shape an object must have in order to be thought of as a bowl; the *material* cause (in Greek: υλικόν αίτιον) is

---

[5]The term they used was *physis* (in Greek: φύσις), a term derived from verb φύω that meant *bring forth, produce*, etc. The root is cognate with words like physics (a direct derivation) and future (via the latin *futūrus*, that meant *about to be*).

[6]For a fuller discussion of Aristotle's theory of causality, see W. K. C. Guthrie, *Aristotle, an Encounter* (Cambridge: Cambridge University Press, 1981), pp. 223–233, 235–240. See also Wihelm Windelband, *A History of Philosophy: With Especial Reference to the Formation and Development of Its Problems and Conceptions* (New York: The Macmillan Company, 1901), pp. 143–145; and Andrea Falcon, 'Aristotle on Causality' *The Stanford Encyclopedia of Philosophy* (Spring 2015 Edition), Edward N. Zalta (ed.), https://plato.stanford.edu/archives/spr2015/entries/aristotle-causality/. For Heidegger's discussion of Aristotelian causation, see Heidegger, *Zollikon Seminars*, p. 19. For a more general discussion of Aristotelian physics, see Koyré, *Galileo Studies*, pp. 4–8.

[7]Aristotle's theory is easier to follow if one remembers that the term cause (in Greek: αίτιον) had many different meanings in ancient Greek. It means *responsible for*, but also *principle* or *starting point* (in Greek: αρχή); *motive* or *occasion* (in Greek: αφορμή); and *blame* or *guilt*. More specifically, in Aristotle's theory, cause can be thought as an attempt to interpret or explain an observed change, as an answer to the question *why*. Similar meanings are still present in the modern English term, but their visibility is less prominent, especially when considering questions of causality in the context of scientific research.

what a bowl is supposed to be made of (e.g. silver); and the *efficient* cause (in Greek: ποιητικόν αἴτιον) is what is needed in order to actually get a bowl done when all the other causes are known or given—in other words, the craftsman himself. Aristotle also spoke about a fifth type of cause, *incidental* (in Greek: κατὰ συμβεβηκός αἴτιον), which can be seen in action where two or more chains of events unexpectedly intersect; he differentiated between *tuché* (sometimes spelled as *tyché*; in Greek: τύχη), that is, chance in the purposive world of humans, and *automaton* (in Greek: αὐτόματον), that is, non-purposeful concurrence in a sphere of events.[8]

All these were referring to earthly things. For example, applying the concept of the efficient cause to the motion of bodies, Aristotle postulated that if something is moving, it moves because something else is making it move (e.g. by pulling or pushing it). In the ancient world view, any earthly movement will continue in order to reach its *telos* or end, i.e. its final cause. As soon as it reaches it, movement stops. As we discussed earlier, Aristotle's theory of motion was far from perfect, failing, for example, to explain properly the phenomenon of projectile motion.[9] But it did describe satisfactorily the easily observable differentiation between the earthly and the celestial worlds: celestial bodies—e.g. the sun, the stars, the moon—appeared to be moving perpetually in circles. The heavenly world was seen as perfect and eternal. No transformation or change was conceivable there. Celestial motion did not seem to have an "end", in contrast to what appeared to be the case on Earth.

People no longer think of the world in the same way. In the modern, scientific world view, there is no difference whatsoever between what is happening here on Earth and what is happening in the sky. Things do

---

[8]The standard translations, *fortune* for tuché and *chance* for automaton, are confounding rather than clarifying the distinction here. As B. Cassin explains, "*Automaton* refers to any appearance of finality whatsoever; but we speak of *tuché* only when the end lets itself be read in terms of a deliberate choice or decision … that is characteristic of a *praxis*, or a practical agent." (Barbara Cassin, '*Tuché* and *automaton* in Aristotle' [2004], in Barbara Cassin (ed.), *Dictionary of Untranslatables* (Princeton: Princeton University Press, 2014), 534).

[9]See above, p. 3.

not move to reach their "end", and in fact, there is no such a thing as an "end" of motion. Motion will continue unaltered for as long as something (a "force") will cause it to change; this might be a direct force such as gravity or an indirect one such as friction. Crucially, in the modern, scientific world view there is no need for an final cause or a motive. In nature, things do not happen because someone or something causes or wills them to happen. They just happen.

But, if a final cause is not to be postulated, what makes things happen? Take, for example, a phenomenon like free fall. If the motion of objects falling is *not* to be understood by invoking the nature of things, what is that that makes it happen? What makes things fall? This is what Galileo, the first scientist of modernity, set out to understand.

## The Era of Galileo

Contrary to what is commonly accepted, Galileo was not the great experimenter we usually think; his epistemology was just as Archimedean as was that of the ancients: deductive, rational, rigorous, abstract. The difference lay in the three basic assumptions on which his world view was built. They were not the product of his world view, but rather what made it possible.

The first assumption is that there is no difference between earth and the heavens—or, more abstractly, that space and time are homogenous. The second is that change is the result of an ongoing process—and not a disruption brought about by a cause as in the Aristotelian understanding. And the third is the assumption that all processes in nature are governed by laws that can be written as mathematical formulas.

Based on these assumptions, Galileo was able to construct a modern, scientific world view, whereby nature is set up as a homogenous and uniform domain of space and time; points of mass move in space and time in conformity to some natural law; the law, or laws, can be written down as formulas; and the effects of these laws can be calculated.

So, as Koyré writes, Galileo's focus

is not the fact of the fall itself; it is not a matter of discovering the *cause* of the bodies' fall. What he is looking for is the *essence* of the motion of fall. ... The problem is to discover the nature of this kind of motion, its essence, or one might say, its *definition* ... It is this which would constitute ... that fundamental axiom, from which it would then be possible to deduce everything else.[10]

In other words, what Galileo is after is the *law* of free fall.

It is important to recognise here that in this modern world view, fundamental concepts such as space, motion, time and causality are taken for granted. Galileo is not reflecting further on them, even though they are of crucial importance for his enterprise. Galileo is not positing a hypothesis about space or time; he is not *postulating* there are time and space—he accepts it. Heidegger explains:

[Galileo] accepts without question: space, motion, time, and causality. What does it mean to say—I accept something like space? I accept that there is something like space and, even more, that I have a relationship to space and time. This *acceptio* is not arbitrary, but contains necessary relationships to space, time, and causality in which I stand. Otherwise I could not reach for a glass on the table. No one can experiment with these [a priori] assumptions. That there is space is not a proposition of physics. What kind of proposition is it? What does it indicate about the human being that such suppositions are possible for him? It indicates that he finds himself comported to space, time, and causality from the beginning.[11]

This is to say that Galileo did not reach conclusions about space, time or causality by reflecting inductively on the phenomena he studied. He posits them from the beginning. His assumptions are metaphysical.[12] They provide him with the conceptual scaffolding that is absolutely required for his theories to be at all conceivable, let alone stated.

---

[10]Koyré, *Galileo Studies*, p. 68.

[11]Heidegger, *Zollikon Seminars*, p. 28.

[12]The term metaphysical is meant here in the sense that it has in Aristotle, namely that of a first or fundamental assumption that comes before any specific enquiry.

## Regional Ontologies

Galileo constructs a modern scientific world view based on a number of metaphysical assumptions that he takes for granted. This is the limitation of his conceptual position. This is the limitation of all modern science as well. As an illustration, let us take a look at a relatively recent book of the late cosmologist Stephen Hawking. "What is the nature of reality?" Hawking asks. "Where did all this come from? Did the universe need a creator? ... Traditionally these are questions for philosophy, but *philosophy is dead*. Philosophy has not kept up with modern developments in science, particularly physics".[13] That's indeed a bold and intriguing assertion; here comes his answer:

> Because there is a law like gravity, the universe can and will create itself from nothing ... Spontaneous creation is the reason there is something rather than nothing, why the universe exists, why we exist. It is not necessary to invoke God to light the blue touch paper and set the universe going.[14]

We see here that Hawking understands his own question—"Where did all this come from?"—as a question regarding the possibility of establishing a causal chain. He reassures us that there is no need to invoke God; he invokes the law of gravity instead and the process of spontaneous creation. Hawking claims that philosophy has not kept up with modern science, but fails to see that the only justification for his claim is his assumption that the universe operates according to laws that can be conceived and written down in the form of mathematical formulas. Hawking's formulas are intellectual products of an intelligent agent that has a point of view and operates within time. Time and space, as the framework within which the scientific questioning happens, and mathematisation are taken for granted with no further thought. These are metaphysical presuppositions.

---

[13]Stephen Hawking and Leonard Mlodinow, *The Grand Design: New Answers to the Ultimate Questions of Life* (London: Bantam Press, 2010), p. 5 (emphasis added).

[14]*Grand Design*, p. 180.

Even when modern physics appears to question the very nature of space and time, for example when it describes the Big Bang, the space-time continuum, or the event horizon around a black hole, it takes for granted *both* space and time. Space and time are always tacitly presupposed as the *theatre* where nature and its processes may come about; they are already there as a possibility. The only challenge modern physics acknowledges is regarding mathematical formulation and measurement—for example when it speaks about the curvature of space or about time dilation. Says Heidegger:

> If physicists make judgments about metaphysics, which is quite absurd in itself, then one must demand that physicists first reflect on metaphysical ideas, for instance, this idea about time. Of course, physicists can do this only if they are prepared to go back to the underlying suppositions of physics, and beyond this, to what remains and continues to be standard in this domain as *acceptio* [or presupposition], even when the physicist is unaware of it. It is no accident that in a strict sense modern science's self-critique is lacking today.[15]

For Heidegger, every science, to the extent that it examines entities of a certain, specific type, has its own ontology. It is in such a *regional* ontology that the foundations for each science are to be found. But in Heidegger's view these foundations are themselves founded on a more primordial understanding, an understanding of being, or, as Heidegger refers to it in the context of the Zollikon Seminars, a *fundamental ontology*. He explains:

> Fundamental ontology is not merely the general ontology for the regional ontologies, a higher sphere, as it were, suspended above (or a kind of basement beneath), against which the regional ontologies are able to shield themselves. *Fundamental ontology* is that thinking which moves within the foundation of each ontology. None of these regional ontologies can abandon the foundation.[16]

---

[15]Heidegger, *Zollikon Seminars*, p. 57.
[16]*Zollikon Seminars*, pp. 190–191.

This is all the more so for sciences that study the human psyche. What is being studied—i.e. the psyche—is correlated in a most fundamental way with who does the studying: the observers study themselves, so to speak. Still, there is no such a thing as an unmediated access to one's field of study. There are always assumptions that have already been accepted, either explicitly or tacitly. These assumptions—i.e. these regional ontologies—are of major importance but the fact of their acceptance is systematically overlooked.

> In the perspective of the Analytic of Dasein, all conventional, objectifying representations of a capsule-like psyche, subject, person, ego, or consciousness in psychology and psychopathology must be abandoned in favour of an entirely different understanding. This new view of the basic constitution of human existence may be called *Dasein*, or being-in-the-world.[17]

Furthermore, the problem of modern science is that it confounds measurability and reality. "That which is calculated in advance and that which is measurable—only *that* is real [for science]".[18] It follows that entities with non-measurable properties cannot be direct objects of scientific research since they cannot be represented by some mathematical model. In fact, such entities are either completely discarded or reduced to some of their partial properties as long as those properties are themselves measurable. So, for example, shame or embarrassment is not directly measurable, therefore it cannot be studied scientifically as such. The redness of a face, however, or the circulation of blood, can. Or, alternatively, one can gauge them indirectly with the help of questionnaires or Likert scales.

When a human being comes under the scrutiny of a science, it becomes its *object* and can only be studied as an object. This means that everything that distinguishes a human being from objects that the human being encounters in the world has to be left aside. Modern

---

[17]*Zollikon Seminars*, p. 4.
[18]*Zollikon Seminars*, p. 19 (emphasis added).

science *cannot* study the human being as anything other than an occurrent object. In this respect, it studies the human being as something that it is not—an object—by forcing it to become one.

# On the Givenness of Space

It is not the case that human beings find themselves in an already "open" world which acts as a container of objects. Such a view entails a circularity: it implicitly presupposes that the spatiality of the world has already been disclosed to human beings. But close examination of the phenomenon of space shows that this is not the case. Space is *not* an empty potentiality where the human world might take place. The human being—even better: Dasein—spatialises space in its being-in-the-world, with its body. Or, as Heidegger puts it, Dasein *makes room in space* (in German: einräumen von Raum). The modern scientific view of space as the theatre where natural processes take place is an abstraction, founded upon an originary disclosure of space to Dasein via Dasein's bodiliness:

> The *Dasein of the human being* is *spatial* in itself in the sense of *making room* [in space] and in the sense of the *spatialisation* of *Dasein in its bodily nature*. Dasein is not spatial because it is embodied. But its bodiliness is possible only because Da-sein is spatial in the sense of making room.[19]

Let us consider, for example, a simple action. As I am sitting here, I decide to fetch the glass of water from the table over there. I see the glass, then I stand up, I walk to that table, I stretch my hand, I grasp the glass of water, the coldness of which I can now feel in my hand as I hold it, and then I return to my initial seat. If I consider the whole of this bodily experience, where would I locate my body?

I am sitting here. I look around and using my eyes I take in the place I occupy in this room. When I stretch my hand, I can see where it

---

[19] *Zollikon Seminars*, p. 81.

reaches: it reaches away from my body, but not very far away. If I want to reach further, I can move my body a bit; in this way, I am able to extend my hand's reach. I can also walk. While I was here, I could see the table over there. Now I am walking towards the table. The bodily experience of the place I occupy in this room allows me to reach far beyond the corporeal limits of my body in a very real sense. I am able to see in the clearest way that my body, the embodiment of this Dasein that I myself am, extends beyond the corporeal limits of this same body qua object in a room.

I am at a distance from other objects in the room; I know this because I experience the depth of this room. If I decide to measure the distance between an object in the room and myself, I can do so. What I need to do is simply to count my steps as I walk from here to there. While I am doing that, however, my experience of the room's depth moves with me. At any given moment, my "here" moves with me as I walk over there. Whatever I do, I am always in a place that is "here" for me. I may be able to measure the distance between myself and any other object in the room, but I cannot measure my very experience of the room's depth. What was disclosed to me was the experience— namely, that I am at a (measurable) distance from this or that object; and yet the experience itself is not measurable. As Heidegger puts it, "I [only] measure the distance between two [material] bodies, not the depth opened up in each case by my being-in-the-world".[20]

The body has this double "role" of being both ontic and ontological—in much the same way that the sign (or language) was shown to be both ontic and ontological.[21] Accordingly, space is *not* a framework where Dasein finds its ontic bodiliness but rather something that is ontologically disclosed to Dasein through Dasein's ontic bodiliness. It is the body that discloses space to Dasein, not the other way around. But what is the origin of this disclosure?

Heidegger returned to this question repeatedly. In *Being and Time*, he attempted to derive spatiality from temporality—i.e. starting from

---

[20]*Zollikon Seminars*, p. 82.
[21]See above, pp. 33–35.

the distinction between presence and absence—but later he admitted that this attempt was "untenable".[22] Instead, he connected the question about the origin of space to building and dwelling, activities that should be understood in terms of Dasein's *being-in-the-world*: "Building, by virtue of constructing locales, is a founding and joining of spaces. … Building is closer to the essence of spaces and to the essential origins of 'space' than any geometry and mathematics".[23] In his understanding of space, the fundamental aspect of the concept is that of separation; space is revealed as such when boundaries are put in place, for example when building a wall or raising a roof. It's only then that presence and absence can be thematised.[24]

# On the Givenness of Time

Heidegger's approach to the modern scientific view of time is similar. The conception of time as a linear succession of empty points, each called "now", is taken by modern science as the only "objective" conception of time. But such a conception is a reductive abstraction founded on an originary disclosure of time to Dasein, the richness of which is being ignored.

When one tries to study time phenomenologically one sees that, far from being a succession of empty "nows", time has specific characteristics that reveal it as not empty at all. For Heidegger, the human experience of time involves something—which he designates as "*worldtime*"—that makes itself public in the temporalising of temporality. As he explains, "we designate it thus [as "world-time"] not because it is

---

[22]See Martin Heidegger, 'Time and Being' [1962], in *On Time and Being* (New York: Harper & Row, 1972), 1–24, p. 23.

[23]'Building Dwelling Thinking' [1951], in David Farrel Krell (ed.), *Basic Writings* (London: Routledge, 1978), 343–363, p. 360.

[24]Interestingly, the same idea seems to be suggested by the etymology of the word "space" which comes to English through French from the Latin *spatium*: room, area, distance. The same applies to the Greek word for space, "χῶρος", the etymology of which also suggests a reference to place, partition or separation.

present-at-hand [occurrent] as an entity within-the-world (which it can never be), but because it belongs to the world in the sense which we have interpreted existential-ontologically".[25]

The first characteristic of this experience (i.e. of world-time) can be called *significance*.[26] This refers to the recognition that, in human experience, time is always, and essentially, time *for* something. Its second characteristic is *datability*. Moments of time are datable but this, Heidegger stresses, is not simply to say that they correspond to this or that specific calendar date; rather it means that a specific moment in time, for human beings, is always related to other "moments" in time, never isolated. It may be *before* or *after* such and such, *while* this was happening, *when* that other thing happened, and so on. The third characteristic of world-time is its *extendedness*. We may say "now", but we very rarely—if ever—refer to a temporal point of zero length; any "now" is temporally extended and can occupy any length of time, such as an evening, a season and a historical period. Finally, the fourth characteristic of world-time is its *publicness*. As Heidegger puts it:

> The datable, significant, and extended 'now' is also never a 'now', merely referring to me. … It is a 'now' that is immediately commonly accessible to all of us talking here with each other. … At any given time, the spoken 'now' is immediately received-perceived by everyone present. We call this accessibility of 'now' the *publicness* of 'now'.[27]

These four characteristics of world-time also apply to when we speak of the past and of the future. The past, the future and the present are the three dimensions of time. But these dimensions "are not simultaneous, as with the dimensions of space, but always only sequential. … All three dimensions are equiprimordial, for one never occurs without the

---

[25]Martin Heidegger, *Being and Time* [1927] (Malden, MA: Blackwell Publishers, 1962), p. 467/414.

[26]For what follows in this paragraph, see *Zollikon Seminars*, pp. 42–43, 47.

[27]*Zollikon Seminars*, p. 48.

other. All three are open to us equiprimordially, but they are not open uniformly".[28]

Time for Dasein is first and foremost world-time, that is, temporality. Its characteristics are lost for the scientist who considers the pure now-sequence as the only objective, true time. The scientist makes the uncritical leap from the phenomenon of time, as revealed to Dasein, to a formalisation of what and how time "is". This question is so removed from the actual phenomenon that reflection upon the nature of time becomes for the scientist confounded with a reflection about measurement of time. Just as we saw earlier discussing the question of space, time too is taken for granted as an empty potentiality. Even modern, i.e. non-classical, theories of time, such as Einstein's theory of relativity fail to approach the phenomenon of time in a concrete, non-reductionist way. Their failure remains invisible to modern science. At best, the difference between the original phenomenological disclosure of time and the reductive "objective" time of science is taken to be a question of an objective (i.e. scientific) vs. a *subjective* (i.e. psychological) description.[29] But as soon as we try to conceive time in terms of a "subjective" psychology vs. an "objective" science, we are already within the limited domain of a problematic regional ontology. The actual phenomenon, Dasein's primordial encounter with world-time, has remained obscured and unexamined.

---

[28]*Zollikon Seminars*, p. 48.

[29]Interestingly, the same questions were the subject of a public debate between Einstein himself and the philosopher Henri Bergson in 1922. It ended with a victory for Einstein. "Bergson and Einstein accepted that an essential difference existed between psychological and physical conceptions of time, yet they made different deductions from this. For Einstein, this led him to conclude that 'the time of the philosophers does not exist, there remains only a psychological time that differs from the physicist's.' For Bergson this lesson—that psychological and physical assessments of time were different—made, on the contrary, the philosopher's task even more interesting, especially because no one, not even physicists, could avoid the problem of relating time back to human affairs" (Jimena Canales, *The Physicist and the Philosopher: Einstein, Bergson, and the Debate that Changed our Understanding of Time* (Princeton: Princeton University Press, 2015), pp. 47–48). The fundamental incompatibility of Bergson's and Einstein's conceptualisations of time is more than visible, and it's not easy to see how this debate could end differently. For Einstein, the scientist has the first word since his or her conception of time is seen as "objective", i.e., true; Bergson, on the other hand, would insist about the primacy of the experience of time as a psychological phenomenon, i.e., as something "subjective".

# Body and the Question of Psyche

Alphonse De Waelhens, a Belgian philosopher who was critical of Heidegger, commented at some point that "in *Being and Time* one does not find thirty lines concerning the problem of perception; one does not find ten concerning that of the body".[30] This criticism, factually true as it was, was thought as Heidegger's failure to attend properly to the phenomena of the lived (bodily) experience of the human being. The same would apply to the question of sexual difference and sexuality. Heidegger's avoidance of the subject was seen as a failure and criticised, by Jacques Derrida, as the repetition of an old hierarchical division between the sexes.[31]

In my view, Heidegger's apparent reluctance to talk about the body follows from the fact that it was never his intention to write a phenomenological study of the human being in his or her bodily (ontic) existence, unlike, for example, Maurice Merleau-Ponty. There can be no doubt that the problem of the body, and indeed the problem of sexual difference, is of crucial importance for any understanding of what it is to be human. However, I concur with Kevin Aho when he argues that it is a matter of priorities. "The core motivation of Heidegger's early project [was] not to offer phenomenological investigations into the concreteness of bodily life. Rather it [was] to enquire into the meaning of being of Dasein itself".[32] More specifically, I am in agreement with R. Cerbone, who has pointed out that "one can spell out what it is to be Dasein without reference to sexuality (the body), but one cannot spell out human sexuality (what a human body is) without first explicating what it is to be Dasein".[33]

---

[30]Alphonse De Waelhens, 'Philosophy of the Ambiguous (Preface to the Second French Edition)' in Maurice Merleau-Ponty, *The Structure of Behaviour* (Boston: Beacon Paperback, 1967), xviii–xxviii, p. xix.

[31]See Jacques Derrida, 'Geschlecht: Sexual Difference, Ontological Difference' *Research in Phenomenology*, XIII (1983), 65–83.

[32]Kevin A. Aho, *Heidegger's Neglect of the Body* (Albany: State University of New York Press, 2009), p. 70.

[33]David R. Cerbone, 'Heidegger and Dasein's "Bodily Nature": What Is the Hidden Problematic?' *International Journal of Philosophical Studies*, 8/2 (2000), 209–230, p. 228n15.

For Heidegger, Dasein is considered as ontologically neutral—i.e. as neither masculine nor feminine: "The peculiar *neutrality* of the term 'Dasein' is essential, because the interpretation of this being must be carried out prior to every factual concretion. This neutrality also indicates that Dasein is neither of the two sexes".[34]

Dasein is not to be thought as an impoverished, neutralised and incorporeal, version of a human being. The question of the body is crucial, but not in the trivial (ontic) sense of our having a body and recognising that we are dependent on it; it is rather a question of Dasein's bodiliness as such and not an invitation to think of this body as an object.[35] As indicated above, space is, for Heidegger, something which is disclosed to Dasein through its bodiliness. But the body is never just an occurrent object. "The corporeal thing stops with the skin", he says. But

> when we are here, we are always in relation to something else. Therefore, one might say that we are beyond the corporeal limits. … The bodily limit and the corporeal limit are not quantitatively but rather qualitatively different from each other.[36]

The differentiation between what is bodily and what is corporeal reflects a differentiation between two senses of the word "body" in the German language, namely the quantifiable "material body" (in German: *Körper*) and, on the other, the "lived-body" (in German: *Leib*). This differentiation was first explicitly articulated by Husserl. In Heidegger, the corporeal or material body can be understood as an occurrent thing, while the lived body, as related to an analytic of Dasein, is that what *is* there ("da") of the human being.

The implications of the differentiation between the corporeal body and the lived body are, for example, apparent when we consider

---

[34]Heidegger, 'Time and Being', *On Time and Being*, p. 136.

[35]There are times, however, when it is perfectly acceptable, if not necessary, for a human being to be studied as an object, or, to put it in Heideggerian terms, as an *occurrent* entity—for example, when one needs to measure someone's height and weight, in order to calculate their body/mass index, or when medical attention requires it.

[36]Heidegger, *Zollikon Seminars*, p. 86.

phenomena such as pain. When I have a back pain, where is it in terms of spatial location? Of course, it is somewhere around my back, but does the actual experience of pain involve the material, measurable spatiality of the body? One can have a mental image of one's body, and thus be able to locate spatially a bodily pain, but this picture need not correspond to the material form of one's body. Heidegger points out that medically trained observers

> are educated in anatomy and physiology as doctors, that is, with a focus on the examination of bodies, [and for this reason they] probably look at the states of the body in a different way than the 'layman' does. Yet, a layman's experience is probably closer to the phenomenon of pain as it involves our body lines, even if it can hardly be described with the aid of our usual intuition of space.[37]

And what about the phenomenon of emotional pain? When I feel it in my heart, where is it located exactly? Is emotional pain psychical or is it somatic? Does the question make sense at all? If I am to study pain, where should I look? What about sorrow? Is sorrow *real*? How can it be studied? How can one's sadness be measured? What about blushing from shame and embarrassment? Can blushing be measured? One could say that even though shame or sorrow cannot be directly measured, they can be measured indirectly. For example, if you blush, that means that your face is more red than usual, and this could be quantified by measuring the flow of blood. Or if you feel sad, you might be asked to complete a questionnaire. Now, when we accept that an assessment of, say, sadness is possible by indicating a figure on a scale from 1 to 10, we tacitly accept that being sad is something that is *isomorphic* to a line segment with a specific length of, say, 10 units. Granted, you can indeed answer the questionnaire and indicate a measurement of "how sad", but by doing so you have been unfaithful to the actual phenomenon of sadness, since sadness is not something that extends in just one dimension—or any given number of dimensions for that matter. You have

---

[37] *Zollikon Seminars*, p. 84.

*forced* the phenomenon to conform to concepts and tools which are not fit for the task. That is a sort of conceptual violence, amplified by the overconfidence inherent in the belief that that's the only way one can proceed—i.e. in the belief that whatever cannot be quantified or *reduced* to something quantifiable is not to be studied at all and might as well be discarded as irrelevant or not real. One can see this at work in modern psychiatry, whereby the actual research hypothesis is that we can, and should, only speak about things that we can observe and assess clearly. Suffering is described in terms of *disorders* which are assessed as distance from a statistically established norm. Assessing a person's suffering, then, becomes a question of statistically assessing the conformity to a norm.[38]

"It is imperative", says Heidegger, "to refrain from any possibility of reductionism".[39] The problem, however, is not just about reductionism. One can hear discussions about psychosomatics and psychosomatic ail-ments,[40] and see medical science attempting to describe phenomena that somehow extend to both domains, the domain of the *soma* or body and the domain of *psyche* or soul. In general, an attempt is being made to study the psychic or mental component of certain physical diseases and establish the interplay between the bodily, or soma, and the mental, or psyche. The problem is that these two thematic domains, psyche and soma, are not given in advance. As Heidegger points out, "[They] are determined by the manner each case can be accessed, and in turn, the way of access is determined by the subject matter, hence, by soma and psyche".[41] Any enquiry about the nature of the connections between *psyche* and *soma* is leading us to a dead end if the answer is expected to

---

[38]I have argued this point in 'Body and the Limits of Language: Articulating the Unthinkable' *Psychodynamic Practice,* 24/2 (2018), 113–123.

[39]Heidegger, *Zollikon Seminars,* p. 85. It has to be noted in this connection that Heidegger's argu-ment against reductionism is only applicable to research conducted according to quantitative methodologies. Indeed, recent decades have seen the emergence of an abundance of qualitative research methodologies that purport to gather an in-depth understanding of human behaviour, and the reasons behind them, ensuring that this understanding is firmly grounded on—and reflects—the empirical data collected.

[40]In the English-speaking world today, the field is more commonly known as Behavioural Medicine; part of its related practice is called Liaison Psychiatry.

[41]Heidegger, *Zollikon Seminars,* p. 79.

be on the level of the somatic or the psychological. These are conceptual constructions that belong in the modern, scientific world view and are adopted uncritically. In much the same way as modern physics, which takes *time* and *space* as suppositions and accepts them without raising questions pertaining to its regional ontology of physics, medical science takes *soma* (body) as a given, without for a moment stopping to contemplate its own regional ontology. From the point of view of medical science, the body is an occurrent object, and as such, it (the science) is justified in studying it in its measurability. But this is a very impoverished view of what the body is.

## Certainty, Truth, Science

Two of the conceptual pillars of modern scientific method are the notions of *object* and *objectivity*. These, however, are a relatively recent addition to the history of thought. They belong to the general phenomenon of how something present can manifest itself to the human being. In ancient Greek thought, a thing which is present was thought as a thing that has emerged in itself, according to its *physis,* or nature.[42] After Descartes, things are no longer understood as emerging in themselves; they are now understood as *objects* available to the observing faculties of a thinking *subject.* The direct implication of this change was that the thinking subject was now elevated to the position of the assessor, so to speak, of entities in the world: Whereas before the question was to be able to discern the nature of things, now it is rather to make sure that things are seen and understood (by the observing intellect) with certainty and truth. Which brings us to the question: Where is the source of certainty to be found?

Descartes did not want to rely on the authority of the Bible or the Church and chose to approach the question regarding the foundation of certainty, taking absolute doubt as his starting point. He realised that even then, when doubting everything, one can still ascertain the

---

[42]See above, p. 54n5.

existence of one's own conscious intellect, the consciousness of the sub-ject that is aware of its doubt. This was expressed in his dictum widely known in the form "Cogito ergo sum", which appears in his 1644 work *Principles of Philosophy*. His original statement was "Je pense donc je suis" and appeared first in part IV of his *Discourse on Method*, published in 1637, in French. Both are rendered as "I am thinking, therefore I exist".[43] Descartes does not really deduce a conclusion; rather, he ascer-tains something as revealed to him in his clear intuition. As he explains in his reply to the *Second Objections* to his Meditations,

> when we become aware that we are thinking beings, this is a primary notion that is not derived by means of any syllogism. When someone says, 'I am thinking, therefore I am, or exist', he does not deduce exist-ence from thought by a syllogism, but, recognizes it as something self-evident by a simple intuition of the mind. This is clear from the fact that if he were deducing it by means of a syllogism, he would have to have had previous knowledge of the major premise 'Everything which thinks is, or exists'; yet in fact he learns it from experiencing in his own case that it is impossible that he should think without existing.[44]

Having established its own existence by the very intuition of its thinking, the human intellect can now turn towards the world—understood as being *out there*, as a domain of objects presented to the human intellect qua observing subject. This is the major change of modernity, one that has had major repercussions in our relation to the world. The whole domain of nature is now thought of as a domain of processes involving material things that the human being can encoun-ter. These things are extended in space, or *res extensae* as Descartes calls them, in contradistinction to the other kind of entities that the human being can intuit, which are non-material or mental—*res cogitantes*.

---

[43]See René Descartes, *Selected Philosophical Writings* [1628–1640] (Cambridge: Cambridge University Press, 1989), pp. 36, 162.

[44]Descartes, quoted in Peter Markie, 'The Cogito and Its Importance', in John Cottingham (ed.), *The Cambridge Companion to Descartes* (Cambridge: Cambridge University Press, 2005), 140–173, p. 146.

Things are recast as *objects*, and the human being is recast as a reflecting intellect, an "Ego" that tries to overcome doubt and reach certainty. As Heidegger explains,

> Objectivity is a definite *modification of the presence of things*. A subject thereby understands the presencing of a thing from itself with regard to the representedness. Presence is understood as representedness. ... The fundamental difference lies in the fact that in the former experience something is a being insofar as I represent it. Modern science rests on *the transformation of the experience of the presence of things into objectivity.*[45]

It follows readily, then, that by virtue of their extendedness in space, material things are characterised by their measurable features. But measurability itself is not a characteristic of the thing. Measurability only designates that measurement—a human activity—is possible. "Thus", says Heidegger,

> our speech about measurability refers to something concerning both the [thing] and the human comportment to it. ... Measurability does not belong to the thing, yet it is also not exclusively an activity of the human being. Measurability belongs to the thing as *object*. Measuring is only possible when the thing is thought of as an object, that is, when it is represented in its objectivity. Measuring is a way I am able to let a thing (present by itself) stand over against me, namely regarding its extension, or still better, regarding the how much of its extension.[46]

The human being—a res cogitans—can ascertain the features of material things he or she encounters, by measuring their properties, i.e. by comparing them to the physical properties of other objects that have been studied and have their properties accepted as units for the respective features. This not only involves a significant change in the conception of how a material thing is understood, but also a corresponding

---

[45]Heidegger, *Zollikon Seminars*, p. 99.
[46]*Zollikon Seminars*, p. 98.

change in what is *truth*. This observing intellect, just like Descartes himself, seeks certainty. Certainty needs a solid foundation, and for Descartes, the only truly solid foundation for certainty can be given by science and mathematics. For Heidegger, absolute reliance on mathematics is not tenable, especially if one understands the mathematical to be closely related to the numerical, as Descartes did.

In its formation the word 'mathematical' stems from the Greek τα μαθήματα, which means what can be learned and thus, at the same time, what can be taught; μανθάνειν means to learn, μάθησις the teaching, and this in a twofold sense. First, it means studying and learning; then it means the doctrine taught. … We are long used to thinking of numbers when we think of the mathematical. The mathematical and numbers are obviously connected. Only the question remains: Is this connection because the mathematical is numerical in character, or on the contrary, is the numerical something mathematical? The second is the case.[47]

More generally, modern scientific reliance on mathematical formulas, in all its abstraction, entails a reliance on the numerical, i.e. on measurements that have been made, or can be made on demand. In other words, the mathematics that modern science involves—applied mathematics—is rather limited in comparison with the full scope of mathematics (e.g. set theory, topology, number theory, knot theory). Applied mathematics is by definition limited to a certain ontological region; by accepting that the world, and nature, is a domain of measurable entities and calculable processes, as modern science holds, one overlooks this limitation.

In principle, mathematical things possess the same proof and certainty. This is the reason that the projection of nature as a calculable domain of objects at the same time implies that calculability is understood as mathematical determination. … In this manner of anticipatory projection of

---

[47] *What Is a Thing?* [1935–36] (South Bend, IN: Gateway Editions, 1967), pp. 69–70.

nature as a domain of calculable objects a decision has already been made
… that everything not exhibiting the characteristics of mathematically
determinable objectivity is eliminated as being uncertain, that is, untrue
and therefore unreal.[48]

It would appear that choosing to focus his criticism on applied
mathematics and modern science's reliance on it, Heidegger overlooks or wilfully ignores the variety and scope of the whole domain
of knowledge that we designate as mathematics. However, considering Heidegger's work as a whole, we see that this was a choice rather
than a limitation or sign of carelessness. He was mostly concerned
with is the reduction of truth qua a-letheia to truth as correspondence;
the degeneration of logos—i.e. the openness of being to Dasein—
to propositional logic; and the impoverished understanding of
being-in-the-world as a subject–object relationship.[49] To be sure, in this
way a lot of mathematics is left out. But this is of no consequence here.
What remains crucial in Heidegger's argument is the observation that
scientists—physicists, medical doctors, psychologists—and laymen alike
"have moved uncritically into the technical-scientific way of thinking
and view it as the only one that is valid".[50] For Heidegger, questioning this view should form an important part of the initial elaboration of
the concepts employed by any science that would claim to study human
beings in their concernful engagements with each other and with the
entities they encounter in the world, in their being in time, in their
being healthy or ill. And yet they do not. "We stand before phenomena, which require us to become aware of them and to receive-perceive
them in an appropriate manner. It is no longer up to the physicist, but
only to the philosopher, to say something about what is accepted in this
way".[51]

---

[48]*Zollikon Seminars*, pp. 106–107.
[49]This is the argument of T. Fay, in his *Heidegger: The Critique of Logic* (The Hague: Martinus Nijhoff Publishers, 1977).
[50]Heidegger, *Zollikon Seminars*, p. 51.
[51]*Zollikon Seminars*, pp. 28–29.

# Psychoanalysis in Focus

Heidegger did not have any direct contact with Freud, and it is not known the extent to which he really read him. Throughout the Zollikon Seminars, he made frequent negative allusions to Freud's theories, but sometimes it appears that the Freud he had in mind was Freud as relayed to him by Medard Boss. Be it as it may, Heidegger did not really seem to respect Freud's thought. He thought that psychoanalysis, just like modern science, fails to acknowledge the regional scope of its ontology and neglects to question its presuppositions. Heidegger counted Freud among the proponents of a type of neo-Kantianism, which speaks about the human being in terms of an observing intellect faced with a reality that cannot be known—basically a subject–object relationship that neo-Kantianism as well as Freud take for granted. This basic understanding "specifically neglects to determine the human being's character of being, [the character] of the human being, who radically articulates his being human with language".[52]

Heidegger was most critical of Freud's tacit belief in the explainability of psychical life in causal terms: for Heidegger, Freud assumed that the psychical and the physical domains operate in the same way, and stipulated that the physical domain can be approached in terms of scientific quasi-deterministic laws. However, having observed that there is no such thing as an unbroken explanatory chain in the *conscious mental life* of an individual, Freud had "to invent" the unconscious in order to establish

an unbroken [chain of] causal connections. The postulate is the complete explanation of psychical life whereby explanation and understanding are identified. This postulate is not derived from the psychical phenomena themselves but is a *postulate* of modern natural science. What for Kant transcends [conscious] perception, for instance the fact that the stone becomes warm *because* the sun is shining, is for Freud 'the unconscious'.[53]

---

[52]*Zollikon Seminars*, p. 224.
[53]*Zollikon Seminars*, pp. 207–208.

It is Freud's adherence to a subject–object model of the human being, together with his insistence that the world is presented to the subject's consciousness via object-presentations (i.e. combinations of a thing-presentation and a word-presentation)[54] that prevented him from seeing that being is disclosed to human beings in the clearing—i.e. the open space where being is disclosed to Dasein as truth (a-letheia) in an *event* of appropriation—even before they have developed a consciousness, that is, even before they have developed an awareness of their reflective comportment towards being. In Heidegger's view, the introduction of hypotheses such as that of an unconscious motivation (to explain, e.g., a slip of the tongue or a parapraxis) does little to advance the understanding of the phenomena in question; instead, it distorts them because it involves unexamined prior assumptions. "The matter [attributed to] unconscious intention is an explanation as opposed to a phenomenological interpretation. This explanation is a pure hypothesis that in no way advances the understanding of the phenomenon itself".[55] As Heidegger maintains, the "unconscious" is only needed if one sees the human being as an agent, or observer, operating in the world through a window of consciousness/perception and responding to stimuli coming from "outside". This distinction, however, is not sustained by the phenomena themselves: Heidegger claims that Freud misses the ontological status of Dasein qua being-in-the-world and fails to see that concernful comportment towards beings is only possible when being has already been revealed to Dasein: "Freud simply did not see this clearing; otherwise, he would have succeeded in understanding the consciousness of children. There is a relationship to clearing which need not be 'conscious' and reflected on in the Freudian sense".[56]

Let us take as an example the phenomenon of memory. How do we remember things? How do we forget things? What is the logic behind our accidental forgetting things that we very obviously know? How can we understand parapraxes and other similar lapses of consciousness?

---

[54]See also below, p. 97.
[55]Heidegger, *Zollikon Seminars*, p. 169.
[56]*Zollikon Seminars*, p. 182.

These phenomena were at the heart of Freud's work. We tend to think of remembering as an action of retrieving something and returning it to (our) awareness. And we think of forgetting as a disruption of this action, or as a difficulty in completing it. If this is the case, then "repression" can be the name of a mental function that explains this disruption. As all of this is supposed to be happening in the dark—behind the scenes as it were—the hypothesis of the unconscious is, for Freud, necessary, adequate and legitimate.

And yet, as Heidegger stresses, we fail to see that all this reasoning involves a number of tacit assumptions regarding memory and recall. Freud sees memory as a psychical *container* or *storage*, from which one is supposed to be able to retrieve information at will. This is a very problematic description. In fact, if we look at it closely, we will see that remembering or forgetting is not even the primary phenomenon. There is a difference between *recalling* (in German: *Erinnerung*) and *making-present* (in German: *Vergegenwärtigung*), a difference that reflects different modes of Dasein's comportment towards beings. If we attend to the phenomenon of forgetting closely enough, we will see the primordial phenomenon in terms of "retaining" and "non-retaining". Heidegger explains:

> *Having forgotten* as an inauthentic way of having been, is thus related to that thrown being which is one's own; it is the temporal meaning of that being in accordance with which I *am* proximally and for the most part as-having-been. Only on the basis of such forgetting can anything be *retained* by the concernful making-present which awaits; and what are thus retained are entities encountered within-the-world with a character other than that of Dasein. To such retaining, there corresponds a non-retaining which presents us with a kind of 'forgetting' in a derivative sense. … *Remembering* is possible only on [the basis] of forgetting, *and not vice versa* ; for in the mode of having-forgotten, one's having been 'discloses' primarily the horizon into which a Dasein lost in the 'superficiality' of its object of concern, can bring itself by remembering.[57]

---

[57] *Being and Time*, p. 389/339.

When I forget something, it is because I no longer wish to think about it, and I let it slip away from me; it is not because there is a failure of some sort in a retrieval mechanism or process. A phenomenon such as my leaving something behind—e.g. an umbrella at the hairdresser's—cannot be explained with the help of, say, a repressed motive, as a psychoanalyst would hold; for Heidegger, the grounds for the assertion are invalid.

> Concealment is not the antithesis of consciousness, but rather concealment belongs to the clearing. … Concealment is not a hiding, as is Freud's 'repression', because hiding is a special way and manner of being in the clearing.[58]

Even if it were the case that something unpleasant is avoided by means of my forgetting the umbrella, it is rather that I let myself be absorbed with something else in order to be able to let slip away what is uncomfortable for me.

> The different ways of 'forgetting' are the ways and manners of how something withdraws from oneself, how it conceals itself. When I forget the umbrella at the hairdresser, what is that? I did forget *taking* the umbrella *with me*, but not the umbrella. I omitted it. I did not think of it. I was just concerned with something else. Therefore, here forgetting is a privation of having thought of something. Here, memory [is understood as] recalling something.

> I have forgotten the name of someone I know. I cannot retrieve his name. It no longer comes to mind. It slipped my memory. The name slipped my memory. What slipped my memory is a privation. From where did it slip? From retaining it, from memory. Therefore, this forgetting is the privation of retaining something. In turn, to retain something is a specific form of the relationship toward which I comport myself. It is not a mode of thinking about something because I do not need to think continuously about a name, which I retain. Here memory is [understood] as retaining.[59]

---

[58]*Zollikon Seminars*, pp. 182–183.
[59]*Zollikon Seminars*, p. 168.

In other words, the actual phenomenon in question is that one may choose to retain something in their concernful comportment towards being, or they may let it slip away. The psychoanalyst tries to *explain* in terms of a set of laws, rules and models, while the phenomenologist only attempts to bring the phenomenon to light. "The matter [attributed to] unconscious intention is an explanation as opposed to a phenomenological interpretation".[60] Implied here is the criticism that a psychoanalytic "explanation" already presupposes a subject–object understanding of being-in-the-world. The phenomenon is "explained", i.e. forced to conform to this unexamined presupposition.

Interestingly, a very similar argument was made by Ludwig Wittgenstein who was otherwise well predisposed towards Freud. Wittgenstein had identified a fundamental flaw at the heart of Freud's argument, namely a confusion between a retrospective explanation of a reason on the one hand and a hypothesis about causation on the other. "When we laugh without knowing why", Wittgenstein said during his Cambridge Lectures,

> Freud claims that by psychoanalysis we can find out. I see a muddle here between a cause and a reason. Being clear why you laugh is not being clear about a *cause*. If it were, then agreement to the analysis given of a joke as explaining why you laugh would not be a means of detecting it. The success of the analysis is supposed to be shown by the person's agreement. … The difference between a reason and a cause is brought up as follows: the investigation of a reason entails as an essential part one's agreement with it, whereas the investigation of a cause is carried out experimentally.[61]

Freud operated within the mechanistic/scientific (i.e. Cartesian) world view whereby the human being is to be reduced to an occurrent object and can be studied scientifically. Because of this, he failed to give an adequate account of the human being as a world-forming being and

---

[60]*Zollikon Seminars*, p. 169.

[61]Wittgenstein, quoted in Jacques Bouveresse, *Wittgenstein Reads Freud: The Myth of the Unconscious* (Princeton, NJ: Princeton University Press, 1995), p. 26.

needed to resort to unnecessary hypotheses, the most problematic of which is what Heidegger called the "fatal distinction between the conscious and the unconscious".[62] In short, what is at stake here is first and foremost the concept that is at the very heart of the Freudian project, the unconscious. As William Richardson elaborates,

> If the Freudian unconscious is only the underside of a Cartesian conception of consciousness, conceived as an encapsulated ego-subject, what happens if this Cartesian model is scrapped? Does not the unconscious go too? Of course it does—and that is exactly Heidegger's position. For Dasein is not fundamentally an ego-subject. Dasein is the clearing of being in which all beings (including itself) may appear and reveal themselves as what they are.[63]

It the unconscious has to go, what about other Freudian "entities", then, such as the instincts (or drives)? Freud felt it necessary to introduce them because he wanted to understand (and explain) phenomena such as sexual urge and sexual object choice or other phenomena such as repetition and trauma. For Heidegger, Dasein, in its concernful comportment towards being, is always, and already, "ahead" of him/herself, absorbed in a future potentiality-to-be. Dasein is not *driven* or pushed from behind (by an instinct or drive) but turned towards something ahead. To draw on something like a drive "is already a reinterpretation and an objectification into a process, that is, an improper interpretation".[64] Freud's failure is, therefore, palpable. "If one desires to reduce willing, wishing, propensity, and urge to 'drives' one must first ask the contrary question: Is the human being present within the total construct of Freudian libido theory at all?"[65] In other words, if in this theory drives can be shown to be behind various aspects of human behaviour, is there any room left for human agency?

[62]Heidegger, *Zollikon Seminars*, p. 254.
[63]William J. Richardson, 'Heidegger and Psychoanalysis?' *Naturaleza humana*, 5/1 (2003), 9–38, p. 14.
[64]Heidegger, *Zollikon Seminars*, p. 173.
[65]*Zollikon Seminars*, p. 172.

One can counter here that drives were never meant by Freud to be an all-explaining hypothesis. Heidegger's criticism on this seems to be at least partially based on a misunderstanding. Moreover, one must at least recognise that it was Freud's attention to the clinical phenomena that guided him in his theoretical speculations and not the other way around. Freud did not hesitate to challenge the medical, scientific and philosophical establishments of his time by introducing concepts that ran contrary to conventional knowledge. In addition, Freud never shied away from modifying or abandoning hypotheses and concepts if clinical evidence required him to.[66] However, the main point stands: Freud's metapsychology is an artificial mechanistic construction that fails to question its presuppositions.

Heidegger's critique focuses on the "orthodox", Freudian version of psychoanalysis; it is not difficult to see, however, that it is applicable to almost all post-Freudian varieties of psychoanalysis. Psychoanalysis fails to grasp the totality of the phenomenon of being-in-the-world, which led to its failure to draw out a complete account of the human being in his or her historicity. "The 'psychoanalytic case history' is by no means a history but [an explanation by means of] a naturalistic chain of causes, a chain of cause and effect, and even more, a construct".[67]

# From the Question of Being to Lacan

Heidegger's philosophy represents a turning point in the history of ideas in the 20th century. His challenge to a philosophical tradition that began with the ancient Greeks and reached its highest point of coherence and influence with the emergence of Descartes's cogito was enormous. The form of the challenge, i.e. Heidegger's insistence on rethinking the question of being, was obscure and easy to misconstrue. This did not prevent it from reaching its audience.

---

[66]This of course is not as clear-cut as it seems, as K. Popper has argued. See below, p. 89.
[67]Heidegger, *Zollikon Seminars*, p. 158.

Heidegger was not a clinician, and his criticisms against Freud were not accompanied by his own systematic laying out how a properly founded Dasein-analytic clinic can be put forward. On the other hand, Heidegger's ideas were already making inroads into discussions about psychology, psychopathology and psychotherapy, even before the commencement of the Zollikon Seminars. Concepts, such as Dasein or being-in-the-world, and ideas, such as his on time, temporality and historicity, were gradually understood as very relevant and connected to the work of those who were trying to study and alleviate human suffering. Among the works by the psychiatrists and psychologists who can be said to be more directly influenced by Heidegger's philosophy, Ludwig Binswanger's *Existential Analysis*, or *Daseinsanalysis* (in German: *Daseinsanalyse*) and Medard Boss's own *Daseinsanalysis* (in German: *Daseinsanalytik*), stand apart. Both authors were very open in acknowledging their debt to Heidegger, as the names of their respective theories suggest; both authors had come to Heidegger from a more or less Freudian starting point. Their respective approaches represented direct and explicit attempts to apply Heideggerian insights to psychiatry and psychotherapy, and as Hans Cohn puts it, they stand apart as "the most comprehensive and radical attempts made so far to provide a philosophical answer and alternative to Freud's scientific project".[68]

Heidegger made manifest the limits of the Cartesian subject–object distinction and pointed at what the problem really was—namely, working out what he called the *meaning* of being. He realised that even philosophy was not adequately equipped to penetrate deeper to this problem, and abandoned its traditional concepts such as metaphysics, or fundamental ontology. Heidegger understood that the problem of the meaning of being and its corollaries—the problem of the human being, of truth, of the world—were problems of language, in the sense that language *creates* or *discloses* a world. Heidegger's conception of truth as unconcealment, or disclosure, represented a major rupture, a cut that distanced him from a tradition that saw truth as a simple question of

---

[68]Hans W. Cohn, *Existential Thought and Therapeutic Practice: An Introduction to Existential Psychotherapy* (London: Sage, 1997), p. 4.

ascertaining the agreement of statements with the state of affairs the statements were about. If Galileo's method represented a rupture with the world of the ancients, Heidegger's thought heralds what Badiou calls "the closure of an entire epoch of thought and its concerns".[69]

Many scholars have attempted a phenomenologically informed re-evaluation of basic Freudian conceptions from a non-mechanistic point of view. Maurice Merleau-Ponty, for example, accepted that there *are* indeed mental phenomena in what he called the *limits of consciousness* and spoke about a convergence between phenomenology and Freudian research; Richard Boothby has tried to draw parallels between Freud's metapsychology and phenomenology, via the work of Jacques Lacan; while Robert Stolorow has been working on a post-Cartesian psychoanalysis, drawing heavily on Heidegger's work. Finally, a decidedly Lacanian reading of basic Freudian conceptions has been advocated by Heideggerian scholar and psychoanalyst William Richardson.[70]

Lacan was very aware of all criticisms that Freud's theories attracted but thought they were not enough to warrant an outright dismissal of Freudian thought and its main innovations. He claimed that the spirit of Freud's discoveries had been forgotten or misconstrued, and called for a *return* to him. In the process Lacan formulated his own version of psychoanalysis, which until the end he insisted on calling Freudian rather than Lacanian, he also found that in the process he was distancing himself from a philosophical background which in the beginning had helped him secure the foundations of his reading of psychoanalysis.

Richardson has suggested that we need to return to Lacan, in the same way that Lacan returned to Freud. We need, Richardson wrote, "to

---

[69]Alain Badiou, *Being and Event* [1988] (New York: Continuum, 2005), p. 1.

[70]See Maurice Merleau-Ponty, 'Phenomenology and Psychoanalysis: Preface to Hesnard's *L'oeuvre de Freud*' [1960], in Alden L. Fischer (ed.), *Essential Writings of Merleau-Ponty* (New York: Harcourt, Brace & World, 1969), 81–87; Hermann Lang, Stefan Brunnhuber, and Rudolph F. Wagner, 'The So-Called Zollikon Seminars: Heidegger as a Psychotherapist' *Journal of the American Academy of Psychoanalysis*, 31 (2003), 349–359; 'Heidegger as Psychotherapist'; Frederick J. Wertz, 'The Phenomenology of Sigmund Freud' *Journal of Phenomenological Psychology*, 24/2 (1993), 101–129; Richard Boothby, *Freud as Philosopher: Metapsychology after Lacan* (New York: Routledge, 2001); Robert D. Stolorow, *World, Affectivity, Trauma: Heidegger and Post-cartesian Psychoanalysis* (New York: Routledge, 2011); and Richardson, 'Heidegger and Psychoanalysis?'.

return to the moment of *énonciation* where the speaking subject called Jacques Lacan was at his very best. But this means trying to articulate his un-said, learning to read him as he has taught us to read Freud".[71] This is what I intend to do in the next two chapters.

❖    ❖    ❖

# Bibliography

AHO, KEVIN A., *Heidegger's Neglect of the Body* (Albany: State University of New York Press, 2009).

BADIOU, ALAIN, *Being and Event* [1988], trans. Oliver Feltham (New York: Continuum, 2005).

BOOTHBY, RICHARD, *Freud as Philosopher: Metapsychology After Lacan* (New York: Routledge, 2001).

BOUVERESSE, JACQUES, *Wittgenstein Reads Freud: The Myth of the Unconscious*, trans. Carol Cosman (Princeton, NJ: Princeton University Press, 1995).

CANALES, JIMENA, *The Physicist and the Philosopher: Einstein, Bergson, and the Debate That Changed Our Understanding of Time* (Princeton: Princeton University Press, 2015).

CASSIN, BARBARA, '*Tuché* and *automaton* in Aristotle' [2004], trans. Emily Apter, Jacques Lezra, and Michael Wood, in Barbara Cassin (ed.), *Dictionary of Untranslatables* (Princeton: Princeton University Press, 2014), 534.

CERBONE, DAVID R., 'Heidegger and Dasein's "Bodily Nature": What Is the Hidden Problematic?' *International Journal of Philosophical Studies*, 8/2 (2000), 209–230.

COHN, HANS W., *Existential Thought and Therapeutic Practice: An Introduction to Existential Psychotherapy* (London: Sage, 1997).

DE WAELHENS, ALPHONSE, 'Philosophy of the Ambiguous (Preface to the Second French Edition)' in Maurice Merleau-Ponty, *The Structure of Behaviour* (Boston: Beacon Paperback, 1967), xviii–xxviii.

---

[71]William J. Richardson, 'Psychoanalysis and the Being-Question', in Joseph H. Smith and William Kerrigan (eds.), *Psychiatry and the Humanities, Volume 6: Interpreting Lacan* (New Haven: Yale University Press, 1983), 139–159, p. 157.

DERRIDA, JACQUES, 'Geschlecht: Sexual Difference, Ontological Difference' *Research in Phenomenology,* XIII (1983), 65–83.

DESCARTES, RENÉ, *Selected Philosophical Writings* [1628–1640], trans. John Cottingham, Robert Stoothoff, and Dugald Murdoch (Cambridge: Cambridge University Press, 1989).

FALCON, ANDREA, 'Aristotle on Causality' *The Stanford Encyclopedia of Philosophy* (Spring 2015 Edition), Edward N. Zalta (ed.), https://plato.stanford.edu/archives/spr2015/entries/aristotle-causality/.

FAY, THOMAS A., *Heidegger: The Critique of Logic* (The Hague: Martinus Nijhoff Publishers, 1977).

GUTHRIE, W. K. C., *Aristotle, an Encounter* (A History of Greek Philosophy, VI; Cambridge: Cambridge University Press, 1981).

HAWKING, STEPHEN AND MLODINOW, LEONARD, *The Grand Design: New Answers to the Ultimate Questions of Life* (London: Bantam Press, 2010).

HEIDEGGER, MARTIN, *Being and Time* [1927], trans. John Macquarrie and Edward Robinson (Malden, MA: Blackwell Publishers, 1962).

———, 'Building Dwelling Thinking' [1951] in David Farrel Krell (ed.), *Basic Writings* (London: Routledge, 1978), 343–363.

———, 'Time and Being' [1962], trans. Joan Stambaugh, in *On Time and Being* (New York: Harper & Row, 1972), 1–24.

———, *What Is a Thing?* [1935–36], trans. W. B. Barton Jr. and Vera Deutsch (South Bend, IN: Gateway Editions, 1967).

———, *Zollikon Seminars: Protocols, Conversations, Letters*, ed. Medard Boss, trans. Franz Mayr and Richard Askay (Evanston, IL: Northwestern University Press, 2001).

KOYRÉ, ALEXANDRE, *From the Closed World to the Infinite Universe* (Baltimore: The Johns Hopkins Press, 1957).

———, *Galileo Studies* [1939], trans. John Mepham (Hassocks, Sussex: The Harvester Press, 1978).

———, 'The Origins of Modern Science: A New Interpretation' *Diogenes,* 4/16 (1956), 1–22.

LANG, HERMANN, BRUNNHUBER, STEFAN, AND WAGNER, RUDOLPH F., 'The So-Called Zollikon Seminars: Heidegger as a Psychotherapist' *Journal of the American Academy of Psychoanalysis,* 31 (2003), 349–359.

LOSEE, JOHN, *A Historical Introduction to the Philosophy of Science* (Oxford: Oxford University Press, 2001).

MARKIE, PETER, 'The Cogito and Its Importance' in John Cottingham (ed.), *The Cambridge Companion to Descartes* (Cambridge: Cambridge University Press, 2005), 140–173.

MERLEAU-PONTY, MAURICE, 'Phenomenology and Psychoanalysis: Preface to Hesnard's *L'oeuvre de Freud*' [1960] in Alden L. Fischer (ed.), *Essential Writings of Merleau-Ponty* (New York: Harcourt, Brace & World, 1969), 81–87.

RICHARDSON, WILLIAM J., 'Heidegger and Psychoanalysis?' *Naturaleza humana*, 5/1 (2003), 9–38.

———, 'Psychoanalysis and the Being-Question' in Joseph H. Smith and William Kerrigan (eds.), *Psychiatry and the Humanities, Volume 6: Interpreting Lacan* (New Haven: Yale University Press, 1983), 139–159.

STOLOROW, ROBERT D., *World, Affectivity, Trauma: Heidegger and Post-Cartesian Psychoanalysis* (New York: Routledge, 2011).

TOMBRAS, CHRISTOS, 'Body and the Limits of Language: Articulating the Unthinkable' *Psychodynamic Practice*, 24/2 (2018), 113–123.

WERTZ, FREDERICK J., 'The Phenomenology of Sigmund Freud' *Journal of Phenomenological Psychology*, 24/2 (1993), 101–129.

WINDELBAND, WIHELM, *A History of Philosophy: With Especial Reference to the Formation and Development of Its Problems and Conceptions*, trans. James Hayden Tufts (New York: The Macmillan Company, 1901).

# 4

# Back to Freud, and Beyond

The history of psychoanalysis is roughly divided into two periods, one before and one after the Second World War. They are demarcated by the massive exodus of Freud and other psychoanalysts from Austria and Germany because of the Nazi anti-Jewish policies and persecutions of the 1930s, but also by Freud's own death in 1939. After the war, psychoanalysis was to flourish mainly away from its origins, in the UK and the USA, in France, and also in Latin America. Freud's heirs would each follow their own trajectories, forming different schools according to the answers they were each giving to the theoretical problems they encountered. In Francophone countries, developments would be forever marked by the teachings of Lacan, a psychoanalyst of the so-called second generation whose main work belongs solidly in the second post-Freudian period.

Lacan believed that the spirit and radicality of Freud's work was being misconstrued and strove throughout his career to reverse that trend. Freud's discovery, in Lacan's view, consisted in recognising the extent to which human suffering is dependent on, and subject to, language. His own reading of Freud reached far beyond, but Lacan remained for a long-time true to his pledge to "return to Freud" by reading Freud's

© The Author(s) 2019
C. Tombras, *Discourse Ontology*, The Palgrave Lacan Series,
https://doi.org/10.1007/978-3-030-13662-8_4

texts closely and referring to them again and again. "It is up to you to be Lacanians if you wish", he said, as late as in 1980. "For my part, I am a Freudian".[1]

In contrast to Freud, who claimed that he did not have any particular philosophical aspirations, Lacan was in close contact and dialogue with many of the most important philosophers of his time. He had a particular admiration for Heidegger and was making frequent Heideggerian allusions in his own teaching. He had met Heidegger through a common acquaintance, Jean Beaufret, a young philosopher who contributed a lot to the introduction of Heidegger's thought to the French intelligentsia, and who incidentally was also one of Lacan's analysands. In 1955, Lacan received Heidegger's permission to translate his essay "Logos", which was then published in the first issue of *La Psychanalyse*. Lacan and Heidegger met a few times, the last time being in 1975. Lacan even sent him a signed copy of his *Écrits* and tried, during this last visit, to interest him in the latest formulations of his theories. Apparently, Heidegger remained unimpressed. "It seems to me", he wrote at some point to Medard Boss, "that the psychiatrist needs a psychiatrist".[2]

# Revisiting Freud's Discovery

Freud was not the first to observe that people have dreams, make slips of the tongue, or suffer from perplexing hysterical symptoms. He was not even the first to study them. But he was the first who, after turning his systematic attention to these phenomena, decided that they were meaningful and began studying them as such. He devised a tool in order to break into the logic of these phenomena—namely, free association—and developed a number of hypotheses, models, and

---

[1]Jacques Lacan, 'Overture to the 1st International Encounter of the Freudian Field: Caracas, 12 July 1980', trans. Adrian Price, *Hurly-Burly*, 6 (September 2011), 17–20, p. 18.
[2]Martin Heidegger, *Zollikon Seminars: Protocols, Conversations, Letters*, ed. Medard Boss (Evanston, IL: Northwestern University Press, 2001), pp. 280–281.

theories to understand them, describe them, and decipher their meaning. He developed psychoanalysis.

Freud claimed that psychoanalysis is a science, working with observations, hypotheses, refutations of hypotheses and so on. He considered his a purely scientific endeavour, only directed by his quest for truth, which, he believed, can only be approached with the help of scientific method. He did not have much time for philosophy, and what he saw as philosophy's need to present an all-encompassing and coherent world view, or *Weltanschauung*: "As a specialist science, a branch of psychology—a depth psychology or psychology of the unconscious—[psychoanalysis] is quite unfit to construct a *Weltanschauung* of its own: it must accept the scientific one".[3]

It must have been very disappointing for Freud, then, to see that philosophers of science were prepared to criticise psychoanalysis on the basis that it was not properly scientific. Karl Popper, for example, argued that psychoanalysis cannot possibly be thought of as scientific. Its claims can never be tested (and possibly falsified); psychoanalysis is "simply non-testable, irrefutable".[4] Popper also stressed that psychoanalysis's claim to scientific status cannot count on clinical observations or evidence as proof: "'Clinical observations' like other observations, are *interpretations in the light of theories* …; and for this reason alone they are apt to support those theories in the light of which they were interpreted".[5] Adolf Grünbaum, who in disagreement with Popper thought that psychoanalysis *can* be considered a science, had also argued that psychoanalytical clinical evidence as such can never be an adequate foundation for psychoanalysis' core hypotheses and metapsychology.[6]

---

[3]Sigmund Freud, 'New Introductory Lectures on Psychoanalysis' [1933a], in James Strachey (ed.), *SE vol. 22* (London: Hogarth Press, 1953–1974), 1–182, p. 158.

[4]Karl R. Popper, 'Science: Conjectures and Refutations' [1961], in *Conjectures and Refutations: The Growth of Scientific Knowledge* (London: Routledge, 2002), 43–86, p. 49.

[5]'Science: Conjectures and Refutations', *Conjectures and Refutations: The Growth of Scientific Knowledge*, p. 49n3.

[6]See Adolf Grünbaum, *The Foundations of Psychoanalysis: A Philosophical Critique* (Berkeley: University of California Press, 1984).

The project of scientific verification of psychoanalysis in this manner continues and still attracts some publicity when results are published.[7]

Seen in the light of Heidegger's critique of science, the whole attempt of scientific verification or refutation of psychoanalysis is revealed as unsatisfactory, and its findings are shown to be beside the point. The problem with psychoanalysis is not whether it can or cannot be properly evaluated as a scientific enterprise, but rather that it appears to share with science a number of unexamined basic assumptions that are taken for granted. This, of course, is not to mean that psychoanalysis is beyond the reach of scientific scrutiny, but rather that psychoanalysis, like the other (hard) sciences, fails to question its presuppositions.

## Basic Assumptions of Psychoanalysis

Let us try, in what follows, to approach Freud's concepts as descriptive attempts, as models that aim to represent and clarify the phenomena that constitute the subject matter of psychoanalysis, and its fundamental hypotheses, and not as "real" entities that exist independently from the theory within which they appear.

In his posthumously published *Outline of Psychoanalysis*, Freud states very concisely the basic assumption of psychoanalysis:

> We know two kinds of things about what we call our psyche (or mental life): its bodily organ, and scene of action, the brain (or nervous system), and on the other hand, our acts of consciousness which are immediate data and cannot be further explained by any sort of description.

---

[7]A relatively early attempt to evaluate psychoanalytic claims by means of a meta-analysis of all relevant scientific research was made by Paul Kline, with inconclusive but favourable results. See Paul Kline, *Fact and Fantasy in Freudian Theory* (London: Methuen & Co, 1972). A more recent example is the ongoing *Tavistock Adult Depression Study*, a randomised controlled trial at the NHS, attempting to establish whether long-term psychoanalytic psychotherapy provides lasting relief to patients suffering from treatment-resistant depression. See Peter Fonagy et al., 'Pragmatic Randomized Controlled Trial of Long-Term Psychoanalytic Psychotherapy for Treatment-Resistant Depression: The Tavistock Adult Depression Study (TADS)' *World Psychiatry*, 14/3 (09/25/2015), 312–321.

Everything that lies between is unknown to us, and the data do not include any direct relation between these two terminal points of our knowledge. If it existed it would at the most afford an exact localisation of the processes of consciousness and would give us no help towards understanding them.[8]

So, for Freud, our mental life is a product of a bodily organ, the brain. He accepts that there is, in principle, some sort of correspondence between what is mental (or psychical) and what is bodily (or physical, i.e., the brain as such, the nervous system, etc.); he emphasises, however, that this correspondence does not allow for a reduction of the former to the latter: the localisation of the mental apparatus in the brain does not help us understand the processes of consciousness as such; different tools and hypotheses are needed.[9]

On this assumption, Freud puts forward the two fundamental postulates of psychoanalysis. According to the first, our psychical or mental life is a function of a structured and spatially localised apparatus: "Mental life is the function of an apparatus to which we ascribe the characteristics of being extended in space and of being made up of several portions".[10] According to the second, there are aspects of psychical life which are unconscious, i.e., not included in what we can be aware of in our so-called conscious processes:

Conscious processes do not form unbroken sequences which are complete in themselves. … There are physical or somatic processes which are concomitant with the psychical ones and which we should necessarily have to

---

[8]Sigmund Freud, 'An Outline of Psychoanalysis' [1940a], in James Strachey (ed.), *SE vol. 23* (London: Hogarth Press, 1953–1974), 139–208, pp. 144–145.

[9]The question of space is never fully thematised in Freud's work. Spatial metaphors are constant in Freud's work, however. He speaks about the depths of mental life, about the surface of the mental apparatus, or about the displacement of libido—to give just a few examples. Still, space for Freud is the empty theatre where entities are able to manifest their extendedness. The extendedness as such is not properly questioned. See, for example, in one of his very latest writings: "Space may be the projection of the extension of the psychical apparatus. No other derivation is probable. Instead of Kant's a *priori* determinants of our psychical apparatus. Psyche is extended; knows nothing about it" ('Findings, Ideas, Problems', *SE vol. 23*, p. 300).

[10]'An Outline of Psychoanalysis', *SE vol. 23*, p. 145.

recognise as more complete than the psychical sequences, since some of them would have conscious processes parallel to them but others would not.[11]

The concept of the unconscious is, for Freud, both "necessary" and "legitimate"—necessary in the sense that it provides a proper understanding of various mental phenomena; legitimate because its introduction does not involve any arbitrary steps, at least not more than the ones involved in introducing the concept of consciousness.[12]

These two postulates together suffice as a foundation for the whole psychoanalytic enterprise. The localisation postulate allows Freud to develop a model of this "mental apparatus", which, with the help of his second postulate, regarding the unconscious, is freed from the constraints of the fragmented nature of the "immediate data of consciousness".

Freud's thought is novel in three different ways.

The first regards his recognition that *mental life* and *consciousness* are not synonymous terms. Mental life, just like psychical life, flows in a continuous manner, while the flow of the immediate data of consciousness is ridden with discontinuities or gaps. Freud hypothesised that these discontinuities can be considered as reflections of entities that are absent (from consciousness) and suggested that they can be considered as having a meaning, in much the same way that a gap where a book is missing from a bookshelf may tell us something about the bookshelf or its owner.

Freud's second innovation is his hypothesis that in principle all mental phenomena can be thought of as meaningful in ways that involve the individual concerned: a dream you have is a dream that concerns and involves *you*. A slip of the tongue is a slip of *your own* tongue.

---

[11]'An Outline of Psychoanalysis', *SE vol. 23*, p. 175.

[12]'The Unconscious' [1915e], in James Strachey (ed.), *SE vol. 14* (London: Hogarth Press, 1953–1974), 159–215, p. 166. Freud thought, however, that the unconscious is more than just a useful concept. He considered it to be a mental entity that very possibly had a biological counterpart in the brain, as his parable regarding a mythical "most simplified" living organism might indicate. See 'Beyond the Pleasure Principle' [1920g], in James Strachey (ed.), *SE vol. 18* (London: Hogarth Press, 1953–1974), 1–64, pp. 26–27.

The actual details of the explanation, and the hypotheses these details involve, are almost irrelevant as long as we recognise that there was something in those phenomena that has something to do with *you*. Accordingly, Freud's third and most important innovation is to be found in the very tool he devised to explore these discontinuities—free association. Its design implies that, in Freud's view, the only one who might be holding a key for interpreting mental phenomena is the individual involved, and that this key involves talking in a process that bears an unmistakable similarity with the dialectic method invented by Socrates.[13] Freud saw that talking—i.e. speech and language—is involved not only in the treatment and alleviation of suffering but crucially in the formation and logic of symptoms too.[14] The implications of this were enormous.

If speech is a powerful enough tool to deal with psychic suffering, this is so because it allows discontinuities and gaps in the chain of the immediate data of one's consciousness to be retroactively worked through and interpreted. This seems to indicate that what we call consciousness may be much more potent than is immediately evident. But how? This was not so clear. When Freud decided to attend more closely to the phenomenon of consciousness, he struggled.[15] He attempted to

[13]As Bernard Burgoyne suggests, Freud appears to have taken up Socratic dialectic from a translation he made in 1879 of a text by John Stuart Mill. See Bernard Burgoyne, 'Autism and Topology', in Bernard Burgoyne (ed.), *Drawing the Soul: Schemas and Models in Psychoanalysis* (London: Karnac, 2000), 190–217, p. 197.

[14]While in Paris, in 1888, Freud had written a paper in which he made a comparative study of hysterical and organic paralyses. His main finding was that hysteria behaves according to the patient's lay conceptions and beliefs of how the body operates. He discovered, that is, that the hysteric's body suffered in ways dictated by ideas—i.e. language—and not by anatomy: "*In its paralyses and other manifestations, hysteria behaves as though anatomy did not exist or as though it had no knowledge of it*. ... Hysteria is ignorant of the distribution of the nerves .... It takes the organs in the ordinary, popular sense of the names they bear: the leg is the leg as far as its insertion into the hip, the arm is the upper limb as it is visible under the clothing". (Sigmund Freud, 'Some Points For a Comparative Study of Organic and Hysterical Motor Paralyses' [1888], in James Strachey (ed.), *SE vol. 1* (London: Hogarth Press, 1953–1974), 157–172, p. 169).

[15]A paper on *Consciousness* was supposed to be part of the 12 planned papers on *Metapsychology*. Of these 12 papers, only five were published. The manuscripts of the other seven were not found, even though it is known that they had been written. See Ernest Jones, *Sigmund Freud, Life and Work, Vol. 2: Years of Maturity, 1901–1919* (London: Hogarth Press, 1955), pp. 208–209; and Peter Gay, *Freud: A Life for Our Time* (New York: W. W. Norton & Company, 1998), p. 373.

break free from this difficulty by moving away from the conscious vs. unconscious dichotomy, and introducing a more elaborate, structural model of the mind, comprising an *ego*, an *id* and a *super-ego*.

In summary, Freud's discovery comprised three interconnected points: (a) all aspects of one's psychical life can be thought of as meaningful for the individual involved; (b) there are aspects of what we consider to be psychical that are not immediately available to conscious inspection; (c) the body can suffer in ways dictated by language. Points (a) and (b) opened to him the potential of formulating theoretical models of how this non-conscious agency works; point (c) confirmed that speech and language is powerful enough to make us ill, but also to help us heal.

## "Retroaction" and the Concept of Time

Freud does not argue for a complete causality of the mental processes, nor does he claim that certain psychical material will invariably bring about specific psychic phenomena. It is rather that you can take any current manifestation of mental life and retrospectively trace it back to origins which have been obscured (or "repressed"). In the process, you effect a change in the older material by allowing it to express itself once more. This is what psychoanalysis, as a therapeutic method, does. It allows one to revisit the past.[16]

Retroaction, that is, the idea that a change in one's psychic life can be effected retroactively, was one of Freud's most important insights. The original German term, *Nachträglichkeit*, has been rendered in the

---

[16]To be precise, at rare points, Freud does indeed seem to be claiming that the laws he discovers can have predictive power. See, for example, in his *Psychopathology of Everyday Life*: "My hypothesis is that this ... is not left to arbitrary psychical choice but follows paths which can be predicted and which conform to laws". (Sigmund Freud, 'The Psychopathology of Everyday Life' [1901], in James Strachey (ed.), *SE vol. 6* (London: Hogarth Press, 1953–1974), vii–296, p. 2). Much more often, however, he talks about reconstruction, retrospective interpretation, or tracing back. It might well be the case that Freud would have liked to make the stronger determinism claim but could only find justification to argue for the weaker one.

*Standard Edition* of Freud's work as *deferred action*. Freud first introduced it in his so-called *Project for a Scientific Psychology* in 1895, in
order to refer to those psychic phenomena where an event or a series
of events exercises some kind of retroactive influence on the effects of
something that has happened in the past.[17] He employed it repeatedly
in his clinical work, but perhaps not so often in his later theoretical
work. It can be seen at work in Freud's understanding of how psychoanalysis works, as well as in other theoretical constructions, such as in
the so-called *secondary revision*, a process of dream work whereby people
attempt to retroactively smooth out the gaps they observe when they
recount one of their dreams. Most importantly, it can be seen at work in
analysis itself.

Retroaction and secondary revision are related phenomena and bring
up the question of time.

In thinking about time, Freud seemed to be concerned with two
different problems, the first being the origins of our conscious awareness and perception of time, and the other regarding the time-related
functions of the mental apparatus as such, its internal clock so to speak.
In connection to the first question, Freud believed that the concept of
time, the one that we hold in our consciousness, is a construction: "The
processes of the system *Ucs.* [Unconscious]", he wrote, "are *timeless*; that
is, they are not ordered temporally, are not altered by the passage of
time; they have no reference to time at all. Reference to time is bound
up, once again, with the work of the system *Cs.* [Consciousness]".[18]

In fact, it is this presumed timelessness that can help explain retroaction and secondary revision as phenomena. If it is possible for
a current event to exercise some kind of influence on a past event,
that can only imply that the mental representations of the events are
indistinguishable with regard to the time of their occurrence: there is
nothing that could make one see which one came first and which one
second. They are only ordered in reference to an interpretative narrative the subject employs in order to include these events in their history.

[17]See 'Project for a Scientific Psychology', *SE vol. 1*, p. 356.
[18]'The Unconscious', *SE vol. 14*, p. 187.

This interpretative narrative is retroactively subject to multiple secondary revisions as needed, with its elements becoming *overdetermined*.

In connection to the second question, that of the "internal clock" of the mental apparatus, Freud developed a functional model of the system *Pcpt.* (Perception) whereby the perception of time is supposed to be derived from the periodicity of its functioning. He argued it is this periodicity that serves as a kind of clocking mechanism, on the basis of the assumption that perception and memory are two mutually exclusive functions.[19]

It is not easy, however, to see how awareness of time can at all be produced by the workings of a clocking mechanism, unless one has already accepted the existence of an observing agent, able to form awareness, that is, if one considers the phenomena in terms of an uncritically accepted subject–object framework. And this point, as we recall, is in the focus of Heidegger's criticism.

## Material and Tools of Psychoanalysis

It is here that I see Lacan entering the picture. Jacques Lacan, a psychiatrist turned psychoanalyst, reads Freud and recognises the enormous potential Freud's ideas unleash for the understanding and alleviation of human suffering. He calls for a *return* to Freud and takes as his starting point the observation that the whole of psychoanalysis—everything: the communications of the analysand, the interventions and interpretations of the analyst, psychoanalytic theories, models, hypotheses and so on— happens within language, that is, with words. Words form the material of psychoanalysis and also are its tools.

---

[19]See 'A Note Upon the "Mystic Writing Pad"' [1925a], in James Strachey (ed.), *SE vol. 19* (London: Hogarth Press, 1953–1974), 225–232. It appears that Freud (who during his studies in Vienna attended Brentano's lectures) was heavily influenced by Brentano's endeavour to develop an epistemological approach on which empirical psychology could be founded. Brentano used the notion of duration to explain how a cognitive mechanism which gathers data from an external world transforms this data into an awareness of time, objects and interactions between objects. Freud's notion of time is linear and, as it has been argued, stems from Brentano's influence. See Joel Pearl, *A Question of Time: Freud in the Light of Heidegger's Temporality* (Amsterdam: Contemporary Psychoanalytic Studies, 2013).

If you open a book of Freud, and particularly those books which are properly about the unconscious, you can be absolutely sure … to fall on a page where it is not only a question of words … but words which are the object through which one seeks for a way to handle the unconscious. Not even the meaning of words, but words in their material aspect.[20]

There is a distinction, Lacan points out, between words, in terms of what they mean, and words, in terms of how they sound—that is, in their "material" aspect. This distinction was very well known to Freud, as evidenced by his speaking, for example, about *object* presentations in consciousness, consisting of a *thing-presentation* and a *word-presentation*.[21] In order to understand it better and build on this distinction, Lacan invites us to look upon the work done in the early twentieth century by the Swiss linguist Ferdinand de Saussure. Saussure described language as a system of linguistic signs, that is, of signifying entities (which he called *signifiers*) that carry a meaning (which he called *signifieds*). For Saussure, the connection between a signifier (the sound of the world as a signifying entity) and a signified (the meaning that the signifier holds) is arbitrary but stable. The two are intimately united. He thought that for humans sharing the same language, the most important part of a linguistic sign is its meaning, i.e., that what is conveyed by the sign to other human beings sharing the language. All interaction and communication between humans takes place on a domain of inter-connected and inter-referenced meanings, but only becomes possible by the exchange of signifiers.[22]

---

[20]Jacques Lacan, 'Of Structure as an Inmixing of an Otherness Prerequisite to Any Subject Whatever' [1970], in Richard Macksey and Eugenio Donato (eds.), *The Structuralist Controversy: The Languages of Criticism and the Sciences of Man* (Baltimore: The Johns Hopkins University Press, 2007), 186–200, p. 187.

[21]See Freud, 'The Unconscious', *SE vol. 14*, pp. 201–204; and 'The Ego and the Id', *SE vol. 19*, pp. 20–23. See also above, p. 76.

[22]Saussure was not the only linguist who attempted to study linguistic signs systematically. Others approached the same phenomena choosing different but largely equivalent terms. Luis Hjelmslev, for example, instead of signifier and signified chose the terms *expression* and *content*; while for Roman Jakobson preferred *signans* and *signatum*, respectively. These concepts are forms of a dyadic formula whereby something stands for something else. Charles Sanders Peirce chose

Following Freud, Lacan focused on the material aspect of words. His crucial insight was that the mental phenomena studied by Freud involve processes that can be thought as operating on the raw material of linguistic signs—i.e. on signifiers—and their interconnections. Accordingly, he reversed Saussure's picture, asserting the primacy of the signifier over the signified. In Lacan's understanding, to use a language means that you have constructed a personal network of interconnected signifiers which runs parallel to a network of interconnected meanings (or signifieds). These interconnected signifiers comprise a chain which Lacan called "signifying chain". He described the meeting points between the two networks (i.e. the couplings between some key signifiers and signifiers) as *quilting points* (in French: *points de capiton*), a term borrowed from upholstery.[23] Lacan used it to create a metaphor in order to show how the network of signifiers is only loosely attached to the network of meanings. In the normal flow of one's life events, signifiers are added all the time and meanings shift slightly but continuously; their respective networks are in a constant flux and continuously transform themselves almost imperceptibly.

> Everything radiates out from and is organized around [a key] signifier, similar to these little lines of force that an upholstery button forms on the surface of material. It's the point of convergence that enables everything that happens in this discourse to be situated retroactively and prospectively.[24]

---

a triadic formula, distinguishing between *representamen* (the entity that represents or signifies something, equivalent to signifier), *interpretant* (the interpretation or meaning of representamen), and *object* (the entity that is referenced or represented by representamen). See Winfried Nöth, *Handbook of Semiotics* [Bloomington and Indianapolis: Indiana University Press, 1995], pp. 42–44, 84–91.

[23]Bruce Fink chooses to render it as *button ties*.

[24]Jacques Lacan, *The Seminar of Jacques Lacan, Book III: The Psychoses* [1955–56], ed. Jacques-Allain Miller (New York: W. W. Norton & Company, 1993), p. 268.

The quilting points—i.e. a number of specific key signifiers, different from one person to the other—are less prone to change and serve as a scaffolding of sorts for the overall structure of a person's psychic space.

## Signifiers and the Origins of Meaning

But what kind of an entity is a signifier? What can constitute a signifier? The answer is: anything—as long as it can be consistently recognised and distinguished from a background. More specifically, as far as linguistic signifiers are regarded, a signifier can be anything as long as it is pronounceable by a human. Signifiers are diacritical in nature but never exist on their own; they can be thought of as autonomous entities only within the particular signifying chains to which they belong. In fact, a signifier should be considered as a complex entity, comprising parts, each of which might be found to be part of different, completely independent signifying chains.[25] Each signifier and each and every one of its constitutive parts are distinguished from one another via their minimum differences, or, in Roman Jakobson's terminology, their "distinctive features".[26]

> The structure of the signifier is, as is commonly said of language, that it is articulated. This means that its units … are subject to the twofold condition of being reduced to ultimate differential elements and of combining the latter according to the laws of a closed order. These elements, the decisive discovery of linguistics, are phonemes; we must not look for any phonetic constancy in the modulatory variability to which this term applies, but rather for the synchronic system of differential couplings that are necessary to discern vocables in a given language.[27]

---

[25]See below, p. 103n34, and 191n8. For a further discussion of the signifier, see pp. 190–193.

[26]See Roman Jakobson and Morris Halle, *Fundamentals of Language* [1955] (The Hague: Mouton Publishers, 1980), pp. 31–49.

[27]Jacques Lacan, 'The Instance of the Letter in the Unconscious' [1957], in *Écrits* (New York: W. W. Norton & Company, 2006), 412–441, p. 418/501.

Lacan's insight regarding the primacy of the signifier is compatible with a simple observation about our world: language is a human creation. It was not delivered to human beings after having been created by some other, non-human entity; it is the collective product of a long history of human interactions, a history of hundreds of thousands of years. Human beings have created language, but each and every human infant is born into a linguistic world that is not of his or her making, was there from before and will continue to be there long after any individual's demise. This linguistic world is completely unintelligible to the human infant when first immersed in it, since the human infant does not have any means to "know" what the sounds exchanged by his or her carers "mean", or even that they do "mean" something. The question, that is, is not what the signified, or meaning, of a given sound is, but whether a meaning is to be expected, whether there *is* meaning as such. Accepting that this indeed is the case, i.e. that *there is meaning*, is an event of monumental importance for the human infant, the inaugurating event of *becoming* a subject of language.[28] Of course human beings have no way to establish in a strict and unambiguous way what the meaning of a given linguistic entity is—i.e. what the signified of a given signifier is—other than by reference to other linguistic entities (signifiers). This can be understood in the literal sense whereby a word can only be defined, explained, clarified or enriched by reference to other *words*. This even applies to words whose meaning can be approximated by an act of pointing or showing.

---

[28]The expression *subject of language*, when used in reference to a human being, is intended to indicate that this human being is a *speaking* human being—i.e. a human being that has already been introduced to language. It has to be pointed out, of course, that I am not talking here about an isolated event as such. Introduction to language—that is, being exposed to a language and learning how to speak it—is a lengthy and complicated process that is studied by disciplines such as developmental psychology, neuropsychology and linguistics. From a *structural* point of view, however, to be introduced to language is more like crossing a threshold, like opening a door, and it is in this sense that I call it an event.

Any chain of signifiers must be thought of as having a starting point, an origin, a signifier that sets it all in motion, so to speak. By convention, this signifier is called a master or unary signifier. Every other signifier in this specific signifying pathway can, less or more directly, be connected back to its master signifier, but this (local) master signifier cannot be connected back to anything. At the origin of the whole signifying network, then, there is a main master signifier that facilitates—and indeed guarantees—it and whose importance for the individual lies not in its meaning (its signified) but in the fact that it is there.

Free association allows the analysand to map these pathways and bring the junctures, or intersections, between signifying chains to light. The whole process enables the analysand to discern the quilting points that form the scaffolding of their own network of signifiers and to slightly reshuffle the associated network of meanings. For Lacan, Freud's discovery consisted in recognising that a person's symptoms are articulated and conform to pathways between key signifiers within that person's mental life. Freud had postulated the system *Ucs.*, *or* unconscious, to account for the fact that these dependencies—i.e. pathways of interconnection between signifiers—are not immediately visible to the person involved. Seen in this way, psychoanalysis is a method that allows a person to reformulate their own personal networks of meanings by revealing their interconnections with the underlying network of signifiers.

"What I call the effect of the signifier", Lacan says in 1970, "does not correspond at all to the signified that linguistics grasps, but well and truly to the subject".[29] In fact, the subject is revealed in the way the signifiers are interconnected within the subject's own signifying network. We can even say that the subject is represented by the interconnected signifiers. Lacan uses this as a definition of a signifier. "My definition of the signifier (there is no other) is as follows: a signifier is what represents the subject to another signifier".[30]

What about of the unconscious in all this?

---

[29]Jacques Lacan, 'Préface à l'Édition des Écrits en Livre de Poche' [1970], in J.-A. Miller (ed.), *Autres Écrits* (Paris: Éditions du Seuil, 2001), 387–391, p. 390 (my translation).

[30]'Subversion of the Subject', *Écrits*, pp. 693–694/819.

# The Lacanian Unconscious

As we saw, the unconscious is one of the most heavily contested concepts in psychoanalysis. For Freud, it was a necessary and legitimate concept, very possibly corresponding to an entity that had a biological counterpart in the brain. But this was a speculation. If Heidegger's criticism is to be taken seriously, then the Cartesian conception of consciousness has to be scrapped, and the unconscious has to go too.[31] The question, therefore, is unavoidable: When psychoanalysis claims that it works with the unconscious, what does this mean? What is the unconscious? What is its ontological status?

This is what Jacques-Alain Miller had in mind when he asked Lacan in 1964 to say more about his ontology.[32] For Lacan, the question should *not* be understood in terms of whether the unconscious exists or doesn't. The workings of an "unconscious" are not manifested in what *is* there, but in what is *not* there. The unconscious is a function that can be observed by the discontinuities it introduces in what would otherwise be a rather ordinary chain of mental events. You see it in a slip of the tongue or memory, in a dream, in a symptom: these are points where the chain breaks. In this, the disrupted continuity of a chain, you'll find the unconscious. Answering J. A. Miller, Lacan said:

> The gap of the unconscious may be said to be *pre-ontological*. I have stressed that all too often forgotten characteristic ... of the first emergence of the unconscious, namely, that it does not lend itself to ontology. Indeed, what became apparent at first to Freud, to the discoverers, to those who made the first steps, and what still becomes apparent to

---

[31]See above, pp. 75–76, 80.
[32]Jacques Lacan, *The Seminar of Jacques Lacan, Book XI: The Four Fundamental Concepts of Psychoanalysis* [1964–65], ed. Jacques-Allain Miller (New York: W. W. Norton & Company, 1998), p. 29. According to M. Marini, Miller's actual question was "Does your notion of the subject imply an ontology?" (Marcelle Marini, *Jacques Lacan: The French Context* (New Brunswick, NJ: Rudgers University Press, 1992), p. 130).

anyone in analysis who spends some time observing what truly belongs to the order to the unconscious, is that it is neither being, nor non-being, but the unrealized.[33]

Words or names are forgotten, confused, mixed up or replaced, but there is a logic to how this happens: existing pathways connecting signifiers are somehow disabled and new pathways take their place. This process has a structure, and its effects, the *formations* of the unconscious as Lacan calls them, make themselves known as a *structure*.[34] Hence, the famous Lacanian motto: *The unconscious is structured like a language*. For Lacan, therefore, the unconscious is never seen as an entity that exists as such; strictly speaking, it's not even a function or a process. "Unconscious" is the name we give to the structure that manifests itself as a discontinuity or gap in a signifying chain and gives rise to a number of replacement pathways. The unconscious invites the subject to make a choice, whether one will own the meaning carried by this

---

[33]Lacan, *Seminar XI*, pp. 29–30.

[34]As an illustration of this point, we can take the famous Signorelli incident, reported by Freud. (See Freud, 'The Psychopathology of Everyday Life', *SE vol. 6*, pp. 2–14). Freud finds himself unable to remember the name of the painter Signorelli while talking with a fellow passenger during a trip in Bosnia and Herzegovina. Instead, the names Botticelli and Boltraffio come to his mind. Free associating later on the key signifiers involved, Freud connects Botticelli and Boltraffio with Bosnia. From there he thinks of Bosnia and Herzegovina, the place where this incident took place, and of the appellation Herr which in German means Sir or Lord. This in turn brings to his mind the Italian equivalent of Herr, i.e. Signor, and all its religious connotations; finally, the name Boltraffio brings to his mind the town of Traffoi, which in turn allows him to recall something professionally embarrassing that happened there. Freud's explanation was that there was something embarrassing which he'd like to avoid thinking of, and also a reluctance to talk about religious matters in a conversation with someone he did not personally know. Both the embarrassment and the reluctance are reflected in this particular incident: the reluctance to speak about religious matters ("Signor") having "caused" the replacement of the original name (Signorelli); and the embarrassment (associated with Traffoi) having found its way in the name Boltraffio. We observe that the name Signorelli apart from its ordinary signification—namely, the famous painter bearing this name—becomes, in the specific case of Freud, a compound signifier, comprising two parts, *signor* and *elli*; the first evokes religious questions through the signifier *Herr*, the German translation of *signor*, while the second evokes Botti*celli*. In his report, Freud does not tell us whether these are the only two signifying chains he can produce in association with the name Signorelli. He reports these two but he might have had a myriad other in his mind. See also below p. 191n8.

or that manifestation of the unconscious. Lacan expressed this very clearly: "The status of the unconscious ... so fragile on the ontic plane, is ethical".[35]

Lacan's understanding of the Freudian unconscious is to a large extent compatible with what Freud himself thought—to a large extent, but not completely. Freud showed a willingness to connect it with some sort of underlying biological structure of the brain, but Lacan was not willing to follow him there. "Does this mean that I hope to include the concepts introduced historically by Freud under the term unconscious? No, I don't think so. The unconscious, the Freudian concept, is something different".[36] This difference became more and more visible, to the extent that in 1978 we see Lacan saying that it was Freud who invented "this admittedly wild story, that we call the unconscious; and the unconscious is perhaps a Freudian delusion. It explains everything but, as articulated very well by someone called Karl Popper, it explains a bit too much. It is a conjecture with no refutation".[37] And on another occasion, again in 1978: "[If the unconscious is] what one constructs with language, it is a *fraud*: the free association of ideas relies on the haphazard; it is haphazardly that we proceed in order to free someone from what is called the symptom".[38]

## An Identity from the Mirror

The human being is brought into a world and presented with a demand that cannot be met. Becoming a subject of language, means becoming subjected to a framework of worldliness that language incorporates. By becoming occupied by language, you are unavoidably alienated: What is yours, and yours only—ownmost or authentic as Heidegger would put it—can only be seen and become expressible in a language given to

---

[35]Lacan, *Seminar XI*, p. 33.

[36]*Seminar XI*, p. 21.

[37]'Conclusions' [1978] *Lettres de l'Ecole Freudienne*, 2/25 (1979), 219–220, p. 219 (my translation).

[38]Lacan, quoted in Marini, *Lacan*, p. 248.

you ready-made, created by *others*. The subject of language is a split or *divided* subject.

Freud did not use such terms. In his structural model of the mental apparatus, Freud spoke about the *ego*, the *super-ego* and the *id*. The Freudian ego was always thought as a go-between of sorts, an intermediary agency that manages the relations and exchanges between the "individual" and an "external" reality. In this decidedly Cartesian conceptual framework, the individual human being is born with the potential to construct an identity—or ego—in a process akin to the process of identification, whereby a person takes on or idealises attributes from other important individuals in his or her life. The templates par excellence are the parents: the child identifies with them and strives to make his or her own ego similar to the Ideal Ego that he or she assumes they possess. For Lacan, just as for Freud, the infant's ego cannot be thought to even exist prior to this identification process: the ego as such is a product of a long structuring process. For both the ego is split, just as the subject is split. But the ego is not identical with the subject.

One of Lacan's earlier contributions to psychoanalysis was the *mirror stage*. He had borrowed and subsequently transformed the notion from the psychologist Henri Wallon, and spoke about it as early as in 1936, at the 14th International Psychoanalytic Congress in Marienbad.[39] It all has to do with the biological fact that the human infant is born prematurely. This is a human particularity: during a comparatively long period after birth, the human infant is not able to survive if left without appropriate care. During this early stage, his or her socialisation consists of a series of interactions involving the human face and its expressions, and other visual, vocal, and tactile cues. According to Lacan, it is only through his or her identification with the image of another human being that the infant obtains an image of his or her body and a sense of self. This sense of self is illusionary, a product of a series of overlapping identifications and appropriations; the identity obtained is a made-up, a patchwork identity, that gives the subject of language a *semblance* of unity. As Lacan puts it, "we must absolutely define the ego's imaginary

---

[39]See Elisabeth Roudinesco, *Jacques Lacan* (New York: Columbia University Press, 1997), p. 111.

function as the unity of the subject who is alienated from himself. The ego is something in which the subject cannot recognise himself at first except by alienating himself".[40]

The hypothesis of a mirror stage allowed Lacan to discuss concretely the structuring process at the end of which the human being is able to position themselves as acting agents within the framework of worldliness that their language incorporates. Furthermore, and most importantly, it allows us to see that what we call a subject of language is *not* synonymous with the human being as Descartes saw it. When a person says "I want this", this "I" serves as the placeholder of the enouncing *subject*. However, this enouncing *I* is *not* identical to the speaking being qua subject.[41] To put it differently, even though the terms "subject", "person", "individual", etc., can all refer to the very same human being, they are not equivalent, synonymous or interchangeable in their respective uses. Consequently, Lacan's take on the Cartesian cogito is radically different from Descartes's own. For Lacan, the subject's existence ("I am") cannot be founded on the subject's reflective certainty ("I am thinking"). As Lacan puts it, "I am thinking where I am not, therefore I am where I am not thinking".[42]

Let us try to unpack this a bit more.

## The Three Registers of Experience

As a biological organism, the human being operates and interacts with the world in ways that are determined by the organism's structure and physiology. We can say that the human being is thrown in the world as "is", i.e., as a biological organism. For the purposes of what I am trying to describe here, we do not need any special understanding of the particular interactions involved. The only extraneous notion I need is that

---

[40]Jacques Lacan, 'The Symbolic, the Imaginary, and the Real' [1953], in *On the Names-of-the-Father* (Cambridge: Polity Press, 2013), 1–52, p. 24.

[41]As we said, it's not identical with the Freudian Ego either.

[42]Lacan, 'Instance of the Letter', *Écrits*, p. 430/517.

of structure. The phenomena I refer to can be thought as events pertaining to structures and their interactions. Structural events are occurrences pertaining to coupling between different structures.[43] Whatever happens in the environment has repercussions on the body's state at any given moment. For example, light falls on the eye and the eye's pupil contracts; or a source of heat will cause a reaction by the nervous system which will be translated to a movement of specific muscles that will result in a movement which will bring a lessening of the excitation, or discomfort, caused by the heat. And so on and so forth. Talking generally, the world qua environment in which the organism is immersed is the source of all kinds of structural changes to the organism.

The human infant who is thrown in the world is unavoidably participating in some structural events: the world has effects on the body, it is the source of structural events for the body, and the infant cannot but be subjected to them.[44] Developing further the hypothesis of a mirror stage, and recognising that all the early identifications and early relations of an infant with their parents or carers that the mirror stage pertains to share a connection with image, in the sense of an actual or a mental picture, Lacan put forward the suggestion that they constitute a special register in the organisation of the psyche. It would not be possible to speak about identification unless there is an original entity that can be discerned and identified with. Furthermore, an identification that has taken place itself entails a more or less sustained alteration of a certain balance: if an entity is identified with another entity, either as a

---

[43]I am referring here to the concept of *structural coupling*, which I am borrowing from the work of the Chilean biologists H. Maturana and Fr. Varela. They defined it as "a phenomenon that takes place whenever a plastic composite unity undergoes recurrent interactions with structural change but without loss of organization, which may follow any changing or recurrent structural configuration of its domain of interactions (medium)". (Humberto R. Maturana and Francisco J. Varela, *Autopoiesis and Cognition: The Realization of the Living* (Dordrecht: D. Reidel Publishing Company, 1980), p. xxi). See also Humberto R. Maturana, *Biologie der Realität* (Frankfurt am Main: Suhrkamp, 1998), pp. 104–105. I find this concept particularly useful because it allows us to describe the interactions of a living organism with the environment, without resorting to teleological hypotheses regarding functions and purposes of bodily organs and/or subsystems.

[44]This is also the case with the human foetus for a number of months during the later stages of pregnancy. For example, research indicates that while in the womb foetuses do react to their mother's voice.

whole, or in any of its specific aspects, this can only mean that the latter can stand as a "pointer" to the former, either as a whole or in some specific aspect, and a structure is formed—a dynamic, fluid structure.[45] The very decision to describe this as a register—rather, say, as an agency or a function—could be thought of as reflecting Lacan's insight that it involves a certain temporal constancy and allows for the emergence of increasingly complicated structures. The name he chose for it was *imaginary*, playing on the linguistic connection of the words image and imagination, and stressing its connection to an image.

Being inscribed in the imaginary register is a structuring process. As such it makes possible the emergence of a further register comprising the more solidly structured elements of the imaginary, together with the ways in which they act as pointers to each other. This further register is the register of the *symbolic*. It is retroactively constructed out of elements of the imaginary that exhibit a temporal persistence and start acting as pointers to other elements of the imaginary that also exhibit a temporal persistence—a "subset" of the imaginary, if we may call it thus.[46]

The emergence of the symbolic register is spontaneous but not instantaneous. It's a structuring process that may be exemplified in the process of the acquisition of language—a process that is also spontaneous but not instantaneous. However, it is not limited to it. One could say that language is a specific subset of the symbolic register. The symbolic comprises signifiers, interconnected in signifying chains or networks. In other words, it initially contains those elements of the imaginary that are taken by the human being to represent something to

---

[45]We can understand this process in terms of Peirce's theory of the sign (see above, p. 97n22). The pointer can be thought of as a *representamen*; what is pointed to as an *object*. Both the "pointer", as well as what is "pointed to", can change in time, some of them more readily than others. Importantly, identification, as a process, is less primordial than the process of "becoming a pointer to".

[46]I am using the term "subset" in a figurative rather than a strict mathematical sense. The symbolic can be said to be a subset of the imaginary only to the extent that it comprises temporarily persistent elements of the latter which become pointers, i.e. become signifiers. It can be thought, nevertheless, as much more extensive than the imaginary since apart from simple elements is also contains relationships between elements qua signifiers, that is chains, or networks of interconnected signifiers.

him or her. The human infant has his or her own signifiers and incorporates them in his or her own signifying networks in the course of time. What is being represented, how a given sign is being "interpreted"— namely, its meaning—is initially private in the sense that it has no bearing to any external framework of reference. Gradually, however, it tends to conform to the network of interconnections that a given language represents.

Now, if the imaginary register is that which the infant can construct out of his or her experience via the help of the image of (an) Other—I am referring here to the mirror stage—and if the symbolic register is a subset of the imaginary that comes about when the human being enters "the significative system of interhuman relations as such",[47] then a question may be raised regarding their origins. This is where we can locate the third register that Lacan postulated, that of the *real*. The real, in accordance with what has been described heretofore, can be defined as the register of all the structural events pertaining to the body—in effect, a register of all interactions of the body, and changes effected to it within its domain of interactions.

We have, therefore, "three quite distinct registers that are essential registers of human reality",[48] the real, the imaginary and the symbolic. There have been considerable debates in regard to their actual conceptual content especially regarding the register of the real. Admittedly, in the beginning at least, Lacan used the term "real" almost interchangeably with the term "reality", giving rise to "blatant contradictions" as Lorenzo Chiesa writes.[49] Gradually, the differentiation between the two became more unambiguous and more pronounced, and the importance of the real grew from the 1960s onwards. François Roustang, however, a former student of Lacan who became one of his more severe critics, has accused him of being deliberately obscure and incoherent, and of introducing a contradictory term that "simply does not exist … or it simply does not exist as a concept, since it can go on drifting in all

---

[47]Lacan, 'The Symbolic, the Imaginary, and the Real', *On the Names-of-the-Father*, p. 27.

[48]'The Symbolic, the Imaginary, and the Real', *On the Names-of-the-Father*, p. 4.

[49]See Lorenzo Chiesa, *Subjectivity and Otherness* (Cambridge, MA: The MIT Press, 2007), p. 126.

directions".[50] In contrast, according to Tom Eyers the real has been a central, determining the concept of Lacan's work, each stage of the theoretical development of which can be understood as attempts to delineate it more precisely.[51]

In my view, both the imaginary and the symbolic register would be completely unfounded if the real had not been already tacitly postulated as the necessary background from which they emerge. As I indicated above, the real can be defined as the register of all the structural events pertaining to the body; in effect, the real can be thought of as the register of how reality—the term "reality" is used here in the sense of both worldly and bodily reality—is received by the individual human being in question. "I am saying the real and not reality", Lacan explains in 1959, "because reality is constituted by all the halters that human symbolism, in a more or less perspicacious fashion, passes around the neck of the real in so far as it makes of them the objects of its experience".[52] So, for example, an unexpected loud bang on our door in the night might be thought of as real in terms of waveforms and decibels, but it can only be part of *our* real insofar as it wakes us up. It becomes part of our own world (or *reality*) the moment we are drawn to account for it (e.g. by saying or thinking something like, "there was a loud bang—someone must be at the door"). In a similar vein, an unexpected bodily discomfort, such as a sharp ache in the arm, is part of *our* real and can become a part of our *reality* when overlaid by a framework of explanations that would allow us to include it.[53] Seen in this way, the concept of the real can show its coherence in a way that would otherwise be impossible to achieve if one were to try to make sense of all of Lacan's different attempts to elucidate it directly, from the ground

---

[50]François Roustang, *The Lacanian Delusion* (New York: Oxford University Press, 1990), pp. 101–102.

[51]See Tom Eyers, *Lacan and the Concept of the 'Real'* (Basingstoke, Hampshire: Palgrave Macmillan, 2012).

[52]Jacques Lacan, *The Seminar of Jacques Lacan, Book VI: Desire and Its Interpretation* [1958–59] (www.lacaninireland.com), p. 342 (translation slightly modified).

[53]It is in exactly this sense that Marcelle Marini writes that "language, the signifier, the letter, logic, the phallus, the Name-of-the-Father, etc., all become superimposed on the real and send it back to the position of the inaccessible". Marini, *Lacan*, p. 72.

up, so to speak. In other words, I am suggesting to recognise that a *circle of understanding* is involved here, not very dissimilar to the one that Heidegger considers indispensable to philosophical thinking: we cannot have a clear understanding of what makes Lacan introduce the real unless we have a first rough conception of what the real *might* be.

Lacan thought of the real as something that is gradually giving way, so to speak, to the imaginary and the symbolic—as the raw material out of which the imaginary and the symbolic are constructed, or the core that remains.[54] Nonetheless, the real can never be fully taken over by the imaginary and symbolic registers, and it is in this sense that we see Bruce Fink writing that "the real is perhaps best understood as *that which has not yet been symbolised*, remains to be symbolised, or even resists symbolisation".[55] Rather than just a background against which the other two registers emerge, the real is really a scaffolding framework—the most basic register of the psychic imprint of structural events involving the living body in its domain of interactions. It is in this that its fundamental difference from what we ordinarily call reality, lies.

Lacan's introduction of the three registers is undoubtedly one of his best-known innovations to psychoanalytic theory, and one that sets his point of view apart from that of other post-Freudian theories. It has obvious clinical implications, but also offers a coherent ontological frame for the emergence of the speaking being. There were those, however, who were not convinced.

Jacques Derrida, for example, claimed that the "tripartition" imaginary/real/symbolic entails a rigidity in connection to how the symbolic

---

[54]See, for example, lesson VII of *Seminar I*, where Lacan speaks about the "original chaos" of the real, out of which the (imaginary) Ego may be born, and the position of the (symbolic) subject may be secured. (Jacques Lacan, *The Seminar of Jacques Lacan, Book I: Freud's Papers on Technique* [1953–54], ed. Jacques-Allain Miller (New York: W. W. Norton & Company, 1988), pp. 73–88.) Lacan returns to the question repeatedly until towards the end of his teaching. As late as in 1976 he refers to the real as "a core around which thought embellishes". As he points out, "the mark as such of this real is that it doesn't tie on to anything. This at least is how I conceive the real". (*The Seminar of Jacques Lacan, Book XXIII: The Sinthome* [1975–76], ed. Jacques-Allain Miller (Cambridge: Polity Press, 2016), p. 104).

[55]Bruce Fink, *The Lacanian Subject: Between Language and Jouissance* (Princeton, NJ: Princeton University Press, 1997), p. 25.

is conceived and thus runs the danger of becoming an "unmodifiable transcendental or ontological structure",[56] i.e. a structure with no phenomenological merit. He suggested that the only way around this conceptual problem would be to undermine or deconstruct the rigidity of the symbolic order by "unsewing" it with the help of what Derrida includes under the rubric of "dissemination".[57] Derrida has a point regarding the danger of potential rigidity of the real/imaginary/symbolic structure, but I think that his general disagreement reflects a limitation of his own understanding of the emergence of the symbolic rather than the limits of the concept itself. Even though we cannot approach the real unless we start from the symbolic, the case is that the imaginary and the symbolic come out of the real and not the other way around. It is imprecise to consider the real as that register that ends up comprising all that has been impossible to be included in the symbolic; the real is not the result of an incomplete process of symbolisation, but rather the other way around. It all starts with the real; at the end, the real still contains all what is *not yet* in the imaginary or the symbolic. Still not, and not yet. In other words, we need to keep our focus on the circle of understanding involved.

Slavoj Žižek, on the other hand, has suggested a rereading of the concept of the real, claiming "that there are at least three notions" of it; he argues that "the very triad of real, symbolic and imaginary is in a way mapped onto or projected into the real itself" producing "[a] real Real, [an] imaginary Real and [a] symbolic Real"; he even extends this idea further to the other registers, describing the knotting between the real, imaginary and symbolic as a three-dimensional configuration, with "each of these categories … mapped onto all the others. … [They] are really intertwined in a radical sense; like a crystal structure in which the different elements are mapped onto and repeat themselves within each category".[58] In total, Žižek envisages nine different variations of the

---

[56]Jacques Derrida, *Positions* [1972] (Chicago: The University of Chicago Press, 1981), p. 113n46.

[57]See *Positions*, pp. 83–87.

[58]Slavoj Žižek and Glyn Daly, *Conversation with Žižek* (Cambridge: Polity Press, 2004), pp. 68, 69. See also Slavoj Žižek, *On Belief* (London: Routledge, 2001), p. 82.

three registers, a combination of each one with each and every one. The idea is appealing, especially because of its internal symmetry, but I cannot see its usefulness. In my view, the main purpose behind Lacan's differentiation between the three registers was to enable three things: the structural modelling of the processes that are taking place in the human psyche as a result of the immersion of the body in the world, the construction of an imaginary identity (mirror stage), and the subjection to language. In other words, Lacan's purpose was predominantly clinical. It is difficult to see the clinical relevance of Žižek's innovation.

## Jouissance and the Signifierisation of the Real

With the real conceived of as the register of structural events pertaining to the body, we would need an additional term to denote these events in regard to the experience of the human being involved. This term is "jouissance". It comes from the French verb *jouir*, "enjoy", and indeed, it was in this sense, *enjoyment*, that Lacan first used it, before gradually allowing its scope to broaden. The term is now usually left untranslated in order to prevent the tendency to regard it as synonymous to enjoyment.[59] Lacan first introduced jouissance in *Seminar V* (1957–1958), where he defined it in contradistinction to the concept of desire.[60] He returned to it again and again, modifying it ever so slightly as he considered it in terms of the clinic and elaborated its interconnections with the imaginary, the symbolic and the real.[61]

[59]According to N. Braunstein, the confusion of jouissance with satisfaction that can sometimes be observed, can be traced to the confusing subtitle given to a subsection of a particular lesson in *Seminar VII* (*The Seminar of Jacques Lacan, Book VII: The Ethics of Psychoanalysis* [1959–60], ed. Jacques-Allain Miller (London: Routledge, 1992), p. 205). See Néstor A. Braunstein, 'Desire and Jouissance in the Teachings of Lacan', in Jean-Michel Rabaté (ed.), *The Cambridge Companion to Lacan* (Cambridge: Cambridge University Press, 2003), 102–115, pp. 104–105.

[60]Jacques Lacan, *The Seminar of Jacques Lacan, Book V: Formations of the Unconscious* [1957–58], ed. Jacques-Allain Miller (Cambridge: Polity Press, 2017), pp. 235–252.

[61]Jacques-Allain Miller has identified six different "paradigms" in Lacan's treatment of the concept of jouissance. They follow one another and replace each other more or less chronologically. See Jacques-Allain Miller, 'Les six Paradigmes de la Jouissance' *La Cause Freudienne*, 43 (1999), 7–29; http://www.causefreudienne.net/wp-content/uploads/2015/04/JAM-Six-paradigmes-jouissance.pdf.

Jouissance can be approached from several different angles, but the most straightforward one would be to consider it at the level of the real. Taking our lead from Lacan's teaching in 1972–1973, we can think of jouissance as representing the events pertaining to the various configurations of structural coupling of the body in the world.[62] Whatever happens to the body gives rise to specific bodily effects, many of which are registered in the real. *Jouissance* (of the body) is the name one can give to such effects. In other words, if the real is the register of all bodily structural events, jouissance can be seen as that which is registered—the *imprint*, so to speak, of these events for the individual involved. An event of the body is not just the outcome of the functioning of the body qua biological organism in structural coupling; it is not to be confused with the stimuli that the body receives and processes. It's rather a concurrence of specific bodily states that can be distinguished, either at the moment of occurrence or retroactively—that is a mark, or a *letter*.

The concept of jouissance is Lacanian, and it is not to be found in Freud's theories. However, it could be thought as vaguely related to "libido" and "stimulus". For Freud, the task of the nervous system is to master external and internal stimuli. Libido is thought as being able to be cathected onto people and things in the external world, or in phantasy.[63] We could account for all these phenomena by referring, instead, to "jouissance". However, there is a notable difference. Jouissance, by definition, is more basic, more primordial than the other two. It is pre-linguistic, or in fact *non*-linguistic, since, as we saw earlier, it is only connected to the register of the real. This is meant in the sense that jouissance is an effect of the body. Speaking in 1966, Lacan is quite clear on this:

---

[62]See, for example, the points where Lacan describes "the jouissance of the body ... as asexual" and explains that he identifies "the reason for the being of signifierness in jouissance, jouissance of the body" (Jacques Lacan, *The Seminar of Jacques Lacan, Book XX: Encore, On Feminine Sexuality, the Limits of Love and Knowledge* [1972–73], ed. Jacques-Allain Miller (New York: W. W. Norton & Company, 1998), pp. 6, 71). For the concept of signifierness see below, p. 139.

[63]In Freud's conceptualisation, the assumption that what is internal is distinct from what is external is not properly examined. It is because of this that he finds necessary to qualify between external and internal stimuli, as well as between the external world and phantasy.

What I call jouissance—in the sense in which the body experiences itself—is always in the nature of a tension, in the nature of a forcing, of a spending, even of an exploit. Unquestionably, there is jouissance at the level at which pain begins to appear, and we know that it is only at this level of pain that a whole dimension of the organism, which would otherwise remain veiled, can be experienced.[64]

To take a concrete example, one can take the case of a new-born infant. Feeding, be it from the breast or from a bottle, is clearly an important procedure for the infant—if only in terms of biological sustenance. However, the baby has no control over it and is completely "at the mercy" of its carer. During unsignifierised actual feeding, the human infant can be expected to experience all kinds of things, some pleasurable, some (perhaps) not. The exact details of what the baby experiences cannot be known. What is crucial here is that all these events *are* jouissance. Now, this procedure is repeated, more or less regularly. The baby becomes accustomed to expect to be fed more or less regularly and lives this event together with some other events—for example, the appearance of a friendly face, or certain sounds. A certain jouissance accompanies these events and becomes linked or "bound" to them and, as such, taken out of circulation, so to speak.[65] The similarity of this process to the process, described by Freud, of the investment or cathexis of libido upon objects is not coincidental. However, in contrast to Freud's libido theory whereby libido can be invested upon, or withdrawn from, objects, Lacan's signifierised jouissance is "lost".

The most important aspect of jouissance is its connection to the signifier and to the signifying process. As we described earlier, some parts of the real become somewhat more stable through a process of retroactive identifications—a process whose pivotal stage is the mirror stage—which leads to the emergence of the imaginary and symbolic registers. Putting jouissance in the picture, we can see that the process

---

[64]Lacan, quoted in Braunstein, 'Desire and Jouissance', *The Cambridge Companion to Lacan*, p. 103.

[65]This is not to be taken literally, of course. What it means is that a certain jouissance becomes conditioned to the events it accompanies and cannot be disassociated.

corresponds to a *binding, moulding* or *crystallisation* of jouissance. Both the imaginary and the symbolic can be thought as crystallised, signifierised jouissance, that *corpsifies* the body—in the sense that it turning is into a corpse, a cadaver.[66] As Lacan had said before, "the symbol first manifests itself as the killing of the thing, and this death results in the endless perpetuation of the subject's desire".[67]

Signification, as such, brings a kind of order to the jouissance of the body: the world is much safer when its effects on the body (i.e. jouissance) can be incorporated into a network of signifiers. In their dealings with the world, human beings create more and complex networks of interconnected signifierised jouissance within which they dwell. The subject of language and the world it lives in are products of the signifierisation process. It is, in Lacan's words, "this emergence which, just before, as subject, was nothing, but which, having scarcely appeared, solidifies into a signifier".[68]

The world that the subject of language inhabits is a world revealed and guaranteed by the symbolic order and the signifier. It is a shared world, in the sense that each and every one of us is subjected to a symbolic order which was established beforehand; but it is also a private world in the sense that each and every one of us, as a subject, is adding their own panoply of signifiers and retroactively creating their own signifying network. This distinction between private and public has some usefulness only when one considers the structure of psychic life from a distance, *macroscopically* so to speak. When one looks closer at the phenomena, it becomes irrelevant. Our own private world is never completely private and our own, but also never completely shared and public.[69] There is a tension between what is private and what is shared that resembles the tension between authenticity and inauthenticity in

---

[66]See Lacan, 'Radiophonie', *Autres Écrits*, p. 409.

[67]'Function and Field', *Écrits*, p. 262/319. Lacan's conceptualisation of signifierisation as the killing of the thing was inspired by A. Kojève's commentary on Hegel.

[68]*Seminar XI*, p. 199.

[69]The argument here is similar to Wittgenstein's *Private Language Argument*. See Ludwig Wittgenstein, *Philosophical Investigations* [1945] (Oxford: Basil Blackwell, 1986), §244–271.

Heidegger.[70] Jacques-Alain Miller has pointed out that for Lacan "the exterior is present in the interior. The most interior … has, in the analytic experience, a quality of exteriority".[71] Lacan tried to represent this tension with the help of mathematical entities such as the Möbius strip or the Klein bottle. As Kazushige Shingu explains,

as a first approximation, we can say that that which is said in psychoanalysis is spoken *within* the subject who is doing the talking. It seems, therefore, as though a boundary exists between these things and the external, social life that the subject experiences from day to day. But in fact, the unconscious, which seems so clearly to be a place hidden within this internal discourse, is also a kind of secret passage leading back to the outside world. By slipping out through this passage, the subject manages to see herself from the outside, and gains the ability to speak of herself. The unconscious is thus structured like a Möbius strip; if you follow the inside to its very end, you find yourself on the outside.[72]

## Emergence of Desire

The process of signifierisation of jouissance is never complete. There is always a part of jouissance that remains unbound, i.e. unsignifierised. This jouissance is experienced "as" something that does not really belong in the subject's world, as out-worldly. It is indeed out-worldly since, as we said earlier, a world is only constituted via the installation of the signifier. These leftovers of jouissance cause the human being to *oscillate*, so to speak, between meaning and anxiety. A way to understand anxiety, then, is to see it as the generic name we can give to all jouissance that

---

[70]See above, p. 40.

[71]Jacques-Alain Miller, 'Extimité' [1985–86], in Mark Bracher et al. (eds.), *Lacanian Theory of Discourse: Subject, Structure, and Society* (New York: New York University Press, 1994), 74–87, p. 76.

[72]Kazushige Shingu, *Being Irrational: Lacan, the Object a, and the Golden Mean* [1995] (Tokyo: Gakuji Shoin, 2004), p. 159.

does not quite fit in a network of signifiers. Obviously, in accordance with what we have already said, jouissance always begins like this.[73]

Any event of the body and its associated jouissance can be a potential signifier. It becomes a signifier when it obtains the character of a pointer to another signifier, i.e. when it becomes part of a network of elements. Until this happens, an event of the body is just unsignifierised jouissance—a trauma, so to speak, or a source of anxiety or tension. Sometimes a tension is discharged, and in this respect, the event can be experienced as pleasurable.[74] It is only after the installation of the signifier that the human being can really consider this or that surge of jouissance as pleasure: an event is not pleasurable or unpleasurable on its own: it only becomes such when considered within the network of interconnected signifiers that constitute the experience of this particular human being. In other words, there is very little in jouissance that would allow an observer to know whether this or that event of the body will be thought of as pleasant or unpleasant by the subject. Something that might be very pleasant for one might be considered as unpleasant or completely unwelcome by the other. What is pleasant or unpleasant is not so self-evident or clear for the speaking being. It's not a question of something that can be "objectively" measured or understood. Among the members of a community, of course, some common ground can be thought to exist, reflecting that part of each member's world that is shared. This is less and less the case, though, when we examine different or distant cultural communities.

As discussed earlier, a side effect of the process of signifierisation is that the signifierised jouissance is removed from circulation, is "deactivated", so to speak. Where once there was an effect because of a body event, there is now a signifier as a pointer to it; the actual effect (i.e. the jouissance of the body event) is now unavailable. The pointer does not

---

[73]Jacques-Alain Miller describes this aspect of jouissance as *jouissance One*, stressing that at the beginning at least, it can do without the other. See Miller, 'Six Paradigmes', p. 25.

[74]Compare, here, Freud's attempt to speak about the origins of the pleasure principle. He outlined it in terms of mounting or discharging a tension resulting from a stimulus: "Unpleasurable feelings are connected with an increase and pleasurable feelings with a decrease of stimulus". Freud, 'Instincts and Their Vicissitudes', *SE vol. 14*, pp. 120–121.

really replace the missing jouissance; that is, it does not create a similar effect—or *any* effect, for that matter. It only opens the possibility of the emergence of a second layer (or register) of interconnectable entities: the imaginary. In other words, signifierisation of jouissance is a process that corresponds to the emergence of the imaginary and the symbolic, as well as to the emergence of *desire*, where by desire we mean the urge to return to an original jouissance which is not available anymore.[75] It has to be stressed that the term "desire" is used here in an ontological rather than an ontic sense, i.e., without any reference to *what* is desired, what it means to desire, or how desire is articulated.

At the heart of the subject of language is a lack, something absent, something that is not available and cannot be pointed at. It can only be referred to. What is lacking is the referent of the signifier, the object that is pointed to, by it. Also, there are other events of the body (already registered in the real) which have not been included in the network of signifiers: anxiety, for example; or orgasm. When a signifier is established, when jouissance is made into signifiers, there is always a leftover, a "remainder" jouissance that has not yet been signifierised. Signifierised jouissance is always *pointing* to an absence, namely the absence of what is being signified. This means that, for every speaking being, the very activity of speaking brings to the fore an absence (or a lack, as Lacan would put it). The corollary of lack is desire. Any signifier that points to an absence—i.e. to a lack—refers to a desire which is caused by the remainder (not-yet-signifierised) jouissance, or to its object. Lacan calls this object *a*:

That is to say that [object a], the object of desire, in its nature is a residue, is a remainder. It is the residue which the being with which the

---

[75]In other words, desire does not come out from some primitive (unconscious) depths of the psyche where it was lying hidden. As Lacan says, "there is a desire because there is unconscious, that is to say language which escapes the subject in its structure and effects, and because there is always on the level of language something beyond consciousness, which is where the function of desire can be situated". (Lacan in 1966, quoted in Dany Nobus, 'A Matter of Cause: Reflection on Lacan's "Science and Truth"', in Jason Glynos and Yannis Stavrakakis (eds.), *Lacan & Science* (London: Karnac, 2002), 89–118, p. 103).

speaking subject is confronted as such leaves to any possible demand. And this is the way that the object re-joins the real. This is how it participates in it.[76]

Lacan considered object *a* to be one of his important contributions to psychoanalysis. The concept's conceptual origin can be found in Karl Abraham's conception of the part object and in Winnicott's transitional object. Lacan had "invented" it, as he said in his *Seminar XXI* (1973–74),[77] to clarify the distinction between an object which is desired and a *virtual* object, that is logically required by the very structure of desire as its *formal cause*.[78] "Object *a*", Lacan said, "is a function I invented in order to designate the object of desire. Small *a* is what Winnicott calls the transitional object".[79] It is, in other words, an abstract placeholder, an empty vehicle that makes the emergence of desire possible.[80] The motivating force for its function comes from the remainder (not yet signifierised) jouissance, which in a way becomes what Lacan called a *surplus* jouissance (in French: *plus-de-jouir*). In a manner parallel to Marxist theories of value,[81] the imaginary and the symbolic are thought to represent more jouissance than the jouissance originally crystallised in them in the process of signifierisation. The subject of language is alienated from the original jouissance but is now under the sway of the surplus jouissance represented by the imaginary and the symbolic.

This discussion brings up the question of the drive.

---

[76]Lacan, *Seminar VI*, pp. 341–342.

[77]See *The Seminar of Jacques Lacan, Book XXI: Les Non-Dupes Errent* [1973–74] (www.lacaninireland.com), pp. 212–13.

[78]See 'Position of the Unconscious', *Écrits*, p. 721n4/850; and 'Science and Truth', *Écrits*, p. 733/863. For the concept of *formal* cause, see above, p. 54.

[79]'At the *Institut Français* in London (3 February 1975)' [1975], trans. Dany Nobus, *Journal for Lacanian Studies*, 3/2 (2005), 295–303, p. 301.

[80]For a discussion, see Fink, *Lacanian Subject*, pp. 83–97, and also Shingu, *Being Irrational*.

[81]In Marxist theory of value, surplus value is the amount of value that is added to a product by human labour, without being reflected in the wages paid to the worker for the work done. Since workers are *alienated* from the product of their labour—i.e. they do not own it—the production of surplus value is thought as the "work" of capital (in the sense of a return of investment).

# Instincts, Drives and Beyond

The *drive* is one of Freud's most easily misunderstood concepts. Freud's German term was *Trieb*, which was originally translated as *instinct*—a choice that might have had some justification then but gave rise to confusion, especially given its biologistic connotations. The meaning Freud gave to the term was that of a motivating force or factor that would account for the observation that living creatures seem to be compelled to behave in certain ways.

The theory of the instincts [or drives] is so to say our mythology. Instincts are mythical entities, magnificent in their indefiniteness. In our work we cannot for a moment disregard them, yet we are never sure that we are seeing them clearly. You know how popular thinking deals with the instincts. People assume as many and as various instincts as they happen to need at the moment—a self-assertive instinct, an imitative instinct, an instinct of play, a gregarious instinct and many others like them. People take them up, as it were, make each of them do its particular job, and then drop them again. We have always been moved by a suspicion that behind all these little ad hoc instincts there lay concealed something serious and powerful which we should like to approach cautiously.[82]

For Freud the drive is thought:

as a concept on the frontier between the mental and the somatic, as the psychical representative of the stimuli originating from within the organism and reaching the mind, as a measure of the demand made upon the mind for work in consequence of its connection with the body.[83]

This distinction, between mental and somatic, stems from Descartes and is, as we said above, at the heart of Heidegger's criticism. But that is only one aspect of the problem. Freud differentiated between two major groups of drives, the ones that have something to do with "life"

---

[82]Freud, 'New Introductory Lectures', *SE vol. 22*, p. 95.
[83]'Instincts and Their Vicissitudes', *SE vol. 14*, p. 112.

(or Eros) and the ones that have something to do with "death" (or Thanatos). He speculated that they reflect a deeper state of affairs within the universe. The life drive would refer to the tendency of certain processes to create more and more complicated structures, such as life itself; while the death drive would refer to processes that undo or counteract the first. Having until then considered the pleasure principle to be the main driving force behind any human (and animal) action, Freud introduced the death drive in order to account for some clinical phenomena that could not fit with it. The aim of the pleasure principle was thought to be the reduction of tension. However, there were some phenomena, all falling under the rubric of a compulsion to repeat, that did not seem to conform to it. For example, why would a dream in a case of traumatic neurosis make the dreamer return to the traumatic event? If there *is* such a thing as a pleasure principle, then the best strategy for the traumatised dreamer would be to repress the traumatic material altogether. Obviously, that would indicate that there is something at play that is *beyond* the pleasure principle.[84]

The whole problematic brings to the fore major conceptual questions, especially in regard to the ontological status of instincts or drives. Are they mere descriptive abstractions of behaviours (or tendencies for behaviour), or do they reflect the existence of hidden forces at play? Freud clearly thought the latter.[85] But in this way he becomes vulnerable to Heidegger's criticism.

Lacan, on the other hand, tried to sidestep the issue. In *Seminar XI*, he tried to combine the two drives into one. He located death at the

---

[84]See 'Beyond the Pleasure Principle', *SE vol. 18*.

[85]Cf. Freud's explanation of his epistemological position in connection to his hypotheses: "I try in general to keep psychology clear from everything that is different in nature from it, even biological lines of thought. For that very reason I should like at this point expressly to admit that the hypothesis of … instincts … rests scarcely at all upon a psychological basis, but derives its principal support from biology. But I shall be consistent enough to drop this hypothesis if psycho-analytic work should itself produce some other, more serviceable hypothesis about the instincts. So far, this has not happened. … Since we cannot wait for another science to present us with the final conclusions on the theory of the instincts, it is far more to the purpose that we should try to see what light may be thrown upon this basic problem of biology by a synthesis of the *psychological* phenomena". ('On Narcissism', *SE vol. 14*, pp. 78–79).

level of the signifier, since, as we saw above, the signifier renders jouissance lifeless, it deadens, corpsifies the body.

> The distinction between the life drive and the death drive is true in as much as it manifests two aspects of the drive. But this is so only on condition that one sees all the sexual drives as articulated at the level of significations in the unconscious, in as much as what they bring out is death—death as signifier and nothing but signifier, for can it be said that there is a being-for death?[86]

There is a crucial similarity in how the drives are conceived of in Freud and Lacan, namely that they are thought as some kind of background motivating factors. In Freud, they are conceived of as being like force fields that change anything that falls within their scope of influence, while for Lacan they are more like *vectors* that connect one signifier to another. But here, on the other hand, lies the main difference between the two conceptualisations. The Freudian concept is ontic—in the sense that Freud sees in it a manifestation of a principle of biology—while the Lacanian concept is, as Lacan himself suggests, *ontological*:

> The *Trieb* [or drive] can in no way be limited to a psychological notion. It is an absolutely fundamental ontological notion, which is a response to a crisis of consciousness that we are not necessarily obliged to identify, since we are living it.[87]

We can see, now, that the ontic conceptualisation of the drive, one of the most important concepts of Freud's metapsychology, becomes less necessary and a bit out of place when one brings on the discussion the notions of jouissance, signifierisation, object *a* (qua remainder) and surplus jouissance (qua product of the alienation of the human being in the process of becoming a subject of language). It is not because it's no longer important, at least on an ontic level, but rather because its function may be ontologically provided in a different way. Is it the case,

---

[86]Lacan, *Seminar XI*, p. 257.
[87]*Seminar VII*, p. 127.

then, that we no longer need to take it as fundamental? Is it the case that in a post-Freudian metapsychology, the concept of a drive can be put aside as ontologically redundant?

◈    ◈    ◈

# Bibliography

Braunstein, Néstor A., 'Desire and Jouissance in the Teachings of Lacan', trans. Tamara Francés, in Jean-Michel Rabaté (ed.), *The Cambridge Companion to Lacan* (Cambridge: Cambridge University Press, 2003), 102–115.

Burgoyne, Bernard, 'Autism and Topology' in Bernard Burgoyne (ed.), *Drawing the Soul: Schemas and Models in Psychoanalysis* (London: Karnac, 2000), 190–217.

Chiesa, Lorenzo, *Subjectivity and Otherness* (Cambridge, MA: The MIT Press, 2007).

Derrida, Jacques, *Positions* [1972], trans. Alan Bass (Chicago: The University of Chicago Press, 1981).

Eyers, Tom, *Lacan and the Concept of the 'Real'* (Basingstoke, Hampshire: Palgrave Macmillan, 2012).

Fink, Bruce, *The Lacanian Subject: Between Language and Jouissance* (Princeton, NJ: Princeton University Press, 1997).

Fonagy, Peter, et al., 'Pragmatic Randomized Controlled Trial of Long-Term Psychoanalytic Psychotherapy for Treatment-Resistant Depression: The Tavistock Adult Depression Study (TADS)' *World Psychiatry*, 14/3 (09/25/2015), 312–321.

Freud, Sigmund, 'Beyond the Pleasure Principle' [1920g], trans. James Strachey, in James Strachey (ed.), *SE vol. 18* (The Standard Edition of the Complete Psychological Works of Sigmund Freud; London: Hogarth Press, 1953–1974), 1–64.

———, 'The Ego and the Id' [1923b], trans. James Strachey, in James Strachey (ed.), *SE vol. 19* (The Standard Edition of the Complete Psychological Works of Sigmund Freud; London: Hogarth Press, 1953–1974), 1–66.

———, 'Findings, Ideas, Problems' [1938], trans. James Strachey, in James Strachey (ed.), *SE vol. 23* (The Standard Edition of the Complete

Psychological Works of Sigmund Freud; London: Hogarth Press, 1953–1974), 299–300.

———, 'Instincts and Their Vicissitudes' [1915c] in James Strachey (ed.), *SE vol. 14* (The Standard Edition of the Complete Psychological Works of Sigmund Freud; London: Hogarth Press, 1953–1974), 109–140.

———, 'New Introductory Lectures on Psychoanalysis' [1933a] in James Strachey (ed.), *SE vol. 22* (The Standard Edition of the Complete Psychological Works of Sigmund Freud; London: Hogarth Press, 1953–1974), 1–182.

———, 'A Note Upon the "Mystic Writing Pad"' [1925a], trans. James Strachey, in James Strachey (ed.), *SE vol. 19* (The Standard Edition of the Complete Psychological Works of Sigmund Freud; London: Hogarth Press, 1953–1974), 225–232.

———, 'On Narcissism: An Introduction' [1914c], trans. James Strachey, in James Strachey (ed.), *SE vol. 14* (The Standard Edition of the Complete Psychological Works of Sigmund Freud; London: Hogarth Press, 1953–1974), 67–102.

———, 'An Outline of Psychoanalysis' [1940a], trans. James Strachey, in James Strachey (ed.), *SE vol. 23* (The Standard Edition of the Complete Psychological Works of Sigmund Freud; London: Hogarth Press, 1953–1974), 139–208.

———, 'Project for a Scientific Psychology' [1895] in James Strachey (ed.), *SE vol. 1* (The Standard Edition of the Complete Psychological Works of Sigmund Freud; London: Hogarth Press, 1953–1974), 281–391.

———, 'The Psychopathology of Everyday Life' [1901], trans. James Strachey, in James Strachey (ed.), *SE vol. 6* (The Standard Edition of the Complete Psychological Works of Sigmund Freud; London: Hogarth Press, 1953–1974), vii–296.

———, 'Some Points For a Comparative Study of Organic and Hysterical Motor Paralyses' [1888] in James Strachey (ed.), *SE vol. 1* (The Standard Edition of the Complete Psychological Works of Sigmund Freud; London: Hogarth Press, 1953–1974), 157–172.

———, 'The Unconscious' [1915e], trans. James Strachey, in James Strachey (ed.), *SE vol. 14* (The Standard Edition of the Complete Psychological Works of Sigmund Freud; London: Hogarth Press, 1953–1974), 159–215.

Gay, Peter, *Freud: A Life for Our Time* (New York: W. W. Norton & Company, 1998).

Grünbaum, Adolf, *The Foundations of Psychoanalysis: A Philosophical Critique* (Berkeley: University of California Press, 1984).

HEIDEGGER, MARTIN, *Zollikon Seminars: Protocols, Conversations, Letters*, ed. Medard Boss, trans. Franz Mayr and Richard Askay (Evanston, IL: Northwestern University Press, 2001).

JAKOBSON, ROMAN AND HALLE, MORRIS, *Fundamentals of Language* [1955] (The Hague: Mouton Publishers, 1980).

JONES, ERNEST, *Sigmund Freud, Life and Work, Vol. 2: Years of Maturity, 1901–1919* (London: Hogarth Press, 1955).

KLINE, PAUL, *Fact and Fantasy in Freudian Theory* (London: Methuen & Co, 1972).

LACAN, JACQUES, 'At the *Institut Français* in London (3 February 1975)' [1975], trans. Dany Nobus, *Journal for Lacanian Studies*, 3/2 (2005), 295–303.

———, 'Conclusions' [1978] *Lettres de l'Ecole Freudienne*, 2/25 (1979), 219–220.

———, 'The Function and Field of Speech and Language in Psychoanalysis' [1953], trans. Bruce Fink, Héloïse Fink, and Russell Grigg, in *Écrits* (New York: W. W. Norton & Company, 2006), 197–268.

———, 'The Instance of the Letter in the Unconscious' [1957], trans. Bruce Fink, Héloïse Fink, and Russell Grigg, in *Écrits* (New York: W. W. Norton & Company, 2006), 412–441.

———, 'Of Structure as an Inmixing of an Otherness Prerequisite to Any Subject Whatever' [1970] in Richard Macksey and Eugenio Donato (eds.), *The Structuralist Controversy: The Languages of Criticism and the Sciences of Man* (Baltimore: The Johns Hopkins University Press, 2007), 186–200.

———, 'Overture to the 1st International Encounter of the Freudian Field: Caracas, 12 July 1980', trans. Adrian Price, *Hurly-Burly*, 6 (September 2011), 17–20.

———, 'Position of the Unconscious' [1960], trans. Bruce Fink, Héloïse Fink, and Russell Grigg, in *Écrits* (New York: W. W. Norton & Company, 2006), 703–721.

———, 'Préface à l'Édition des Écrits en Livre de Poche' [1970] in J.-A. Miller (ed.), *Autres Écrits* (Paris: Éditions du Seuil, 2001), 387–391.

———, 'Radiophonie' [1970] in J.-A. Miller (ed.), *Autres Écrits* (Paris: Éditions du Seuil, 2001), 403–447.

———, 'Science and Truth' [1966], trans. Bruce Fink, Héloïse Fink, and Russell Grigg, in *Écrits* (New York: W. W. Norton & Company, 2006), 726–745.

———, *The Seminar of Jacques Lacan, Book I: Freud's Papers on Technique* [1953–54], ed. Jacques-Allain Miller, trans. John Forrester (New York: W. W. Norton & Company, 1988).

————, *The Seminar of Jacques Lacan, Book III: The Psychoses* [1955–56], ed. Jacques-Allain Miller, trans. Russel Grigg (New York: W. W. Norton & Company, 1993).

————, *The Seminar of Jacques Lacan, Book V: Formations of the Unconscious* [1957–58], ed. Jacques-Allain Miller, trans. Russell Grigg (Cambridge: Polity Press, 2017).

————, *The Seminar of Jacques Lacan, Book VI: Desire and Its Interpretation* [1958–59], trans. Cormac Gallagher (Unauthorised translation from unpublished manuscript: www.lacaninireland.com).

————, *The Seminar of Jacques Lacan, Book VII: The Ethics of Psychoanalysis* [1959–60], ed. Jacques-Allain Miller, trans. Dennis Potter (London: Routledge, 1992).

————, *The Seminar of Jacques Lacan, Book XI: The Four Fundamental Concepts of Psychoanalysis* [1964–65], ed. Jacques-Allain Miller, trans. Alan Sheridan (New York: W. W. Norton & Company, 1998).

————, *The Seminar of Jacques Lacan, Book XX: Encore, On Feminine Sexuality, the Limits of Love and Knowledge* [1972–73], ed. Jacques-Allain Miller, trans. Bruce Fink (New York: W. W. Norton & Company, 1998).

————, *The Seminar of Jacques Lacan, Book XXI: Les Non-Dupes Errent* [1973–74], trans. Cormac Gallagher (Unauthorised translation from unpublished manuscript: www.lacaninireland.com).

————, *The Seminar of Jacques Lacan, Book XXIII: The Sinthome* [1975–76], ed. Jacques-Allain Miller, trans. A. R. Price (Cambridge: Polity Press, 2016).

————, 'The Subversion of the Subject and the Dialectic of Desire in the Freudian Unconscious' [1960], trans. Bruce Fink, Héloïse Fink, and Russell Grigg, in *Écrits* (New York: W. W. Norton & Company, 2006), 671–702.

————, 'The Symbolic, the Imaginary, and the Real' [1953], trans. Bruce Fink, in *On the Names-of-the-Father* (Cambridge: Polity Press, 2013), 1–52.

MARINI, MARCELLE, *Jacques Lacan: The French Context*, trans. Anne Tomiche (New Brunswick, NJ: Rudgers University Press, 1992).

MATURANA, HUMBERTO R., *Biologie der Realität*, trans. Wolfram Karl Köck (Frankfurt am Main: Suhrkamp, 1998).

MATURANA, HUMBERTO R. AND VARELA, FRANCISCO J., *Autopoiesis and Cognition: The Realization of the Living* (Dordrecht: D. Reidel Publishing Company, 1980).

MILLER, JACQUES-ALLAIN, 'Extimité' [1985–86], trans. Françoise Massardier-Kenney, in Mark Bracher, et al. (eds.), *Lacanian Theory of Discourse: Subject, Structure, and Society* (New York: New York University Press, 1994), 74–87.

————, 'Les six Paradigmes de la Jouissance' *La Cause Freudienne*, 43 (1999), 7–29; http://www.causefreudienne.net/wp-content/uploads/2015/04/JAM-Six-paradigmes-jouissance.pdf.

NOBUS, DANY, 'A Matter of Cause: Reflection on Lacan's "Science and Truth"' in Jason Glynos and Yannis Stavrakakis (eds.), *Lacan & Science* (London: Karnac, 2002), 89–118.

NÖTH, WINFRIED, *Handbook of Semiotics* (Bloomington and Indianapolis: Indiana University Press, 1995).

PEARL, JOEL, *A Question of Time: Freud in the Light of Heidegger's Temporality*, trans. Amir Atsmon and Joel Pearl (Amsterdam: Contemporary Psychoanalytic Studies, 2013).

POPPER, KARL R., 'Science: Conjectures and Refutations' [1961] in *Conjectures and Refutations: The Growth of Scientific Knowledge* (London: Routledge, 2002), 43–86.

ROUDINESCO, ELISABETH, *Jacques Lacan*, trans. Barbara Bray (New York: Columbia University Press, 1997).

ROUSTANG, FRANÇOIS, *The Lacanian Delusion*, trans. Greg Sims (New York: Oxford University Press, 1990).

SHINGU, KAZUSHIGE, *Being Irrational: Lacan, the Object a, and the Golden Mean* [1995], trans. Michael Radich (Tokyo: Gakuji Shoin, 2004).

WITTGENSTEIN, LUDWIG, *Philosophical Investigations* [1945], trans. G. E. M. Anscombe (Oxford: Basil Blackwell, 1986).

ŽIŽEK, SLAVOJ, *On Belief* (London: Routledge, 2001).

ŽIŽEK, SLAVOJ AND DALY, GLYN, *Conversation with Žižek* (Cambridge: Polity Press, 2004).

# 5

# Lacanian Metapsychology

Until the end of his life, Lacan insisted that he was a Freudian. Perhaps this should be understood in the same way that we would understand Einstein if he said that he remained a faithful Newtonian; Freudian psychoanalysis might be said to be included in the Lacanian version of it, but the latter comprises much more than the former. For example, whereas Freud tried until the end of his teaching to defend psychoanalysis' position within the sciences, Lacan positions psychoanalysis at a vantage point that allows it to *discuss* science rather than *be* a science. Still, in Lacan's view psychoanalysis does not offer a new fundamental ontology or a new epistemology. Psychoanalysis *can* speak about other discourses, as it can speak about itself; but it never ceases to be one of *possible* discourses. In this sense, an attempt to formulate a post-Freudian—that is, Lacanian—metapsychology seems to involve a circularity. It is useful, however, as it denotes an ontological thematisation of a set of ontic (i.e. clinical) observations.

As discussed in previous chapters, the basic assumption of the whole Freudian enterprise is that the human psyche is seen as an intrinsically deterministic "mental apparatus" that can be studied scientifically: mental phenomena can, in principle, be explained, in the sense that there is

© The Author(s) 2019
C. Tombras, *Discourse Ontology*, The Palgrave Lacan Series,
https://doi.org/10.1007/978-3-030-13662-8_5

a (discoverable) reason why things happen in this or that way. We saw also that for Heidegger Freud was trapped in a subject–object world view and adopted uncritically ideas from the natural sciences, distorting the very phenomena he was trying to explicate. Conjecturing that something is a reason for a given state of affairs does not mean that it has *caused* this state of affairs: the premise (or conclusion) of a mental determinism remains unsubstantiated and arbitrary. In the light of these criticisms, Freud's theory emerges as rather unstable, without solid foundations.

Let us take one step back.

# The Subject of Psychoanalysis

Psychoanalysis would not be possible at all if people were not able, ready or willing to consider the objects it studies—the manifestations of mental life—as objects that *can* be studied at all. Take dreams, for example. People have always been fascinated by dreams, but the idea that dreams follow a certain internal logic—albeit unknown—was novel at the time of Freud. To be sure, Freud was not the first scientist to take dreams seriously. But as his *Interpretation of Dreams* testifies, he was the first who systematically attempted to outline and decipher their logic.

Acknowledging that Freud's method is Cartesian, Lacan stressed the fact that the Freudian subject—i.e. the human being as understood by Freud—is, just like the Cartesian one, a subject that seeks certainty but cannot find it. Certainty is not a straightforward issue for the Freudian subject, because there is always something—a dream, a slip of the tongue, a neurotic symptom or something like this—that gives reasons for doubt. For Freud, the source of this disconcerting "something" is the unconscious. Just like Descartes, who establishes the certainty of his existence by virtue of the fact that he doubts, that is, he thinks, Freud, in his own search for certainty, postulates the unconscious.

"It's no coincidence", Lacan says, "that psychoanalysis appeared well after the appearance of … scientific discourse. Psychoanalysis does not cease to have a relation with the scientific discourse. They are of the same nature".[1] Psychic phenomena would not be perceived as warranting further investigation, were it not for Descartes's revolution. This, of course, does not mean that they were unobserved before Descartes; the point rather is that before Descartes such phenomena were taken as evidence of external interventions or interactions; they were thought of as omens or divine messages carrying secret meanings.

> I am saying, contrary to what has been trumped up about a supposed break on Freud's part with the scientism of his time, that it was this very scientism … that led Freud, as his writings show, to pave the way that shall forever bear his name. … The subject upon which we operate in psychoanalysis can only be the subject of science.[2]

A subject of science, here, is neither a subject that adopts scientific methods—i.e. a scientist—nor the human being as a subject of scientific research. It is, rather, the subject that is surprised by the products of their own psyche, which the subject considers as concerning themselves. It is the doubtful Cartesian subject who is perplexed—and sometimes disturbed—by something of their own: a subject "captured and tortured by language".[3] Freud's originality was that he first took these mental phenomena to be individual products of the mind of this or that individual human being, as manifestations of the suffering of a specific individual. These individuals, the *subjects* of psychoanalysis, were invited, by Freud, to reflect upon their own suffering, via a dialectical process of questions and answers. At the root of Freud's invitation was his belief that the subject himself or herself holds the keys to the meaning of his or her "unconscious formations". This invitation is the prerequisite but also the precondition for psychoanalysis. Crucially, it presents the speaking being

[1]Jacques Lacan, 'At the *Institut Français* in London (3 February 1975)' [1975], trans. Dany Nobus, *Journal for Lacanian Studies*, 3/2 (2005), 295–303, p. 297.
[2]'Science and Truth' [1966], in *Écrits* (New York: W. W. Norton & Company, 2006), 726–745, pp. 728/857–729/858.
[3]*The Seminar of Jacques Lacan, Book III: The Psychoses* [1955–56], ed. Jacques-Alain Miller (New York: W. W. Norton & Company, 1993), p. 243.

with a challenge. It's up to the speaking being whether the challenge will be taken up or not.

The recognition of this (Cartesian) connection between the subject of psychoanalysis and the subject of science renders the whole issue of the scientificity of psychoanalysis somewhat irrelevant: the subject of science allows the subject of psychoanalysis to come about, and this, in turn, makes psychoanalysis as a field possible: "Psychoanalysis is to be taken seriously, even though it is not a science. ... It is a practice that will last as long as it will last, it is a practice of chit-chat. ... This does not prevent analysis from having consequences: it says something".[4] It's only then that we become able to outline the emergence of the subject of science and see science as a *discourse*—the term "discourse" (in Lacanian theory) denoting, as we shall see, the structure of a subject's engagement within a network of signifiers.

## Law and Cause in Psychoanalysis

In the ancient world picture, change was thought as an imperfection of the human world and was contrasted to the eternal perfection of the celestial world. As we saw earlier, in Aristotle's understanding all change observed in a chain of purposive (earthly) events was the result of one or more causes; he distinguished between the *material*, the *effective*, the *formal* and the *final* cause.[5] This predominantly anthropocentric world view was not acceptable to Descartes. Intending to establish absolute certainty without resorting to the authority of human institutions like the church, Descartes inaugurated the programme of modern science by ridding it of anything subjective. Scientific knowledge was to be formulated as a set of concrete concepts, relationships, interactions and processes. This was the ideal of Freud too.

---

[4] *The Seminar of Jacques Lacan, Book XXV: The Moment to Conclude* [1977–78] (www.lacaninireland.com), p. 1.
[5] See above, pp. 54–55.

Lacan, building on Freud's work, sees the psyche as comprising inter-connected signifiers. The specificities of these interconnections are not determined beforehand. They are being laid *retroactively*, so to speak, as new signifiers are "added" and are connected to earlier signifiers—after the fact, or *après-coup*, as Lacan had it.[6] This is an effect of what Lacan called the *law of the signifier*. The fact that the linking is only established retroactively renders this law non-predictive. You cannot outline the course these interconnecting pathways *will* take. You can only back-trace pathways already laid down. A law conceived in this way needs to be distinguished from a *cause*. The law of the signifier is not a law of causality; a signifier is not thought to be a "cause" of another signifier. It just *describes* the sequence of a series of states of affairs in such a way that there is no gap between them. "Think of what is pictured in the law of action and reaction", Lacan says.

There is here, one might say, a single principle. One does not go without the other. The mass of a body that is crushed on the ground is not the cause of that which it receives in return for its vital force—its mass is inte-grated in this force that comes back to it in order to dissolve its coherence by a return effect. There is no gap here, except perhaps at the end.[7]

In an attempt to enrich Freud's belief in the determinism of the men-tal apparatus with reintroducing the human being as an agency, Lacan in his *Seminar XI* drew parallels between his understanding of psychical causality and Aristotle's conception of *incidental* cause, by connecting the law of the signifier with the Aristotelian *automaton*, and the chance interruption or gap in the signifying chain with *tuché*.[8] The subject is always under the sway of the law of the signifier; what-ever is his or her very own is manifested as a surprise, a discontinuity, a

---

[6]*Après-coup* is Lacan's translation of Freud's "Nachträglichkeit", or retroaction. See also above, pp. 94–96.
[7]Jacques Lacan, *The Seminar of Jacques Lacan, Book XI: The Four Fundamental Concepts of Psychoanalysis* [1964–65], ed. Jacques-Allain Miller (New York: W. W. Norton & Company, 1998), p. 22.
[8]See above, p. 55.

gap. It is there that the agency is to be found. Of course, this gap is just a gap, an empty placeholder that could have been occupied by a signifier which is now missing (or replaced). A signifier is never in isolation. An entity can be a signifier only to the extent that it is interconnected within a network of similar entities. But such a network can only be meaningful, i.e. *non*-automatic, if it involves a choice. A choice is where the subject enters the picture. The subject is what is represented in an interconnection between signifiers in as much as this interconnection is non-automatic, i.e. unexpected. Seen in this way, the signifier can be understood as the cause of the subject. The subject, Lacan says,

> is not the cause of himself; he bears within himself the worm of the cause that splits him. For his cause is the signifier, without which there would be no subject in the real. But this subject is what the signifier represents, and the latter cannot represent anything except to another signifier.[9]

It's perhaps interesting to note here that in *Seminar XX* Lacan returns to Aristotle's four causes in order to present the signifier as the cause of jouissance:

> The signifier is the cause of jouissance. Without the signifier, how could we even approach that part of the body [that gave rise to jouissance]? Without the signifier, how could we centre that something that is the material cause of jouissance? However fuzzy or confused it may be, it is a part of the body that is signified in this contribution. Now I will go right to the final cause, final in every sense of the term because it is the terminus—the signifier is what brings jouissance to a halt. ... The efficient, which Aristotle proposes as the third form of the cause, is nothing in the end but the project through which jouissance is limited. ... And the embrace, the confused embrace wherein jouissance finds its cause, its last cause, which is formal—isn't it something like grammar that commands it?[10]

---

[9]Lacan, 'Position of the Unconscious', *Écrits*, p. 708/835. The term "real" in this quote should be understood in the sense of reality, rather, than of the real qua register of human experience.

[10]*The Seminar of Jacques Lacan, Book XX: Encore, On Feminine Sexuality, the Limits of Love and Knowledge* [1972–73], ed. Jacques-Allain Miller (New York: W. W. Norton & Company, 1998), pp. 24–25.

In other words, the signifier is that which allows jouissance to be revealed to the speaking being. Without jouissance, there would be no signifier. It's only because one is under the sway of the signifier that jouissance can be an issue. The signifier, in other words, involves a circularity. Jouissance is crystallised as signifier and, in the process, it comes into view be*cause* of the signifier.

## Signifierness and Signifying Chain

When speaking about the law of the signifier, one refers to the law that governs the ways in which signifiers are linked to each other in a chain. These *horizontal* associative dependencies of signifiers are complemented by *vertical* structures of dependency that govern the ways different signifying chains are connected one with another, allowing for a jump, so to speak, from one chain of signifiers to another.[11] These "jumps" can happen in different ways. The two more basic mechanisms are recognised as metaphor and metonymy. In the former, signifiers can be made to stand for other *signifiers*, and in the latter, signifiers can be made to stand for other *signifieds*. Thus, from an initial state where a signifier $S_1$ was associated with signified $s_1$ and a signifier $S_2$ was associated with signified $s_2$, we now have (a) a signifier $S_2$ standing for a signifier $S_1$ and hence for its signified $s_1$ (metaphor); and (b) signified $s_2$ being now associated with signifier $S_1$ instead of signifier $S_2$ (metonymy). In other words, in metaphor the signified of a signifier $S_1$ is *transferred* to a signifier $S_2$, while in metonymy a signified $s_2$ is no longer represented by $S_2$ and is now *renamed* to $S_1$. One could say, then, that in metaphor we have the transfer of a meaning (signified), while in metonymy the change of a name (signifier).[12] The mechanism is the same and results to the formation of a network of signifiers that, depending on circumstantial factors, can be anything, from very loose to very tight. It is crucial

---

[11]The differentiation between horizontal and vertical dependencies should be understood here in a figurative way.

[12]It is interesting to note here that, indeed, in Greek the word metaphor ("μεταφορά") means "transfer" and the word metonymy ("μετωνυμία") means "renaming".

to see here that even though both metaphor and metonymy are defined and understood in terms of their effects on meaning, their functioning is independent of meaning.

Metaphor allows us to understand how a signifying network can be enlarged, by the production of new signifying pathways.

> We must define metaphor by the implantation in a signifying chain of another signifier, by which the one it supplants falls to the rank of the signified, and as a latent signifier perpetuates there the interval by which another signifying chain can be grafted onto it.[13]

In other words, the structure of metaphor allows the subject to escape the restrictions of a signifying chain, by substituting a signifier (of a particular signifying chain) with another signifier (of a different signifying chain).[14] The main tool of psychoanalysis, free association, works by allowing the subject to follow the different pathways as they are opened at every metaphoric or metonymic juncture. Lacan goes one step further, suggesting that even symptom s are products of a metaphoric mechanism:

> Metaphor's two-stage mechanism is the very mechanism by which symptoms, in the analytic sense, are determined. Between the enigmatic signifier of sexual trauma and the term it comes to replace in a current signifying chain, a spark flies that fixes in a symptom—a metaphor in which flesh or function is taken as a signifying element—the signification, that is inaccessible to the conscious subject, by which the symptom may be dissolved.[15]

---

[13]Lacan, 'Ernest Jones', *Écrits*, p. 594/708.

[14]This creative aspect of metaphor has not remained unnoticed by contemporary American pragmatist philosophers like R. Rorty. As he writes, "to think of metaphorical sentences as the forerunners of new uses of language, uses which may eclipse and erase old uses, is to think of metaphor as on a par with perception and inference, rather than thinking of it as having a merely 'heuristic' or 'ornamental' function". (Richard Rorty, 'Philosophy as Science, Metaphor, Politics' [1986], in *Essays on Heidegger and Others: Philosophical Papers, Volume 2* (Cambridge: Cambridge University Press, 1991), 9–26, p. 14).

[15]Lacan, 'Instance of the Letter', *Écrits*, p. 431/518.

One of the effects of the metaphoric structure is that it induces a signifying effect by making one signifier step in, so to speak, in the place of another signifier. What we would need here, then, is some insight relating to the inaugural moment during which a first metaphor is established. By postulating an "inaugural moment", I make an implicit reference to a starting point in what is a signifying chain or a temporal sequence. Of course, this is only to be understood figuratively. It is not the case that there is only *one* signifying chain, nor that there is only *one* temporal sequence. Similarly, one can speak about the *first* metaphor only in a strictly figurative way.

Building on Freud's observation of the little game his grandson invented to account for the periodic presence and absence of his mother,[16] which could not but be a source of anxiety that he would have to master in some way, Lacan argues that the matter is not just a question of a basic biological need (namely feeding) that has to be attended to. The infant has a need and demands the fulfilment of this need. By the very fact that an Other can satisfy needs—or can choose not to—the infant finds itself in a position of lack. There is anxiety when the mother, or carer, is away and there is joy (or pleasure) when the mother is there. The child needs to master these extremes, and in this, it is helped by a *third* pole different from the two poles of the child and the mother. This third pole comes into play as the (possible) reason for the mother's absence and is designated by Lacan as the *Name-of-the-Father, no-of-the-Father* (in French: *nom-du-père* and *non-du-père* respectively) or paternal function. It serves as a limiting point for the omnipotence of the mother (or carer): if the mother is away, this can only be because she too *lacks* something.

One needs to keep in mind here that these processes are not following some kind of predetermined script. They serve more as illuminating hypotheses rather than accurate descriptions of events. So, when talking about the mother lacking something, this is to be understood

---

[16]See Freud's account of his grandson's game "o-o-o-o" and "da" ("fort", and "da") in Sigmund Freud, 'Beyond the Pleasure Principle' [1920g], in James Strachey (ed.), *SE vol. 18* (London: Hogarth Press, 1953–1974), 1–64, pp. 14–15.

figuratively—in the sense that it is never possible to indicate exactly *what* is it that the mother, or anyone else for that matter, lacks. It is rather a statement about the human condition. The mother of this example—and each and every speaking being in general—is founded on a lack: speaking beings are desiring subjects.[17] Lacan uses the term *phallus* to designate the signifier of this lack.

> The phallus as a signifier provides the ratio [in French: *raison*] of desire (in the sense in which the term is used in 'mean and extreme ratio' of harmonic division). I shall thus be using the phallus as an algorithm … The fact that the phallus is a signifier requires that it be in the place of the Other that the subject have access to it. But since this signifier is there only as veiled and as ratio [*raison*] of the Other's desire, it is the Other's desire as such that the subject is required to recognize—in other words, the other insofar as he himself is a subject divided by the signifying *Spaltung*.[18]

The phallus, then, is thought as the imaginary object of what the mother wants (i.e. lacks); as such it becomes the signifier of this lack and inaugurates the whole network of signifiers that constitutes subjectivity and reveals (or represents) the divided subject. Discussing the dynamics of these early phenomena, Freud used the term "Oedipus complex" to designate a child's preference and attachment to the parent of the opposite sex. According to the orthodox Freudian theory, the boy wants the mother but is met with a prohibition by the father, who makes it clear that the mother is off-limits. Lacan looks at the Oedipal dynamic in terms of a dialectic of being the phallus or *having* it, i.e. in terms of one's position vis-à-vis the mother's desire. What Freud called castration, i.e. the limiting of one's access to the mother qua desired object, is seen by Lacan not as a threat or danger but, reversely, as a (reassuring) symbolic limit to the mother's omnipotence. In short, the phallus is the signifier of a lack; a network of signifiers is created as a metaphor of lack; and the divided subject is represented by its network of signifiers.

---

[17]See also above, pp. 117–120.

[18]Lacan, 'Signification of the Phallus', *Écrits*, pp. 581–582/693. *Spaltung* is the term Freud used to indicate the *splitting* or division of the ego because of internal conflicts.

If, following Lacan, we use the symbol $\mathbf{S}$ to designate the divided subject and $S_1 \to S_2$ to designate the interconnection between signifiers, and then, the relation between the two can be written as follows:

$$\frac{S_1 \to S_2}{\mathbf{\$}}$$

This connecting structure, a scaffolding so to speak, represents the subject in his or her individuality. It is equivalent to Lacan's referring to the subject of language—i.e. the divided subject—as represented by a signifier to another signifier and will be helpful for the discussion of Lacan's discourse theory.

Meaning comes as a secondary effect of the fact that there are elements of some sort that can become pointers to other elements. As such, they are potentially signifiers and can form a signifying network. Lacan calls this *signifierness* (in French: *signifiance*). Signifierness, in other words, is the name we give to the phenomenon than an entity can become signifier. The differentiation between signifier and signified is a secondary one, stemming from the phenomenon that an entity qua signifier can stand for another entity qua signified: at the beginning, there were no signifieds as such. Any given signified was *originally* a signifier belonging in another chain of signifiers (the term "originally" understood here in a structural rather than a temporal sense). In many respects, a signified is *still* a signifier belonging to a different signifying chain. Signifierness, that is, is a general case of the metaphoric function: something stands for something else.[19]

---

[19]In *Seminar XX*, Lacan had commented that the function of the phallus is "not unrelated" to the bar between the signifier and the signified—were it not for which "nothing about language could be explained by linguistics. Were it not for this bar above which there are signifiers that pass, you could not see that signifiers are injected into the signified" (*Seminar XX*, pp. 34, 40). Lacan's suggestion can perhaps be understood in the sense that the bar represents that which allows us to see that there are signifiers beyond (or, perhaps, *over*) the signified—in other words, the bar is representing the effect of signifierness, and as such, it allows us to see language in its material aspect, namely beyond (or before) signifierness. That, as Lacan says, is "not unrelated" to the function of the phallus: it is because of a process akin to that of metaphor that the second signifier obtained the structural position of what we call signified. This process is what Lacan calls function of the phallus, and it is in this sense that the phallus can also be understood as the metaphor of desire (as lack).

Lacan's description of the Freudian unconscious in terms of gaps and discontinuities in a signifying chain allows him to consider psychopathology from a structural point of view, rather than one focusing on symptomatology. Symptoms are no longer seen as the most distinctive aspect of one's "illness" or "disorder", but rather as products of the specificities of one's own network of signifying chains; this is a *structured* network, reflecting a specific instance of psychic structure. As soon as it is installed, the network of signifiers obtains an anchoring point that supports the stability of the whole network. The name-of-the-Father is the key in the whole process of stabilising a steady network of signifiers. If this is not established, then the stability is precarious. The question of diagnosis, then, emerges as a question of differentiation between structural traits, rather than a question of clinically observable defining features judged against an accepted notion of normality.[20]

# The Corporeality of Language: Lalangue

Linguists claim that the connection between signifier and signified is arbitrary, but also stable. However, our discussions so far allow us to see that the connecting pathway between an entity qua signifier and an entity qua signified has a "metaphoric" logic—which means that it is not arbitrary as such. This logic, however, is lost. We are no longer able to see what the primary "metaphor" was, and because of that the

---

[20]So, to give just an example, in what we call "psychotic structure" the network of signifiers fails to contain anxiety. The experience of the psychotic subject seems to involve the continuous renegotiation of the signifying network, via ad hoc imaginary identifications, in order to make up for its insufficient stability. This works most of the times. There are moments, however, in which this is no longer possible. In such moments, the network of signifiers is ripped and the subject itself is deconstructed. These would be the triggering moments of a clinically observable psychosis. The literature regarding a Lacanian clinic is quite extensive. See, for example, Joël Dor, *The Clinical Lacan* (Northvale, NJ: Jason Aronson, 1997); Bruce Fink, *A Clinical Introduction to Lacanian Psychoanalysis: Theory and Technique* (Cambridge, MA: Harvard University Press, 1997); Paul Verhaeghe, *On Being Normal and Other Disorders: A Manual for Clinical Psychodiagnostics* (New York: Other Press, 2004); and Darian Leader, *What Is Madness?* (London: Hamish Hamilton, 2011).

signifying interconnections appear as arbitrary. Arbitrariness, in other words, is only apparent and comes as a result of the lost pathways of metaphoric interconnections.[21]

We saw how Lacan described the loose attachment of the network of signifiers to the network of signifieds as the quilting point. As we see now, signifieds and signifiers are entities of the same kind, the only differentiation between the two being their structural position as the two poles of a "lost" metaphoric connecting pathway. Because of the phallic function, a signifier's connection to another signifier appears as if it is stabilised, allowing the second signifier to emerge as if it was the meaning of the first. The two signifiers are then connected with a quilting point and the different position they occupy gives rise to this elusive distinction between signifier and signified. The quilting point itself becomes an index of this differentiation.

Elaborating on the quilting point, Lacan suggested that the concept can be thought of as a translation of the ancient Stoic "expressible" or "say-able" (in Greek: λεκτόν).[22] He emphasised that the Stoics used the term "signifier" to refer to what, for them, is "most primordial" in language, and likened his own object a as "the major incorporeal of the Stoics".[23] In this sense, Lacan's theory of language is materialist, or corporeal, in much the same way as the theory of the Stoics.

---

[21]It should be noted here that this is a phenomenon that happens at both a synchronic axis and a diachronic axis—synchronic in the sense of the individual and diachronic in the sense of a whole language as a structured system.

[22]See Jacques Lacan, 'Préface à l'Édition des Écrits en Livre de Poche' [1970], in J.-A. Miller (ed.), *Autres Écrits* (Paris: Éditions du Seuil, 2001), 387–391, p. 390. The Stoics had advocated a materialist theory of the mind, and their conception of the say-able was intended to explain how something immaterial (incorporeal) like meaning can come out of something material that can bear a meaning (a signifier). For them, a signifier, which is always a material, or corporeal, entity, was thought of as bonded with the incorporeal world of meaning. This bond was conceived by the Stoics as a product of an act of saying, hence its designation as "say-able". The similarity to Lacan's conceptualisation of the *quilting point* is evident.

[23]See 'The Place, Origin and End of My Teaching' [1967], in Jacques-Alain Miller (ed.), *My Teaching* (London: Verso, 2008), 3–55, p. 36; and also 'Preface' in Anika Lemaire, *Jacques Lacan* (London: Routledge & Kegan Paul, 1977), viii–xv, p. xiv.

Where psychical phenomena are concerned, language and words become materials, building blocks, and their morphological features are as important as, if not more important than, their signifying features. As far as the analysis of psychical phenomena is concerned, "meaningless" fragments of words are just as important as meaningful ones (words and phrases).[24] In order to discuss language and speaking without any reference to meaning, Lacan introduced in 1971 the neologism *lalangue*—a play on the two words, *la langue* (French for language/speech), written as one. He used it to refer to speaking with no regard for what is being spoken about—for example, words taken as their sound, as phonemes, or when babbling or speaking in tongues.[25] Lacan's intention was to stress the bodily, *corporeal* aspect of being engaged in the activity of speaking and, in so doing, to recast as a recursive construction the distinction that linguists usually designate as *duality of patterning*.[26] Signifiers can be thought of as autonomous entities only within the particular signifying chains to which they belong. They comprise parts, each and every one of which can be found to belong in different, completely independent signifying chains.[27] Looking at

---

[24]See above, p. 103n34.

[25]For the most readily available example of lalangue, one could think of a baby playing with linguistic sounds, who might at some point say something like *mah-mah-mah-mah*; it is in the possible reaction of the primary carer that this utterance will become, for this infant, a reference to the carer and obtain the meaning "mother". In other words, from some moment onwards, the babbling *mah-mah* will be taken as the word (or signifier) *mama* and will be accepted as referring to that woman, i.e. to "mother". Other examples of lalangue can be found in the linguistic constructions of dreams, or even in the marginally linguistic constructions observed in cases of echolalia.

[26]This term, introduced by American linguist C. F. Hockett, refers to the fact that language, as a semiotic system, can be seen as organised on two distinct layers, one composed of meaningless elements or phonemes (differentiable sounds that can be pronounced by humans) and a second one composed of meaningful elements such as words and phrases. The French linguist A. Martinet has suggested the term *double articulation*, to describe the same phenomenon. See Winfried Nöth, *Handbook of Semiotics* (Bloomington and Indianapolis: Indiana University Press, 1995), pp. 237–238. This term was also used by G. Deleuze and F. Guattari to describe in very generalised way phenomena of different types of organisation between what they called layers or *strata*. See Gilles Deleuze and Félix Guattari, *A Thousand Plateaus: Capitalism and Schizophrenia* (London: Athlone Press, 1987), pp. 40–44.

[27]Signifying chains and their horizontal or vertical associative dependencies are what philosopher and biologist H. Maturana has in mind when he describes a linguistic domain as "a domain of consensual coordinations of actions or distinctions … [arising as] a particular manner of living-together contingent upon the unique history of recurrent interactions of the

language, qua "lalangue", allows us to focus on its comprising material as material with the potentiality of signifierness, but with no reference to what is signified.

# Knowledge, Truth, Metalanguage

When signifierness and (indirectly) meaning are installed, the signifying network in its horizontal and vertical associative interconnections and dependencies becomes systematic, increasingly cross-referenced and coherent. It becomes what we could describe as *knowledge*, and indeed, this is what Lacan calls it. Knowledge as such is not seen as dependent on the knower or on what is being known. It is that which emerges when signifiers become interconnected in a network:

> Knowledge initially arises at the moment at which $S_1$ comes to represent something, through its intervention in the field defined … as an already structured field of knowledge. And the subject is its supposition, its *hypokeimenon*, insofar as the subject represents the specific trait of being distinguished from the living individual. The latter is certainly its locus, where the subject leaves its mark, but it isn't of the same order as what is brought in by the subject, by virtue of the status of knowledge.[28]

An implication of this is the differentiation between the human being as a specific living individual and the human being in its dwelling in language and knowledge—that is, the human being as a subject of language and knowledge. The *locus* of the subject is always the living individual, but its structural position has nothing to do with the structural position of the living individual.

---

participants during their co-ontogeny". (Humberto R. Maturana, 'The Biological Foundations of Self Consciousness and the Physical Domain of Existence', in *Beobachter: Konvergenz der Erkenntnisttheorien?* (München: Wilhelm Fink Verlag, 1992), 47–117, p. 92).

[28]Jacques Lacan, *The Seminar of Jacques Lacan, Book XVII: The Other Side of Psychoanalysis* [1969–70], ed. Jacques-Alain Miller (New York: W. W. Norton & Company, 2007), p. 13.

Pursuing this line of enquiry further, the question of truth is brought to the fore. Just as knowledge is seen as something broader than what the everyday term denotes, truth also is presented in terms not related to our common understanding.

In his 1970 television interview, which was later published as *Television*, Lacan begins like this: "I always speak the truth. Not the whole truth, because there's no way to say it all. Saying it all is literally impossible: words fail. Yet it's through this very impossibility that the truth holds onto the real".[29] Truth is related to speaking. As soon as I speak, I speak the truth (or, perhaps, truth is spoken through me). Truth, then, means that I accept that I am the subject of language.

Lacan draws on Freud's discussion of the function of negation, and his observation that the judgement as to whether a state of affairs holds true or not is subsequent to a more primordial *affirmation* or acceptance (in German: *Bejahung*) on the part of the subject. "In a general way ... the condition such that something exists for a subject is that there be *Bejahung*, this *Bejahung* which isn't a negation of the negation".[30] For Lacan, however, nothing is revealed to the human being, at least not in the Heideggerian sense; the case is rather that something is *missing* from the human being, and in the place of this lack, the divided subject emerges as a speaking being. Speaking represents an affirmation. Truth is something that is said in words (i.e. in a language); truth cannot be whole (because words fail); and truth is connected to the real—i.e. the source of the symbolic (and of words, for that matter).

Lacan's conception of truth, then, is closely related to his assertion that there is no metalanguage. Metalanguage is a term of logic and linguistics that describes a language in which statements about another language can be formulated. In A. Tarski's theory of truth, a distinction is made between an *object language* (containing statements where some state of affairs is described or postulated) and a *metalanguage*, which

---

[29]'Television' [1970], in Joan Copjec (ed.), *Television* (New York: W. W. Norton & Company, 1990), 1–46, p. 3.

[30]*The Seminar of Jacques Lacan, Book I: Freud's Papers on Technique* [1953–54], ed. Jacques-Allain Miller (New York: W. W. Norton & Company, 1988), p. 58.

contains statements *about* the object language.[31] Not so for Lacan. He claims that in human language there is no vantage point from which one can assert the truth value of a statement or a proposition. You can never escape the level of the language in which you speak: "No authoritative statement has any other guarantee … than its very enunciation … I formulate this by saying that there is no metalanguage that can be spoken, or, more aphoristically, that there is no Other of the Other".[32] And elsewhere:

> Everything that can be said of truth, of the only truth—namely, that there is no such thing as a metalanguage, … no language being able to say the truth about truth, since truth is grounded in the fact that truth speaks, and that it has no other means by which to become grounded.[33]

It could be said, then, that for Lacan truth is conceptualised in terms of the affirmation of the subject's engagement with a signifying chain. It is seen, in other words, as that what allows the contours of this engagement to be outlined.[34]

Now, the assertion that there is no metalanguage has further major implications. If truth is only grounded on the fact that it speaks (through the subject), and if, following Heidegger, we accept truth as a-letheia and revelation of being, then the position of being itself becomes unstable. In fact, Lacan goes so far as to claim that here is no being. As Lacan explains,

---

[31]Alfred Tarski, a Polish logician and mathematician, had developed this semantic conception of truth by drawing on Aristotle's insights and also on the medieval view of truth as the correspondence of a thing to the intellect. See Alfred Tarski, 'The Semantic Conception of Truth' [1944], in Maria Baghramian (ed.), *Modern Philosophy of Language* (Washington, DC: Counterpoint, 1999), 44–63. As Jaakko Hintikka explains, for Tarski "a truth definition can be given for a language only in a stronger metalanguage". (Jaakko Hintikka, *The Principles of Mathematics Revisited* (Cambridge: Cambridge University Press, 1996), p. 15). See also above, p. 36.

[32]Lacan, 'Subversion of the Subject', *Écrits*, p. 688/813.

[33]'Science and Truth', *Écrits*, pp. 736–737/867–868.

[34]Cf. Lacan's discussion of truth in four different guises: as the efficient cause of magic; as the final cause of religion; as the formal cause of science; and as the material cause of psychoanalysis. (See 'Science and Truth', *Écrits*, pp. 740–743/871–875.) This discussion leads to, and was superseded by, his more elaborate theory of discourses. See below, pp. 151–155.

when I say [there is no metalanguage], it apparently means—no language of being. But is there being? ... What I say is what there isn't. Being is, as they say, and nonbeing is not. There is or there isn't. Being is merely presumed in certain words—'individual', for instance, and 'substance'. In my view, it is but a fact of what is said.[35]

Lacan's conceptualisation of truth as affirmation in the absence of metalanguage brings to the fore the question regarding the foundations of truth and its connection with time: if there is no such a thing as a metalanguage, and if no statement has any other guarantee than its enunciation, then truth as such is rendered unstable, impossible or irrelevant. Can there be a guarantee for truth? Or, does it all mean that truth is impossible, and everything goes? Lacan offers no specific solution to this. We will need to turn for help elsewhere.[36] But before that, let us first focus on the question of time.

## Logical Time and Temporality

As a prerequisite for order to approach a metapsychological understanding of time, we would need to conceptually differentiate between clocking the passage of time as a function of the human body as such (circadian rhythms, etc.) and of awareness of the passage of time on the level of our dealings with the world. Receptiveness to the periodicity of bodily functions and receptiveness to the difference between presence and absence represent the absolute minimum for the biological organism, but they are not adequate to account for our concernful dealings

---

[35] *Seminar XX*, p. 118. Of course, this does not mean that there are no beings. One needs to keep in mind Heidegger's ontological difference; otherwise, this whole conceptualisation runs the risk of becoming a set of mumbo jumbo.

[36] A potential solution might be given by methodologies closely related to efforts in modern logic to escape the limitations of the distinction between an object language and a metalanguage, as, for example, in Jaakko Hintikka's work. Hintikka has developed a first-order logic in which truth is defined and expressed with no need to refer to a metalanguage. He accomplishes this in terms of a game-like iterative (or recursive) process. According to Hintikka, his solution can be extended to natural languages as well. I will return to this below, pp. 200–203.

with a world within time. Time needs to exist at some lower (ontic) level in order to have a living organism with or without the ability to enter the world of language, which would then unveil ontological time to the human being. We can only postulate this "lower", ontic time when we have already entered the world unveiled to us by language. A circle is once again visible here.

Time is implicitly connected with signifierness. It is required by the very nature of the signifier: in order to have a signifier, we need to be able to distinguish entities, i.e. to differentiate something from its background; in addition to this, we need to be able to differentiate between presence and absence, in the sense that for something to be pointed to we need to somehow be able to discern and register it. These two aspects of reckoning with the world are central and unavoidable parts of signifierisation as a process. So, for example, the very first signifiers for the human infant would be related to the mother and the body (voice, gaze, breast, faeces). It is clear, here, that an inability to register and discern these differences would make it impossible for the human being to become a subject of language. This does not mean that this particular human being would lose the ability to live. Life, at the level of the biological mechanisms involved, would continue without major issues. But the world inhabited by this human being would be an impoverished and solitary one, not shared with other humans.

Sharing of the world with other humans is at the heart of Lacan's argument about the emergence of logical or intersubjective time. Writing in 1945, he used the parable of a puzzle to show how, by means of a progression of logical steps, a progression of temporal moments is also implicitly created, resulting in the emergence of an intersubjective time as a by-product of a coordinated symbolic human interaction.[37]

---

[37]In this "sophism", as he called it, three prisoners are invited to solve a logical puzzle. Timing is crucial, because the first to solve the puzzle will be the first (and only one) to gain his freedom. The puzzle is designed in such a way that one cannot arrive at the solution in one step. Each of the prisoners needs to decide their own actions in connection with the others' actions. In this way, Lacan is able to distinguish between three different aspects of time modulation: (a) the "Instant of the Glance"; (b) the "Time for Comprehending"; and (c) the "Moment of Concluding". This modulation allows him to describe how the subjective sense of time (the hesitation of each prisoner in the story) is de-subjectified by the collective action of all three prisoners, resulting in the emergence of what Lacan calls "objective" time. See Lacan, 'Logical Time', *Écrits*, pp. 167–173/204–211.

For Lacan, the structure of the psyche is a set of timeless pathways connecting signifiers together—timeless, in the sense of obtaining outside of time constraints. The present is related to speaking. Speaking discloses time to the speaking being by the very fact that the elements of a speech act (phonemes, words, sentences) cannot be delivered simultaneously.[38] Time—or rather, temporality—remains, for Lacan, a linguistic construction, that is, a product of language, overlaid on the "now", i.e. on the moment at which we speak. This formulation brings up a distinction between time qua duration and time qua temporality. Duration, as such, is a compound notion, comprising the temporal aspect of presence and the temporal aspect of speaking. Both speaking (as sound) and presence, as the theatre of potentiality of distinctions, reveal themselves to the human being in the real, that is, they do not need the signifier; it is rather the signifier that comes from them—just as the imaginary and the symbolic come from the real. This reflects a distinction between duration—a time interval in the real—and temporality, i.e. a scaffolding of time relations in the imaginary and the symbolic. The very phenomenon of presence only becomes visible as such when the signifier is installed. You need the signifier in order to discern a presence, but a presence cannot be thematised in the absence of a signifier. We can say: the signifier makes a presence ex-sist.[39]

The symbolic order is a static, motionless structure. It is a network of pathways that interconnects meaning-enabled elements. The symbolic, just like the Freudian unconscious, is timeless. It is irrelevant whether certain signifiers are "older" than others; the very notion of the "age" of a signifier is in fact a nonsense as far as the subject is concerned. The only pointers to temporal relations between signifiers are provided by their place within the whole signifying network, by the pathways that interconnect them and by the obstacles along those pathways. The relation to temporality of animals or pre-verbal humans—i.e. infants— is fundamentally different. All living beings *are* in time, as living,

---

[38]I have elaborated this argument elsewhere. See Christos Tombras, 'Kicking Down the Ladder: Language, Time, History' *Journal of the Centre for Freudian Analysis and Research*, 19 (2009), 119–137, pp. 127–129.

[39]For the term ex-sist, see above, p. 28n18.

biological organisms, but only those who can share a world as revealed in the shared intersubjective coordination of human interaction can also partake in temporality. In the words of Lacan:

> At a time when the whole of philosophy is engaged in articulating what it is that links time to being, … it is quite simple to see that time, in its very constitution, past-present-future (those of grammar) refers itself to the act of the word—and to nothing else. The present is the moment at which I speak and nothing else. It is strictly impossible for us to conceive of a temporality in an animal dimension. Namely in a dimension of appetite. The abc of temporality requires even the structure of language.[40]

These temporalising interconnecting pathways are constantly "renegotiated" and may bring alterations to the temporal relations pointed to by them—a process of retroaction that Freud first recognised.[41] The temporal essence of speaking—its temporality—is never lost. It is there when a speech act takes place, and it is there when it is reflected upon. Moreover, it is still there when a speech act is constructed or rehearsed, i.e. during the process of thinking. It doesn't really matter if we think in order to say something, or if we just think because we think. All thinking is discursive, and time is always involved in thinking, as it is involved in speaking or listening. When I speak about thinking, here, I mean conscious thinking, i.e. thinking of which the thinking subject is fully aware. However, this is not the only kind of thinking, as

---

[40]Jacques Lacan, *The Seminar of Jacques Lacan, Book VI: Desire and Its Interpretation* [1958–59] (www.lacaninireland.com), p. 203.

[41]Adrian Johnston has argued that Lacan fails to reconcile the timelessness of the unconscious (as postulated by Freud) with his own attempt to derive temporality from the symbolic (logical time), and claims that the problem persists until the end of Lacan's teaching, i.e. even until after Lacan decided to turn to mathematics and topology. See Adrian Johnston, *Time Driven: Metapsychology and the Splitting of the Drive* (Evanston, IL: Northwestern University Press, 2005), pp. 55–57. His argument is weakened if, as suggested here, one considers Lacan's conceptualisation of duration as time in the real and of temporality as a scaffolding of imaginary and symbolic time relations. Timelessness, in Freud's sense, is not irreconcilable with Lacan's "temporal logic": the installation of temporal logic (i.e. the installation of the signifying chain) gives rise to the emergence of signification and opens a place for the unconscious. It is exactly because Lacan is able to discern a temporal logic in his conceptualisation of the unconscious that he can describe the formations of the unconscious as gaps in a signifying chain.

Freud discovered. "Thinking" happens in the unconscious, too. But that thinking is recombinatory, rather than discursive, and does not involve time. A dream is "presented before consciousness as an object of perception",[42] i.e. it is not recounted. For the dreaming subject, it is the process of *secondary revision* that brings a narrative form to dream material.[43]

Similarly, historicity itself comes about by a kind of secondary revision. I am using the term to denote the observation that human beings have an awareness of coming *from* somewhere, and going *to* somewhere, i.e. they have a history and tend to let this history inform their future. History would not exist without time or, rather, without *awareness* of time and temporality. However, the step from temporality to historicity is not a self-evident one. To have a history, you need something more than just time. You need something that would give a perspective within the symbolic—a signifier that would set the symbolic in motion, so to speak. This signifier would create arrows that would point towards what is not here yet. In a way, it would provide a direction and a sense. Lacan does not hold a fixed position in connection with this question. Early on, he connects this to *logical time*. Then, he brings up Heidegger and Heidegger's conceptualisation of death. Following Heidegger, he conceives this ontologically and connects it with Freud's death drive:

> The death instinct essentially expresses the limit of the subject's historical function. This limit is death—not as the possible end date of the individual's life, nor as the subject's empirical certainty, but, as Heidegger puts it, as that 'possibility which is the subject's ownmost, which is unconditional, unsurpassable, certain, and as such indeterminable'—the subject being understood as defined by his historicity.[44]

But then he moves away from Heidegger and, as we saw above, brings in the structure of language itself. At the end of his teaching, he

---

[42]Sigmund Freud, 'New Introductory Lectures on Psychoanalysis' [1933a], in James Strachey (ed.), *SE vol. 22* (London: Hogarth Press, 1953–1974), 1–182, p. 21.

[43]See also above, p. 95.

[44]Lacan, 'Function and Field', *Écrits*, pp. 261–262/318.

connects the question of temporality to topology. In his final (twenty-sixth) seminar, *Topology and Time* (1978–79), he speaks about a correspondence between topology and psychoanalytic practice, which, as he says, exists in time. But Lacan is already too old and too tired. He never gives more than a very small number of indications of what he means. As Marini writes, the seminar is unpublishable and shows clearly the "stumbling block" of his theorising.[45]

# Theory of Discourses

The theory of the discourses is introduced in Lacan's teaching relatively late, in *Seminar XVII* (1969–70), as a solution to the question of the subject's engagement with a signifying chain and with the symbolic Other. Lacan describes a discourse as a social link or bond founded on language, a "necessary structure that goes well beyond speech … [and] subsists in certain fundamental relations which would literally not be able to be maintained without language".[46]

Language, in this case, is meant both as the set of linguistic signs, rules and operations that comprise it, and as the set of interactions and relations that language makes possible. The basic structure of a discourse is an extension of a simpler structure representing Lacan's definition of a signifier as that which represents the subject to another signifier.

Signifiers are interconnected within the subject's own network of signifiers

$$S_1 \rightarrow S_2$$

allowing the subject to be represented through their interconnection.

$$\frac{S_1 \rightarrow S_2}{\$}$$

---

[45]See Marcelle Marini, *Jacques Lacan: The French Context* (New Brunswick, NJ: Rudgers University Press, 1992), p. 247. See also Johnston, *Time Driven*, pp. 51–52.

[46]Lacan, *Seminar XVII*, pp. 17, 12–13. *Social link* or *social bond* (in French: *lien social*) is a term borrowed from Saussure, who used it to describe what constitutes the basis of a linguistic group.

This schema has only three legs, so Lacan suggests adding one more, at the bottom right corner, since, as he has explained elsewhere, "a quadripartite structure can always be required in a construction of a subjective ordering".[47] This fourth leg he designates as object $a$, i.e. as the object *cause* of desire.

$$\frac{S_1}{\mathcal{S}} \rightarrow \frac{S_2}{a}$$

This formula "locates a moment".

> It says that it is at the very instant at which $S_1$ intervenes in the already constituted field of the other signifiers, insofar as they are already articulated with one another as such, that, by intervening in another system, this $\mathcal{S}$ which I have called the subject as divided, emerges. ... Finally, we have always stressed that something defined as a loss emerges from this trajectory. This is what the letter to be read as object $a$ designates.[48]

The divided subject emerges as a speaking being, that is, as truth (since speaking represents an affirmation). Truth is revealed when language is spoken, i.e. at the moment that an *agent* (in this case $S_1$, i.e. a master signifier) reaches out to the *other* (in this case $S_2$, i.e. the constituted field of the other signifiers). A discourse is established in reference to an object which is supposed to be at the side of the Other, and operates as the *cause* or that-what-is-*at-stake*. That object can be thought as a *product* or *loss*.[49]

Thus, the four legs of the formula can be described then in their utmost abstraction as follows:

$$\frac{\text{agent}}{\text{truth}} \rightarrow \frac{\text{other}}{\text{product/loss}}$$

These four places are implied as an organising structure in any discourse and reflect a tension between what traditionally—and perhaps

---

[47]'Kant with Sade', *Écrits*, p. 653/774.
[48]*Seminar XVII*, p. 15.
[49]This relates to the concept of surplus jouissance. See above, p. 120.

naively—would be described as *internal* and *external* in a subject's psychic life. A discourse outlines how signifying elements are organised in the field opened by a subject's discursive interactions, *as well* as within a subject's own psychic space as such.

The first arrangement presented above is called the discourse of the master. It is, according to Lacan, "a discourse that is already in the world and thus underpins it, at least the one we are familiar with. Not only it is already inscribed in it, but it is one of its arches".[50] From there, by applying an anti-clockwise quarter-turn operation, Lacan produces three additional arrangements of the terms, each corresponding to a different discursive structure. This operation is purely formal, but Lacan stresses that it is not just accidental:

I have been speaking about this notorious quarter turn for long enough and on different occasions—in particular, ever since the appearance of what I wrote under the title 'Kant with Sade'—for people to think … that there are other reasons for this quarter turn than some pure accident of imaginary representation.[51]

However, he says very little about those other reasons.[52]

In any case, starting from the discourse of the master, and applying the anti-clockwise quarter-turn rotation once, we obtain the university discourse,

---

[50]Lacan, *Seminar XVII*, pp. 14–15.

[51]*Seminar XVII*, p. 14. In *Kant with Sade*, Lacan had constructed a schema with four place holders representing, as he explained, the Sadean phantasy. Further in the text he transformed it by a 90-degrees rotation. See 'Kant with Sade', *Écrits*, pp. 653/774, 657/778. Dany Nobus points out that Lacan had already used this quarter-turn operation in the early 60s but suggests that at that early stage of his thinking, "Lacan himself may have not made much of it". (Dany Nobus, *The Law of Desire: On Lacan's 'Kant with Sade'* (Cham, Switzerland: Palgrave Macmillan, 2017), p. 74n1).

[52]It appears that Lacan has formulated this anti-clockwise rotation as the result of operations involving the application of radical (square root) functions on vectors in a two-dimensional complex ("Argand") plane. (I owe this suggestion to Bernard Burgoyne.) It is possible that Lacan plays on the fact that operations involving complex numbers are symbolic operations on the complex plane that includes an axis of real numbers $x$ with an axis of imaginary numbers $iy$, where $i = \sqrt{-1}$. In this way, the order of the symbols be retained, something that might explain why Lacan does not accept a transformation based on an horizontal or vertical axis of symmetry.

$$\frac{S_2}{S_1} \rightarrow \frac{a}{\$}$$

Then the analyst's discourse,

$$\frac{a}{S_2} \rightarrow \frac{\$}{S_1}$$

and finally, the hysteric's discourse.

$$\frac{\$}{a} \rightarrow \frac{S_1}{S_2}$$

As can be seen, each of these four discourses is the inverse of another one of the four. The inverse of the master's discourse, for example, is the discourse of the analyst (as implied by the original title of *Seminar XVII*, *L'envers de la psychanalyse*, where the four discourses are introduced), while the discourse of the hysteric is the inverse of the discourse of university.[53]

Lacan's discourse theory has found immediate application in clinical practice, with some claiming that it brings predictive strength to an analyst's interpretative choices.[54] It has also been readily adopted by researchers and theoreticians working in the fields of political theory and social and cultural studies, and a lot of important work has been produced as a result. The apparent simplicity of the four formulas, however, facilitated their uncritical adoption and application to all kinds of contexts in such

---

[53]Speaking at Milan University, in 1972, Lacan discussed a fifth discourse, a substitute, as he said, of the master discourse, which he called discourse of the capitalist. To produce it, Lacan suggested a simple inversion of the two left-hand side legs of the master discourse:

$$\frac{\$}{S_1} \rightarrow \frac{S_2}{a}$$

The discourse of the capitalist, he said, "is untenable. ... It works like a clockwork, cannot go better, but in fact it goes too fast, it consumes, it consumes so well that it will consume itself" (Jacques Lacan, 'Du Discours Psychanalytique' [1972], in G. B. Contri (ed.), *Lacan In Italia – 1953–1978 - En Italie Lacan* (Milan: Salamandra, 1978), 32–55, p. 48). Apart from few other mentions, however, he does not return to it in any systematic way, allowing one to suspect that it was a token of political criticism rather than a formal extension of his discourse theory.

[54]See, for example, Paul Verhaeghe, *Does the Woman Exist? From Freud's Hysteric to Lacan's Feminine* (New York: Other Press, 1999), p. 98.

a way that it has become very difficult to judge whether there was any merit in doing so. This was aided by the ambiguous clarity of the names Lacan chose for his four discourses. It might be tempting, for example, to mistake the master's discourse for a discourse of oppression, or to think that scientists engage in the university discourse, or even to believe that most neurotics—but not all of them—are operating within the hysteric's discourse. This, however, is not the case. Each discourse represents a manner of engagement with the symbolic order (or big Other) and *not* the structure of the social field facilitated by it. So, we can say that the discourse of the master describes the emergence of the divided subject through its submission to the symbolic order in a vain attempt to subordinate and keep under control the object cause of desire (a); in the discourse of the university, the established system of knowledge $(S_2)$ becomes an end in itself, resulting to the eclipse of the divided subject; the discourse of the hysteric addresses and challenges the master in disregard of and defiance of established knowledge; and, finally, the discourse of the analyst attempts to bring the divided subject vis-à-vis their own desire, in an attempt to recreate a new, less alienating, master signifier. Within this explanatory framework, it is interesting to note that true scientific thinking is best described by the hysteric's discourse, or to observe how psychoanalysis only becomes possible when desire rather than the master signifier reflects the subject's engagement with knowledge.

Lacan himself preferred to leave open how his formulas are to be used. He pointed out, however, that there is nothing deterministic in the transformation operation that produces the four discourses, i.e. there is no specific order or necessity in how they emerge. Misconstructions were anticipated:

My little quadrupedal schemas—I am telling you this today to alert you to it—are not the Ouija boards of history. It is not necessarily the case that things always happen this way, and that things rotate in the same direction. This is only an appeal for you to locate yourselves in relation to what one can call radical functions, in the mathematical sense of the term.[55]

---

[55]Lacan, *Seminar XVII*, p. 188. For Lacan's referring to "radical functions" see above, p. 153n52.

# Jouissance and the Speaking Body

I wrote earlier about Lacan's introduction of the three registers of experience—imaginary, symbolic and real—and also of jouissance, which we conceptualised as an effect of the world on the body in its structural coupling within this world, an effect that fuels these registers. It is now clear that a more careful consideration of the role of the body as such is needed. First, it is necessary to clarify what is meant by the term "body".

A basic, everyday sense of the term, the one provided by dictionaries for example, takes *body* to mean the complete physical structure of a human being or animal, comprising a head, a trunk, a neck, legs, arms, etc. This description is valid for most intents and purposes as long as the body is taken to be just an object, i.e. an occurrent entity. This means to say that "body"—taken in this simple dictionary sense—is an *ontic* term. It's clear to see, however, that an ontic term is not appropriate when one wants to consider phenomena like the ones studied by psychoanalysis, as this would involve the uncritical adoption of an understanding of both the body as such (i.e. as an occurrent entity) and what it means to be an embodied subject—or to "have" a body, as people usually say.

The term "body" is a construction, a signifier referring to a collection of signifiers that obtains a place in the human world by its interconnections to other signifiers and collections of signifiers; but it is also the agent through which signifiers are possible. The body—the biological organism—is a prerequisite of everything discussed until now. It's only because we have a body—a biological body—that there can be jouissance, and that the register of the real can be populated. But this biological body needs to be contrasted to the body we talk about when we consider our bodily existence as speaking beings—our *language body*, so to speak. In the words of Colette Soler, "one is not born with a body. In other words, the body is not primary. The living being is not the body. ... There is a distinction to be made between the organism, i.e. the living being, on the one hand, and that which, on the other hand, is called the body".[56] Human beings obtain a language body through their introduction to language. In the beginning, the body is experienced as fragmented and chaotic—the source of unsignifierised jouissance, i.e. anxiety. It only starts becoming whole via a process that Lacan described under the rubric of the *mirror stage*. But, as he wrote very early on,

> This illusion of unity, in which a human being is always looking forward to self-mastery, entails a constant danger of sliding back again into the chaos from which he started; it hangs over the abyss of a dizzy Assent in which one can perhaps see the very essence of Anxiety.[57]

Language, as it was indicated earlier, comprises an articulated network of signifierised jouissance. It is because these elements of signifierised jouissance qua signifiers point to other signifiers that the human being can keep the as-yet non-signifierised jouissance under control: the network of signifiers is being installed, and more and more of this non-signifierised jouissance becomes a part of it—that is, becomes increasingly signifierised. Jouissance becomes controllable only when it is "channelled" through a series of imaginary identifications and symbolic signifierisations, the result of which is the construction of an imaginary body and of a corresponding *symbolic body* made of linguistic signifiers. It is in this sense that we can say that the symbolic, or as we called it earlier, language body is very different from the biological body. Its emergence is at the heart of a multitude of clinical and non-clinical phenomena, ranging widely in severity and urgency: from severe cases of schizophrenia and catatonia to bodily dissociations, eating disorders or addictions; from gender discomfort, or body dysmorphic syndromes, to hysterical conversions or various other psychosomatic ailments; and

---

[56]Colette Soler, 'The Body in the Teaching of Jacques Lacan' *Journal of the Centre for Freudian Analysis and Research*, 6 (1995), 6–38, p. 7.
[57]Jacques Lacan, 'Some Reflections on the Ego' *International Journal of Psychoanalysis*, 34 (1953), 11–17, p. 15. See also above, pp. 104–106.

so on and so forth.[58] What all these have in common is the fact that the body of the speaking being is marked and transformed by the symbolic in ways that go far beyond the limits imposed by biology as such. In fact, introduction to the symbolic may have influenced human phylogeny itself.[59] It is as if the body presents the human being qua subject (of language) with an insoluble enigma. The question is far broader from what a simplistic understanding of the important biological and other physiological issues at hand would entail. Questions of survival, sustenance and procreation are common to all living beings as living beings. A human being, considered only at the level of biology, would have to behave in such way as to "guarantee" life to the greatest extent possible. But a human being considered as a speaking being—or *parlêtre*, as Lacan calls it—is concerned about what is happening, because everything that *is* happening—one's world, one's environment, one's body as well—is a potential signifier. In other words, it is not speaking alone that establishes the speaking being, but engagement with the network of signifiers—i.e. language, the symbolic order or else the big Other.[60] It is in this sense that Lacan says that "thought is

---

[58]For a discussion, see Paul Verhaeghe, 'Subject and Body: Lacan's Struggle with the Real', in *Beyond Gender: From Subject to Drive* (New York: Other Press, 2001), 65–97.

[59]In comparison to the chimpanzee, humans are born prematurely. Researchers estimate that human gestation period should be at least double if the human infant was to be born at a neurological development stage comparable to that of a chimpanzee infant. Even though there is no consensus in regard to why this is the case, there are those who argue that it might be connected to the fact that humans are "cultural animals". It appears that such short gestation period, with all it entails, would not be possible if there were no social structures that would provide a safe environment for the infant for the period just after birth until the age of 2–3 years old.

[60]Cf. in this connection what Lacan says about his dog: "I have a dog ... My dog, in my sense and without ambiguity, speaks. My dog has without any doubt the gift of speech. This is important, because it does not mean that she possesses language totally. ... What distinguishes this speaking animal from what happens because of the fact that man speaks ... is that, contrary to what happens in the case of man in so far as he speaks, she never takes me for another. ... By taking you for another, [a] subject puts you at the level of the Other with a big O. It is precisely this which is lacking to my dog: for her there is only the small other. As regards the big Other, it does not seem that her relationship to language gives her access to it". (Jacques Lacan, *The Seminar of Jacques Lacan, Book IX: Identification* [1961–62] (www.lacaninireland.com), pp. 21–22).

jouissance".[61] It is hard to overestimate the philosophical implications of this assertion: if signifiers stem from jouissance, and if all thought *is* jouissance, then the traditional philosophical concept of being loses its place. At least in Lacan's view. As he says, he opposes to this being, "the being of signifierness".[62]

Your body as a signifier represents you qua subject to another signifier. It's not just about *doing something* as such with your body; it's the further issue. What does it mean to have a body? What is the meaning of the body? In reference to what is this meaning established? And what about gender and sexuation?

# Sexuation

The term sexuation refers to how the speaking being comes to acquire a sexual identity. In so far as the symbolic order is a construction involving jouissance, sexuation too involves a construction, i.e. a choice. This question bothered Freud from very early on—when he spoke, for example, about the "polymorphously perverse disposition" of children and tried to account for the differentiation between men and women; or later, when he acknowledged the differing and complicated trajectories of men and women in their attempts to obtain and occupy their respective sexual identity.[63]

In a Lacanian understanding of the issues, the starting point is jouissance. Jouissance, understood as the effect of the world on the body, is undifferentiated: Jouissance *One*, as J.-A. Miller has it.[64]

---

[61]*Seminar XX*, p. 70.

[62]*Seminar XX*, p. 71.

[63]See, for example, Sigmund Freud, 'Three Essays on the Theory of Sexuality' [1905d], in James Strachey (ed.), *SE vol. 7* (London: Hogarth Press, 1953–1974), pp. 123–246; 'Some Psychical Consequences of the Anatomical Distinction Between the Sexes' [1925j], in James Strachey (ed.), *SE vol. 19* (London: Hogarth Press, 1953–1974), pp. 241–258; and "Femininity" in 'New Introductory Lectures', *SE vol. 22*.

[64]See Jacques-Allain Miller, 'Les six Paradigmes de la Jouissance' *La Cause Freudienne*, 43 (1999), 7–29, http://www.causefreudienne.net/wp-content/uploads/2015/04/JAM-Six-paradigmes-jouissance.pdf.

But as soon as the signifier is established, something changes: the human being obtains what we referred to earlier as a symbolic body and occupies, as a sexed being, a position related to this symbolic body. What we call *male* and *female* are constructs of language—and not categories of biology:

> Assuredly, what appears on bodies in the enigmatic form of sexual characteristics—which are merely secondary—makes sexed beings. No doubt. But being is the jouissance of the body as such, that is, as asexual because what is known as sexual jouissance is marked and dominated by the impossibility of establishing as such, anywhere in the enunciable, the sole One that interests us, the One of the relation 'sexual relationship' [*rapport sexuel*].[65]

Which is to say that the sexual relationship is impossible not because there are no human beings engaging in sexual activities but rather that what we refer to as a sexual relationship is a relationship between linguistic—i.e. symbolic—constructs:

> Has it not occurred to you that this 'sexual reality' ... is specified in man in this, that there is no instinctual relation between male and female? ... Man—when man is to be spoken about, I shout out—should be ok just to dream about it. He should be ok just to dream about it because it is quite certain that ... *The* woman doesn't exist. There are women, of course, but *The* woman is but a dream of man.[66]

The signifierisation of (some of the) jouissance imposes a differentiation between *phallic* jouissance and *other* jouissance. The first is linked to the phallus (and hence to the signifier and to signifierness as such), while the other is linked to what is beyond that what can be signified. After the phallus has been introduced, phallic jouissance obtains a special position. In Lacan's words:

---

[65]Lacan, *Seminar XX*, pp. 6–7.
[66]'Conférence à Genève sur le Symptôme' [1975] *Le Bloc-notes de la psychanalyse*, 5 (1985), 5–23, p. 15 (my translation).

To one of these beings qua sexed, to man insofar as he is endowed with the organ said to be phallic—I said, 'said to be'—the corporal sex or sexual organ of woman—I said, 'of woman', whereas in fact *woman* does not exist, woman is *not whole*—woman's sexual organ doesn't tell him anything, except via the body's jouissance. ... Analytic experience attests precisely to the fact that everything revolves around phallic jouissance, in that woman is defined by a position that I have indicated as 'not whole' with respect to phallic jouissance. ... Phallic jouissance is the obstacle owing to which man does not come, I would say, to enjoy woman's body, precisely because what he enjoys is the jouissance of the organ.[67]

Lacan's position is grounded on Freud's own: just like Freud, Lacan takes the castration complex as his starting point; just like Freud, Lacan recognises that being a man or a woman is not a question of biology. Lacan takes one more step by introducing the symbolic dimension of sexuation—that is, by approaching the question of the human being as a sexed being, in terms of the signifier. The concept of jouissance plays a most important role here. Being the source of signifierness, jouissance, which can also be understood here in the narrower sense of sexual *enjoyment* and—as we said—has no direct equivalent in Freud, allows Lacan to discern more clearly the distinction between *phallic* jouissance and *other*—and thus to show in a quasi-concrete manner how the complexities of female sexuality could be approached.

In *Seminar XX*, Lacan provides a schema that represents this configuration (see Fig. 5.1). The formulas on the left-hand side represent the male state of affairs, while those on the right represent the female state of affairs.[68] Transcribed in plain English, the two formulas for men say something like: every x (i.e. every human being) is inscribed in the phallic function ($\forall$x $\Phi$x) provided that there is a limit to that function, i.e. there is at least one *other* human being (x), who is *not* bound by it ($\exists$x $\overline{\Phi x}$). This is nothing very new, really. The formulas represent Lacan's understanding of the paternal function, that is,

---

[68] It should be reminded here that this discussion has nothing to do with the biological sex as such. The symbol x represents a human being with no reference to biological sex.

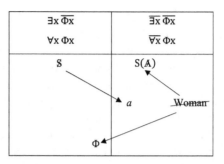

**Fig. 5.1** Formulas of sexuation

castration: every subject is submitted to the phallic function as long as there is a master who is above it and sets the law—namely, the *name-* (or the *no-*) *of-the-father*—imposing it by threat of castration.[69]

The two formulas on the female side tell a somewhat different story. The starting point for the female subject is that there is an ambivalence about the limit to the phallic function. Jouissance is not limited to being merely phallic because—or *since*—there isn't one x who is not subjected to it ($\overline{\exists x\ \overline{\Phi x}}$). If there was one such x, then it would play the role of the omnipotent master, and then, the jouissance of the subject qua *female* would *have* to be under the phallic function (i.e. operating under the threat of castration). That would then bring this particular subject to the male side. To say that for women jouissance is not all phallic is equivalent to saying that the *not whole* of woman is under the phallic function ($\overline{\forall x}\ \Phi x$)—"not whole" being the content of the rather uncommon notation $\overline{\forall}$.[70] To put it differently, contrary to Freud's understanding, Lacan sees that some of the woman is *not* under the threat of castration.

The lower part of the schema describes the position of men and women in connection with desire. Man, qua divided subject, aims at object *a*, which represents the function that causes his desire; it is in

---

[69]See above, p. 137.

[70]Cf. Lacan: "I write $\overline{\forall x}\ \Phi x$, a never-before-seen function in which the negation is placed on the quantifier, which should be read 'not-whole'". Lacan, *Seminar XX*, p. 72.

this sense that we can think of male jouissance as phallic jouissance, i.e. jouissance of the organ. On other side, the woman, written in this crossed-out way to indicate that the woman doesn't exist, aims at either Φ (which indicates the symbolic phallus) or S(Ⱥ) (which indicates the master signifier, a notation roughly equivalent to $S_1$).

This very abstract formulation and its explanation are not intended to be read as some kind of magic mathematical recipe that sorts out the question of sexuation once and for all. It is, however, intended to provide some understanding of this very complicated state of affairs. But, as B. Fink writes, "we need not assume that there is some sort of complete unity or consistency to his [Lacan's] work, for he adds to and changes things as he goes along".[71] Be that as it may, the most important aspect of Lacan's conceptualisation is his determination to thematise in a structural, i.e. ontological manner, the question of sexual difference.[72]

# Borromean Clinic

Like Freud, who used schemata as simpler illustrations of complex ideas from as early as in his *Interpretation of Dreams* up to *The Ego and the Id* and later, Lacan's concern was also to come up with appropriate schematic representations of his theoretical models. In contrast to Freud, however, whose topography, at least according to Lacan, was "not free of awkwardness",[73] Lacan seemed to have higher hopes in his schemas. He had been thinking for some time that topology offers a non-metaphorical way of exploring psychic structures. His hypothesis was that there is a homeomorphism between the actual phenomena he is studying and

---

[71]Cf. here Bruce Fink, 'Knowledge and Jouissance', in Suzanne Barnard and Bruce Fink (eds.), *Reading Seminar XX: Lacan's Major Work on Love, Knowledge, and Female Sexuality* (Albany: State University of New York Press, 2002), 21–45, p. 40.

[72]In contrast to Heidegger, for example, who postulated the ontological neutrality of the Dasein, accepted the ontic reality of sexual difference, but was not able to speak ontologically about it.

[73]Jacques Lacan, 'Overture to the 1st International Encounter of the Freudian Field: Caracas, 12 July 1980', trans. Adrian Price, *Hurly-Burly*, 6 (September 2011), 17–20, p. 18.

his topological models, and that it is, therefore, possible to use them heuristically.

As discussed earlier, the three registers of human subjectivity—imaginary, symbolic and real—are linked to each other, with the imaginary and the symbolic emerging, so to speak, from the real, i.e. the register of the effects of the world on the body. They are all dependent on each other, interconnected, in a psychic whole. The challenge, for Lacan, was to find a way to model this interconnection and interdependence, and to represent it schematically. He was trying to account for two seemingly contradictory features of the three registers: the first is that they all have their origin in unsignifierised jouissance and the second that they become increasingly distinct from each other up to the point where, because of the paternal function, they emerge as independent entities.

In 1972, Lacan came up with the idea that the three registers are intertwined like rings forming a knot. He had a specific kind of knot in mind, called *Borromean*. It was called this because it was found on the coat of arms of the Borromeo medieval banking family, very possibly symbolising the Holy Trinity. It comprises three rings not connected with each other in any way, but arranged so that if one of them is cut, all of them become free.[74] Applying this configuration to the three registers, Lacan envisaged them as a Borromean knot. Each of the registers is represented by a ring, and all three rings are arranged in such a way that if one of them is "cut", all of them become separated—even though not one of them was joined with any other in any way (see Fig. 5.2, left).

It was a promising idea, and Lacan embraced it enthusiastically.[75] His hope was that knot theory, the branch of mathematics that studies knots, would provide clinically relevant and helpful insights. He continued working on the knot theory for the whole of the last part of his teaching, albeit with growing impatience and disappointment for the meagreness of results. "It would be nice", he said in 1976,

---

[74]In knot theory, a *knot* is defined as a curve in space that is closed, while a link is a configuration of several such disjointed curves. In this sense, the Borromean knot should actually be thought as a link.

[75]For the background of Lacan's becoming interested in it in 1972, see Elisabeth Roudinesco, *Jacques Lacan* (New York: Columbia University Press, 1997), pp. 363–364.

**Fig. 5.2**  Borromean knot or link and trefoil knot

if I could manage to get some response, some collaboration, some active interest. It seems to me that it's hard to take an interest in what is becoming a research project. I mean that I am starting to do what the word *research* implies, namely to go around in circles.

There was a time when I used to sound my bugle a bit more. ... These days, however, it's tougher for me to clear my path.[76]

His disappointment only grew. As Dany Nobus writes, attendees at his seminars would see him spending

hours and hours weaving ends of rope and drawing complicated diagrams on small pieces of paper. ... During his seminar of 1978-79 he even silenced his own voice in favour of the practice of writing and drawing, treating his audience to the speechless creation of intricate knots on the blackboard.[77]

This labour did not produce very concrete fruits. It was clear that for Lacan it was very important to have his knots represent something of

---

[76]Jacques Lacan, *The Seminar of Jacques Lacan, Book XXIII: The Sinthome* [1975–76], ed. Jacques-Allain Miller (Cambridge: Polity Press, 2016), p. 74.
[77]Dany Nobus, 'Lacan's Science of the Subject: Between Linguistics and Topology', in Jean-Michel Rabaté (ed.), *The Cambridge Companion to Lacan* (Cambridge: Cambridge University Press, 2003), 50–68, p. 63.

the clinic. In 1976, he commented that "the Borromean knot is not a knot, it's a link. Why not grasp that each of these loops continues in the next in a way that is strictly not distinguished?"[78] In this way, the Borromean knot or link would be transformed into a so-called trefoil knot (see Fig. 5.2, right). Could this offer a way to address the problem regarding the common origin of the three registers? Perhaps. The picture would be an elegant one. Beginning from one "ring" (or torus) comprising unsignifierised jouissance—i.e. the real—a structuring process takes place that allows the emergence of the imaginary and the symbolic, as a trefoil knot, and from there to the final Borromean configuration. The transformation, however, is not a straightforward one, since the trefoil knot has three crossings while the original torus of the real has a crossing number of zero.[79] It is even less easy to see how the transformation of the trefoil knot into a Borromean link can happen. As Lacan was ready to admit:

> I have told you, that this theory of knots is in its infancy, is extremely clumsy. And as it is fabricated, there are many cases where at the sight of simple figures such as the ones that I have made for you on the board, you could not in any way give an explanation for the fact, whether yes or no, the tangle that you have drawn is or is not a knot, whatever may be the conventions that you have given yourself in advance to account for the knot as such. The fact is moreover that there is something that is worth dwelling on. Is it because of an intuition?[80]

Lacan's Borromean models were not met with unanimous acceptance. Two of his students, psychoanalyst D. Lécuru and mathematician D. Barataud, have tried to demonstrate the validity of Lacan's Borromean postulates. They have been unsuccessful. "So far", they wrote in 1982, "we made no progress in this direction, which leads to the observation

---

[78]Lacan, *Seminar XXIII*, p. 71 (translation slightly altered). See also above, p. 164n74.

[79]In knot theory, the crossing number of a knot is its smallest number of crossings. It remains invariant for all equivalent knots.

[80]Jacques Lacan, *The Seminar of Jacques Lacan, Book XXII: RSI* [1974–75] (www.lacaninireland.com), p. 40.

that this postulate is, instead, a dogma, and that it is sustained solely through the faith invested in it".[81]

Moreover, how can we include in this picture our understanding of clinical structures? For example, what is the Borromean equivalent of the diagnostic distinction between psychosis and neurosis? Psychosis is understood as a failure of the paternal function; if the paternal function is the function that guarantees the separation of the three Borromean rings from each other, then psychosis can be understood in terms of an instability of the Borromean knot. In psychosis, the knot *can* be unravelled; in neurosis, this is not possible. In order to account for those cases where a triggering of psychosis appears imminent but is somehow staved off, Lacan suggested that there might be something that can keep the Borromean knot together. He called it *sinthome* (in French: *sintôme*, an older spelling of the word *symptôme*, or symptom) and pictured it as an additional ring that would hold the other three together. The sinthome is thought to occupy for psychotics a place similar to the place the neurotic symptom occupies for neurotics—i.e. it is an attempt at a cure. Lacan chose the older spelling to indicate that the psychotic sinthome is more primordial than the neurotic symptom and undergoes different vicissitudes. As Lacan says, "I have allowed myself to define as a sinthome that which enables the trefoil knot, not to go on forming a trefoil knot, but rather to maintain itself in a position that *looks like* it is forming a trefoil knot".[82] The form of this additional ring (the sinthome) is, as its name implies, circumstantial—in the sense that the way it can manage to preserve the knot can vary widely from individual to individual.

The introduction of the sinthome raises a number of questions in connection with clinical practice. A neurotic symptom is situated somewhere in the three registers and can be taken as a cipher to be deciphered. As Lacan points out, for the neurotic subject "there is consistency between the symptom and the unconscious. Except for the

---

[81]Denis Lécuru and Dominique Barataud, quoted in François Roustang, *The Lacanian Delusion* (New York: Oxford University Press, 1990), p. 99. Their work, "Essai sur quelques raisons d'une lecture borroméenne du symbolique", written in 1982, is available to researchers but remains unpublished.

[82]Lacan, *Seminar XXIII*, p. 77.

fact that the symptom cannot be defined otherwise than by the way in which each one enjoys the unconscious in so far as the unconscious determines it".[83] A psychotic subject, on the other hand, is as if it does *not* have an analysable symptom. It will *not* recognise a symptom as a cipher and will not be able to engage with any invitation by an analyst to decipher it. The sinthome, understood as what holds the three registers together, is thought of as situated outside the three registers as such and is for that reason unreachable by any discourse. For all intents and purposes, then, the psychotic subject is unreachable by analysis. With a psychotic, it would perhaps be preferable to talk of a *treatment* instead of analysis. This is how Jean-Louis Gault puts it:

> In neurosis, the point is to decipher the symptoms, moving from the symbolic to the real. It is this deciphering that the very word 'analysis' aims at. In psychosis, on the contrary, the idea is to go from the real to the symbolic, and to construct a symptom. This is where the term 'treatment' is justified.[84]

Further questions could be raised in connection with its applicability: are sinthomes restricted to psychotic subjects or is there a space to think of them as concepts relevant to neurotics as well? Is the concept really useful at all? Is it justified? Is it necessary?

Such questions bring us to the more general issue of the status of mathematical and topological formalisation in Lacan's work.

## A Method of Discovery or of Exposition?

Considering the later years of his teaching, the reaction of Lacan's followers was mixed. Many dismissed Lacan's use of mathematics, or interpreted it as a metaphor—a prop for the imagination, as it were. Joël

---

[83] *Seminar XXII*, p. 98.

[84] Jean-Louis Gault, 'Two Statuses of the Symptom: Let Us Turn to Finn Again', in Véronique Voruz and Bogdan Wolf (eds.), *The Later Lacan: An Introduction* (Albany: State University of New York Press, 2007), 73–82, p. 79.

Dor, for example, has argued that Lacan's "idiosyncratic use of these topological objects involves a metaphorical illustration" and that "even if they do not constitute the proof of a *mathematisation* of psychoanalytic theory" they can support "the idea of a *matheme* allowing for the transmission of psychoanalysis".[85] Jacques-Alain Miller, on the other hand, insisted that for Lacan topology "is not metaphor, it represents a structure".[86] Others have been overtly negative. In the words of David Corfield, "Lacan never reached the point where his symbolisation could provide sufficient guidance to further theory construction. ... His theory has not been able to achieve the kind of liberation from authorship we see in the mathematical sciences".[87]

In a Q&A session during *Seminar XI*, a member of the audience asked Lacan: "Is topology for you a method of discovery or of exposition?" Lacan responded: "It is the mapping of the topology proper to our experience as analysts, which may later be taken in a metaphysical perspective".[88] In other words, Lacan claimed that topology might, at some point, be able to serve as a metaphysical (or ontological) foundation of the psychoanalytic praxis. His claim would imply that there is a correspondence between two structured systems, one being what we describe as psychic reality and the other being topology. Some years later, Lacan was presented with a question that challenged openly his understanding of the limits of such correspondence:

[Q] May I ask if this fundamental arithmetic and this topology are not in themselves a myth or merely at best an analogy for an explanation of the life of the mind?

---

[85]Joël Dor, 'The Epistemological Status of Lacan's Mathematical Paradigms', in David Pettigrew and François Raffoul (eds.), *Disseminating Lacan* (Albany: State University of New York Press, 1996), 109–121, pp. 117, 120.

[86]Jacques-Allain Miller, 'Mathemes: Topology in the Teaching of Lacan', in Ellie Ragland and Dragan Milovanovic (eds.), *Lacan: Topologically Speaking* (New York: Other Press, 2004), 28–48, p. 35.

[87]David Corfield, 'From Mathematics to Psychology: Lacan's Missed Encounters', in Jason Glynos and Yannis Stavrakakis (eds.), *Lacan & Science* (London: Karnac, 2002), 179–206, p. 189.

[88]Lacan, *Seminar XI*, p. 90.

[A] Analogy to what? 'S' designates something which can be written exactly as this S. And I have said that the 'S' which designates the subject is instrument, matter, to symbolise a loss. A loss that you experience as a subject (and myself too). ... Where is the analogon? Either this loss exists or it doesn't exist. If it exists it is only possible to designate it by employing a system of symbols. In any case, the loss does not exist before this symbolisation indicates its place. It is not an analogy. ... It is not even an abstraction, because an abstraction is some sort of diminution of reality, and I think this is reality itself.[89]

For Lacan, then, topology, as a system of symbols and relations between symbols, is of the same order of existence as that of the subject of language: indeed, the subject of language is a symbol as well, a symbol of a loss. When we speak about reality or about the human being as a divided subject, we are referring to constructions that only belong to the order of the symbolic. It is in this sense that he refuses to accept that the question here is one of analogy. His high hopes for knot theory stem from that, since operations on knots seem to be able to produce results belonging to all three orders, real, imaginary and symbolic. Lacan remained firm in his hypothesis of a correspondence between psychoanalytic clinic and mathematics, and dedicated most of his later seminars on the subject.

Since Lacan's death, this has been taken up by various psychoanalysts and mathematicians. Among them, Bernard Burgoyne, for example, argues for a specific homology—or parallelism—between the domain of mathematics and the domain of what he calls *sexual love*. As Burgoyne explains, the strong version of this "parallelism thesis" appears in one of two forms: "(I) for all structures in the domain of mathematics (where a structure is a number of sentences together with their consequences) there exists a corresponding structure in the domain of sexual love; and (II) for all structures in the domain of sexual love, there exists a

[89]'Of Structure as an Inmixing of an Otherness Prerequisite to Any Subject Whatever' [1970], in Richard Macksey and Eugenio Donato (eds.), *The Structuralist Controversy: The Languages of Criticism and the Sciences of Man* (Baltimore: The Johns Hopkins University Press, 2007), 186–200, pp. 195–196 (translation slightly altered).

corresponding structure in the domain of mathematics".[90] The Freudian theory of defence, for example, could be tested by means of differentiation of structures of separation in topological spaces. Burgoyne writes that "we know four themes where such relations between psychoanalysis and mathematics exist" involving "the concepts of connectivity, compactness, order relation, and separation".[91]

At present, Lacan's hypothesis remains, at best, a hypothesis that has not yet yielded specific results.[92]

## Mathematical Formalisation and Discourse

All reflection about the speaking being takes place in language. But if, following Lacan, we see language as a construction, as a network of interconnected elements that can stand as signifiers, for other elements as signifieds, and if we accept that there is no metalinguistic vantage point from which we can discuss language, i.e. if we accept that there is no Other of the Other, then we see that language cannot "escape" itself—which is to say, language is not able to step "aside", as it were, and study itself. How is it possible, then, to develop a formalisation that would break through the confines of the signifier and play the role of a metalanguage?

Lacan thought of mathematics as involving the manipulation of symbols, or letters, according to certain syntactical rules for their exchanges, transformations and arrangements. Mathematics alone could obey the rules of the symbolic order, with the added privilege that it does not depend on the imaginary individualities of the people involved.

---

[90]Bernard Burgoyne, 'What Causes Structure to Find a Place in Love?', in Jason Glynos and Yannis Stavrakakis (eds.), *Lacan & Science* (London: Karnac, 2002), 231–261, p. 251.

[91]'Place in Love', *Lacan & Science*, pp. 251, 257n53. Burgoyne credits the Hungarian psychoanalyst Imre Hermann as the originator of the idea that psychical structure has its parallel in the domain of mathematics, and adds that Lacan knew of Hermann's work. See 'Autism and Topology', in Bernard Burgoyne (ed.), *Drawing the Soul: Schemas and Models in Psychoanalysis* (London: Karnac, 2000), 190–217.

[92]For an overview of some recent work, see Michael Friedman and Samo Tomšič (eds.), *Psychoanalysis: Topological Perspectives* (Bielefeld: transcript Verlag, 2016).

Likewise, the letters are not imitating any objects or entities of the world. They are completely removed from their origins and from what they had originally represented.

> What is at stake for us is to obtain a model of mathematical formalisation. Formalisation is nothing other than the substitution of what is called a letter for any number of ones. ... Whatever the number of ones you place under each of those letters, you are subject to a certain number of laws—laws of grouping, addition, multiplication etc. ... Mathematisation alone reaches a real—and it is in that respect that it is compatible with our discourse, analytic discourse—a real that has nothing to do with what traditional knowledge has served as a basis for, which is not what the latter believes it to be—namely reality—but rather fantasy.[93]

Lacan's approach to mathematics was far removed from what one ordinarily associates with this term, but it is still mathematics. He allowed himself a liberty in adopting, manipulating and reinterpreting mathematical notation or conventions, a liberty that has confused many of his readers, both followers and opponents. Lacan always presented himself as bemused (or slightly amused) by their confusion and only occasionally appeared less certain. In 1975, for example, during a visit to the USA, he stated, "I have tried to condense, to formulate as regards our practice something that would be coherent. It has led me to wild imaginings that worry me a lot".[94] In general, he did not show any willingness to change his approach in any way.

Mathematisation, in the sense that Lacan understood the term, is not supposed to give us access to reality, as a more traditional understanding of the concepts involved might have wanted it. Lacan sought mathematical formalisation not because the great book of the universe is written in mathematical language (Galileo's argument), but rather because of the access it gives to the real as the register out of which the

---

[93]Lacan, *Seminar XX*, pp. 130–131.
[94]Lacan, quoted in Marini, *Lacan*, p. 242.

imaginary and the symbolic emerge.[95] Lacan did not claim the self-adequacy of mathematics. In his view, mathematics will always need language:

> No formalization of language is transmissible without the use of language itself. It is in the very act of speaking that I make this formalization, this ideal metalanguage, ex-sist. It is in this respect that the symbolic cannot be confused with being—far from it.[96]

Mathematical entities are not thought of as existing independently of the humans using them; mathematical entities were not thought of as comprising the deeper structure of the world—or of the human psyche, for that matter. It is only by speaking that the knots, schemas or formulae that Lacan introduces can step outside their imaginary or symbolic register. In contrast to Galileo's, Lacan's approach was not Platonic: mathematics is not thought as the language of the great book of the universe, but rather that what can represent the workings of the signifying chain.[97] Nor is it neo-Kantian: for Lacan, the intellect is not standing vis-à-vis truth. There is no metalanguage, and yet the human being speaks. In discourse truth, and being, are revealed. As he says, "being … is but a fact of what is said".[98] Ditto for mathematics. It only subsists if we employ it. Mathematics too is but a fact of what is said.

Lacan's position here is remarkably close to Heidegger's when we see him claiming that "Language is the house of being".[99] Not identical, though. Heidegger refers to language in an ontological sense, while Lacan would be suspicious of this ontological sense, since for him language is material, bodily, *corporeal*. For Lacan, more importance is accorded to *saying*—the term understood literally, i.e. as the *action* of

---

[95]It has to be stressed: to the real, and *not* to reality.

[96]Lacan, *Seminar XX*, p. 119.

[97]Cf. in this connection Badiou's statement that "Mathematics *is* ontology—the science of being qua being". See Alain Badiou, *Being and Event* [1988] (New York: Continuum, 2005), p. 4.

[98]Lacan, *Seminar XX*, p. 118.

[99]Martin Heidegger, 'Letter on Humanism' [1947], in William Mcneill (ed.), *Pathmarks* (Cambridge: Cambridge University Press, 1978), 239–276, p. 239.

articulation, with all the movements of the throat, the mouth, the lips involved.[100] *Saying*, seen thus, is always something that pertains to the imaginary register: saying, as such, is inadequate to grasp the phenomena at hand on its own. It obeys an internal logic, namely the logic of the chain of signifiers. But it also *reveals* this logic, it makes it visible: only a *discourse* can allow truth, time and being to ex-sist, without making necessary to resort to metalanguage.

This yet again brings up the question of a circularity. The human being is not in language from the beginning. Lacan's claim is that language plays a fundamental role in opening up the world for the human being, and that the law of the signifier—or, in a more general sense, a discourse—is imposed on any engagement with what is at stake. How is it possible, then, to use language to formulate a discourse *in lieu* of a metalanguage, to avoid falling into the trap of conceptual circularity? This is exactly the same *circle of understanding* that Heidegger had encountered.[101] There is indeed a circle involved when one needs to use language in order to speak about the introduction of the human being to language. There is no way one can avoid this circularity, and in fact, as Heidegger has argued, in trying to avoid it one "misses the decisive issue here, which is an insight into the centre of the circle as such … for the centre only manifests itself as such as we circle around it".[102] Rather than a circle, though, it would be better thought and considered of as a spiral. Some concepts need to be introduced or defined from the beginning—such, for example, are jouissance and the real. Using these concepts, then, one can get a clearer view of the phenomena in question, which in turn will allow one to go back to the original concepts and define them better.

This problem has a further aspect in connection with time. Objective—i.e. intersubjective—time is, according to Lacan, a product

---

[100]Cf. Lacan's early comment, in *Seminar III*, regarding "the discovery that consisted in observing one day that certain patients who complain of auditory hallucinations were manifestly making movements of the throat, of the lips; in other words, they were articulating them themselves". Lacan, *Seminar III*, p. 49.

[101]See above, p. 30.

[102]Martin Heidegger, *The Fundamental Concepts of Metaphysics: World, Finitude, Solitude* [1929–30] (Bloomington: Indiana University Press, 1995), p. 180.

of speaking. If language, i.e. the symbolic, is an end product of a process that begins with the signifierisation of jouissance, then we seem to encounter one more circularity here, namely that time seems to be a product of a process that implicates time at its very core, i.e. signifierisation and the handling of the lack. Signifierisation is a way for the human being to manage what is not there. We saw Lacan claiming that "being is, as they say, and nonbeing is not. There is or there isn't".[103] However, both being there and non-being have time as a prerequisite. Heidegger addresses the problem by introducing the *event*. Lacan accomplishes the same thing by introducing the object *a* as cause of desire, and thematising desire as that which fuels the emergence of signifierness, and bringing in surplus jouissance.[104]

The challenge is, rather, to decide whether it is possible at all to look closely at phenomena that pertain to the speaking being, and, if it is, to find an appropriate way to study them. Lacan's position is tantamount to claiming that mathematical formalisation, especially in set theory and topology, is the only tool that *ex-sists*—i.e. the only tool that can stand beside the phenomena—allowing us to study them for what they are, in an unmediated way. He employs mathematics in an attempt to study the human psyche in the potentiality of its associative chains; his claim is that mathematics provides a robust foundation for the deeper understanding of psychic structures, subjective positions in the world and psychopathology—an understanding that would make possible the development of tools for differential diagnosis, prognosis and treatment.[105]

# From "Anti-philosophy" Back to Philosophy

There has been a lot of discussion regarding Lacan's stance in connection with philosophy. It is taken as a fact now that his turn to mathematics and the increasing obscurity of his teaching signalled a turn

---

[103]Lacan, *Seminar XX*, p. 118.

[104]See above, p. 120.

[105]Lacan, then, uses mathematics in the same way that Heidegger uses phenomenology.

against philosophy—whatever the term "philosophy" is taken to mean. In his later period, Lacan is thought to have been an *anti-philosopher*, but what *this* means is not very clear either. Lacan's first use of the term "anti-philosophy" appears in a 1975 text in which he presented the conditions required for the teaching of psychoanalysis: "Anti-philosophy", he writes,

> this is the name I'd like to give to the investigation of what university discourse owes to its 'educational' supposition. It is not the history of ideas, sad as it is, that will be able to face up to the challenge. A patient collection of all the idiocy that characterizes it will, I hope, allow to highlight it in its indestructible root, in its eternal dream. Of which there is no other awakening if not one's own.[106]

One can clearly see Lacan engaged in an increasingly intense polemic against traditional metaphysics and ontology, and this is exactly what it is: a position of forceful opposition against a tradition of thinking that fails to meet to the challenges it is confronted with. Understood broadly, Lacan's position is just as anti-philosophical as the position of late Heidegger.[107]

In Lacan's view, the main lesson that could be learned from Freud was the importance granted to words, in their material aspect. Looking at it from today's vantage point, Lacan's teaching seems to follow a rather clear trajectory. Having initially focused on phenomena that he would gradually group together under the term "imaginary", he turned after 1953 to language and to the symbolic dimension of human experience, emphasising their centrality to human experience (and, of course, psychoanalysis). The 10 years after 1963 were a period of clarification and recapitulation, during which he focused on terms and concepts he

---

[106]Lacan, 'Peut-être à Vincennes…', *Autres Écrits*, pp. 314–315 (my translation). See also Marini, *Lacan*, pp. 242–243. For a further discussion of Lacan's anti-philosophy, see Adrian Johnston, 'This Philosophy Which Is Not One: Jean-Claude Milner, Alain Badiou, and Lacanian Antiphilosophy' *Journal of the Jan van Eyck Circle for Lacanian Ideology Critique*, 3 (2010), 137–158.

[107]See above, pp. 43–46.

had introduced earlier and elaborated on them. And finally, from 1974 until the end of his life, Lacan returned to the three registers (RSI) in an attempt to study their interrelations further, with the help of topology, knot theory and symbolic logic. This period of increased abstraction was also marked by his increased attention to the concrete reality of the body as the source, and also locus, of the experience of the speaking being.

Thus, Lacan began by studying the human being and its obtaining an identity and a body by submitting to the Other of language and the symbolic, and returned to the body by studying the fundamental role played by the real in what it is to be a human. Lacan's almost exclusive preoccupation with his mathemes and his knots during the latter part of his career was seen by many as a failure. As Roudinesco writes, "his entry into the world of knots led him to the destruction of what the matheme claimed to build. Lacan … finally dissolved into the silent stupor of a Nietzschean aphasia".[108]

Admittedly, his teaching during this last period became more and more opaque—to the point that it appeared to be completely incomprehensible, if not incoherent and mystical. This was exacerbated by the relative absence of concrete results. But it should not, in my view, distract us from Lacan's intention, which was to express issues of signification, history, suffering and symptoms in the most unmediated way possible, in full recognition of the problem that there is no steady ground of metalanguage to facilitate this. To put it in somewhat Heideggerian terms, Lacan was attempting to formulate a fully ontological account of what a *speaking* being is, what its structure is, and how the speaking being relates to other speaking beings in the world they have co-created and shared in discourse. Lacan's project, in other words, was consonant with Heidegger's in more than a few cursory or superficial ways. There is a clear pathway that starts from Heidegger and opens up through Lacan.

◈    ◈    ◈

---

[108]Roudinesco, *Jacques Lacan*, p. 359.

# Bibliography

BADIOU, ALAIN, *Being and Event* [1988], trans. Oliver Feltham (New York: Continuum, 2005).

BURGOYNE, BERNARD, 'Autism and Topology' in Bernard Burgoyne (ed.), *Drawing the Soul: Schemas and Models in Psychoanalysis* (London: Karnac, 2000), 190–217.

———, 'What Causes Structure to Find a Place in Love?' in Jason Glynos and Yannis Stavrakakis (eds.), *Lacan & Science* (London: Karnac, 2002), 231–261.

CORFIELD, DAVID, 'From Mathematics to Psychology: Lacan's Missed Encounters' in Jason Glynos and Yannis Stavrakakis (eds.), *Lacan & Science* (London: Karnac, 2002), 179–206.

DELEUZE, GILLES AND GUATTARI, FÉLIX, *A Thousand Plateaus: Capitalism and Schizophrenia*, trans. Brian Massumi (London: Athlone Press, 1987).

DOR, JOËL, *The Clinical Lacan* (Northvale, NJ: Jason Aronson, 1997).

———, 'The Epistemological Status of Lacan's Mathematical Paradigms', trans. Pablo Nagel, in David Pettigrew and François Raffoul (eds.), *Disseminating Lacan* (Albany: State University of New York Press, 1996), 109–121.

FINK, BRUCE, *A Clinical Introduction to Lacanian Psychoanalysis: Theory and Technique* (Cambridge, MA: Harvard University Press, 1997).

———, 'Knowledge and Jouissance' in Suzanne Barnard and Bruce Fink (eds.), *Reading Seminar XX: Lacan's Major Work on Love, Knowledge, and Female Sexuality* (Albany: State University of New York Press, 2002), 21–45.

FREUD, SIGMUND, 'Beyond the Pleasure Principle' [1920g], trans. James Strachey, in James Strachey (ed.), *SE vol. 18* (The Standard Edition of the Complete Psychological Works of Sigmund Freud; London: Hogarth Press, 1953–1974), 1–64.

———, 'New Introductory Lectures on Psychoanalysis' [1933a] in James Strachey (ed.), *SE vol. 22* (The Standard Edition of the Complete Psychological Works of Sigmund Freud; London: Hogarth Press, 1953–1974), 1–182.

———, 'Some Psychical Consequences of the Anatomical Distinction between the Sexes' [1925j], trans. James Strachey, in James Strachey (ed.), *SE vol. 19* (The Standard Edition of the Complete Psychological Works of Sigmund Freud; London: Hogarth Press, 1953–1974), 241–258.

————, 'Three Essays on the Theory of Sexuality' [1905d], trans. James Strachey, in James Strachey (ed.), *SE vol. 7* (The Standard Edition of the Complete Psychological Works of Sigmund Freud; London: Hogarth Press, 1953–1974), 123–246.

FRIEDMAN, MICHAEL, AND TOMŠIČ, SAMO (eds.), *Psychoanalysis: Topological Perspectives* (Bielefeld: transcript Verlag, 2016).

GAULT, JEAN-LOUIS, 'Two Statuses of the Symptom: Let Us Turn to Finn Again' in Véronique Voruz and Bogdan Wolf (eds.), *The Later Lacan: An Introduction* (Albany: State University of New York Press, 2007), 73–82.

HEIDEGGER, MARTIN, *The Fundamental Concepts of Metaphysics: World, Finitude, Solitude* [1929–30], trans. William McNeill and Nicholas Walker (Bloomington: Indiana University Press, 1995).

————, 'Letter on Humanism' [1947], trans. Frank A. Capuzzi, in William McNeill (ed.), *Pathmarks* (Cambridge: Cambridge University Press, 1978), 239–276.

HINTIKKA, JAAKKO, *The Principles of Mathematics Revisited* (Cambridge: Cambridge University Press, 1996).

JOHNSTON, ADRIAN, 'This Philosophy Which Is Not One: Jean-Claude Milner, Alain Badiou, and Lacanian Antiphilosophy' *Journal of the Jan van Eyck Circle for Lacanian Ideology Critique*, 3 (2010), 137–158.

————, *Time Driven: Metapsychology and the Splitting of the Drive* (Evanston, IL: Northwestern University Press, 2005).

LACAN, JACQUES, 'At the *Institut Français* in London (3 Feburary 1975)' [1975], trans. Dany Nobus, *Journal for Lacanian Studies*, 3/2 (2005), 295–303.

————, 'Conférence à Genève sur le Symptôme' [1975], *Le Bloc-notes de la psychanalyse*, 5 (1985), 5–23.

————, 'Du Discours Psychanalytique' [1972] in G. B. Contri (ed.), *Lacan In Italia - 1953–1978 - En Italie Lacan* (Milan: Salamandra, 1978), 32–55.

————, 'The Function and Field of Speech and Language in Psychoanalysis' [1953], trans. Bruce Fink, Héloïse Fink, and Russell Grigg, in *Écrits* (New York: W. W. Norton & Company, 2006), 197–268.

————, 'In Memory of Ernest Jones: On His Theory of Symbolism' [1959], trans. Bruce Fink, Héloïse Fink, and Russell Grigg, in *Écrits* (New York: W. W. Norton & Company, 2006), 585–601.

————, 'The Instance of the Letter in the Unconscious' [1957], trans. Bruce Fink, Héloïse Fink, and Russell Grigg, in *Écrits* (New York: W. W. Norton & Company, 2006), 412–441.

———, 'Kant with Sade' [1963], trans. Bruce Fink, Héloïse Fink, and Russell Grigg, in *Écrits* (New York: W. W. Norton & Company, 2006), 645–668.

———, 'Logical Time and the Assertion of Anticipated Certainty' [1945], trans. Bruce Fink, Héloïse Fink, and Russell Grigg, in *Écrits* (New York: W. W. Norton & Company, 2006), 161–175.

———, 'Of Structure as an Inmixing of an Otherness Prerequisite to Any Subject Whatever' [1970] in Richard Macksey and Eugenio Donato (eds.), *The Structuralist Controversy: The Languages of Criticism and the Sciences of Man* (Baltimore: The Johns Hopkins University Press, 2007), 186–200.

———, 'Overture to the 1st International Encounter of the Freudian Field: Caracas, 12 July 1980', trans. Adrian Price, *Hurly-Burly*, 6 (September 2011), 17–20.

———, 'Peut-être à Vincennes…' [1975] in J.-A. Miller (ed.), *Autres Écrits* (Paris: Éditions du Seuil, 2001), 313–315.

———, 'The Place, Origin and End of My Teaching' [1967], trans. David Macey, in Jacques-Alain Miller (ed.), *My Teaching* (London: Verso, 2008), 3–55.

———, 'Position of the Unconscious' [1960], trans. Bruce Fink, Héloïse Fink, and Russell Grigg, in *Écrits* (New York: W. W. Norton & Company, 2006), 703–721.

———, 'Preface', trans. David Macey, in Anika Lemaire, *Jacques Lacan* (London: Routledge & Kegan Paul, 1977), viii–xv.

———, 'Préface à l'Édition des Écrits en Livre de Poche' [1970] in J.-A. Miller (ed.), *Autres Écrits* (Paris: Éditions du Seuil, 2001), 387–391.

———, 'Science and Truth' [1966], trans. Bruce Fink, Héloïse Fink, and Russell Grigg, in *Écrits* (New York: W. W. Norton & Company, 2006), 726–745.

———, *The Seminar of Jacques Lacan, Book I: Freud's Papers on Technique* [1953–54], ed. Jacques-Allain Miller, trans. John Forrester (New York: W. W. Norton & Company, 1988).

———, *The Seminar of Jacques Lacan, Book III: The Psychoses* [1955–56], ed. Jacques-Allain Miller, trans. Russel Grigg (New York: W. W. Norton & Company, 1993).

———, *The Seminar of Jacques Lacan, Book VI: Desire and Its Interpretation* [1958–59], trans. Cormac Gallagher (Unauthorised translation from unpublished manuscript: www.lacaninireland.com).

———, *The Seminar of Jacques Lacan, Book IX: Identification* [1961–62], trans. Cormac Gallagher (Unauthorised translation from unpublished manuscript: www.lacaninireland.com).

————, *The Seminar of Jacques Lacan, Book XI: The Four Fundamental Concepts of Psychoanalysis* [1964–65], ed. Jacques-Allain Miller, trans. Alan Sheridan (New York: W. W. Norton & Company, 1998).

————, *The Seminar of Jacques Lacan, Book XVII: The Other Side of Psychoanalysis* [1969–70], ed. Jacques-Alain Miller, trans. Russell Grigg (New York: W. W. Norton & Company, 2007).

————, *The Seminar of Jacques Lacan, Book XX: Encore, On Feminine Sexuality, the Limits of Love and Knowledge* [1972–73], ed. Jacques-Allain Miller, trans. Bruce Fink (New York: W. W. Norton & Company, 1998).

————, *The Seminar of Jacques Lacan, Book XXII: RSI* [1974–75], trans. Cormac Gallagher (Unauthorised translation from unpublished manuscript: www.lacaninireland.com).

————, *The Seminar of Jacques Lacan, Book XXIII: The Sinthome* [1975–76], ed. Jacques-Allain Miller, trans. A. R. Price (Cambridge: Polity Press, 2016).

————, *The Seminar of Jacques Lacan, Book XXV: The Moment to Conclude* [1977–78], trans. Cormac Gallagher (Unauthorised translation from unpublished manuscript: www.lacaninireland.com).

————, 'The Signification of the Phallus' [1958], trans. Bruce Fink, Héloïse Fink, and Russell Grigg, in *Écrits* (New York: W. W. Norton & Company, 2006), 575–584.

————, 'Some Reflections on the Ego' *International Journal of Psychoanalysis*, 34 (1953), 11–17.

————, 'The Subversion of the Subject and the Dialectic of Desire in the Freudian Unconscious' [1960], trans. Bruce Fink, Héloïse Fink, and Russell Grigg, in *Écrits* (New York: W. W. Norton & Company, 2006), 671–702.

————, 'Television' [1970], trans. Denis Hollier, Rosalind Krauss, and Annette Michelson, in Joan Copjec (ed.), *Television* (New York: W. W. Norton & Company, 1990), 1–46.

LEADER, DARIAN, *What Is Madness?* (London: Hamish Hamilton, 2011).

MARINI, MARCELLE, *Jacques Lacan: The French Context*, trans. Anne Tomiche (New Brunswick, NJ: Rudgers University Press, 1992).

MATURANA, HUMBERTO R., 'The Biological Foundations of Self Consciousness and the Physical Domain of Existence' in *Beobachter: Konvergenz der Erkenntisttheorien?* (München: Wilhelm Fink Verlag, 1992), 47–117.

MILLER, JACQUES-ALLAIN, 'Les six Paradigmes de la Jouissance' *La Cause Freudienne*, 43 (1999), 7–29. http://www.causefreudienne.net/wp-content/uploads/2015/04/JAM-Six-paradigmes-jouissance.pdf.

————, 'Mathemes: Topology in the Teaching of Lacan', trans. Mahlon Stoutz, in Ellie Ragland and Dragan Milovanovic (eds.), *Lacan: Topologically Speaking* (New York: Other Press, 2004), 28–48.

Nobus, Dany, 'Lacan's Science of the Subject: Between Linguistics and Topology' in Jean-Michel Rabaté (ed.), *The Cambridge Companion to Lacan* (Cambridge: Cambridge University Press, 2003), 50–68.

————, *The Law of Desire: On Lacan's 'Kant with Sade'* (Cham, Switzerland: Palgrave Macmillan, 2017).

Nöth, Winfried, *Handbook of Semiotics* (Bloomington and Indianapolis: Indiana University Press, 1995).

Rorty, Richard, 'Philosophy as Science, Metaphor, Politics' [1986] in *Essays on Heidegger and Others: Philosophical Papers, Volume 2* (Cambridge: Cambridge University Press, 1991), 9–26.

Roudinesco, Elisabeth, *Jacques Lacan*, trans. Barbara Bray (New York: Columbia University Press, 1997).

Roustang, François, *The Lacanian Delusion*, trans. Greg Sims (New York: Oxford University Press, 1990).

Soler, Colette, 'The Body in the Teaching of Jacques Lacan' *Journal of the Centre for Freudian Analysis and Research*, 6 (1995), 6–38.

Tarski, Alfred, 'The Semantic Conception of Truth' [1944] in Maria Baghramian (ed.), *Modern Philosophy of Language* (Washington, DC: Counterpoint, 1999), 44–63.

Tombras, Christos, 'Kicking Down the Ladder: Language, Time, History' *Journal of the Centre for Freudian Analysis and Research*, 19 (2009), 119–137.

Verhaeghe, Paul, *Does the Woman Exist? From Freud's Hysteric to Lacan's Feminine*, trans. Marc du Ry (New York: Other Press, 1999).

————, *On Being Normal and Other Disorders: A Manual for Clinical Psychodiagnostics*, trans. Sigi Jottkandt (New York: Other Press, 2004).

————, 'Subject and Body: Lacan's Struggle with the Real' in Paul Verhaeghe, *Beyond Gender: From Subject to Drive* (New York: Other Press, 2001), 65–97.

# 6

# An Ontology from Discourse

With *Being and Time* Heidegger set out to raise again the question of being and construct a new, non-Cartesian fundamental ontology. This would serve as the foundation of all other *regional* ontologies— for example, those studied by traditional metaphysics or those of the sciences. This project was abandoned. He ceased conceiving of the question of being as a question of an ahistorical fundamental ontology and began approaching it as a question regarding the historicity of being. Even though the principal themes of his research programme remained unaltered, Heidegger became more and more disillusioned with regard to the possibility of providing comprehensive answers. He stopped using the term "ontology" altogether because he felt it was inadequate and misleading, deciding instead to focus on what he considered to be a major failure of modernity and an imminent danger to Dasein. In his critical discussion of science, psychology in general, and Freudian psychoanalysis, in particular, Heidegger argued against what he saw as their limitations and naivety: psychology, psychiatry and psychoanalysis fail to think critically about their conceptual premises, and therefore, unwittingly obscure and distort the phenomena they purport to study. For him, adopting the modern world view

© The Author(s) 2019
C. Tombras, *Discourse Ontology*, The Palgrave Lacan Series,
https://doi.org/10.1007/978-3-030-13662-8_6

entails disregarding fundamental aspects of Dasein's comportment towards being. Accordingly, he made it his task to bring this question back to the fore. This was the attempt of a moral, or better, of a *deontic* philosopher.

Lacan shared Heidegger's distrust of traditional metaphysics. In his "return to Freud" the Heideggerian perspective was rather evident, even though, unlike Heidegger, Lacan had no interest in constructing a non-Cartesian fundamental ontology as such. With Freud's discovery as his starting point, Lacan turned to language. His research programme was to reread Freud's discovery in such a way that one remains faithful to its novelty, and yet avoids its misconceptions and pitfalls. The human being is a subject of language, a divided subject under the sway of the symbolic order—i.e. the law of the signifier. Language is both that which brings the subject into the human world and that which makes the subject suffer. But first and foremost, language, or rather *speaking*, is a corporeal behaviour, a ritualistic imitation game, a *halter* for jouissance and the real. Language involves signifiers but the signified, or meaning, is always floating, unstable and attributed retroactively. In the beginning, Lacan studied the human being and its attainment of an imaginary identity and a "language" body after submitting to the Other of language and the symbolic. His attention became more and more distant from the study of language, and he turned to mathematics—topology and knot theory—in an attempt to formulate a non-regional post-Freudian metapsychology, which would not be limited by the impossibility of reaching a proper meta-level of description.

Heidegger would still argue that psychoanalysis, even in this "enhanced", Lacanian form, is a limited project. For Heidegger, mathematics in all its shapes and forms can only contribute to a impoverished understanding: if Lacan claims that mathematics stands *transcendentally* vis-à-vis the world, then his position would amount to little more than an uncritical conformity with the modern, Cartesian scientific world view. Lacan's mathematical formalisations should be either dismissed as derivative and ontic, or rejected altogether as fascinating but arbitrary by-products of an artificial neo-Kantian idealism, very possibly Platonic at its root, and very distanced from the phenomena at hand.

Still, as we saw, Lacan's approach was not neo-Kantian or Platonic at all. He did not think of mathematical structures as existing independently of the humans using them. Mathematics, knot theory, and topology were for him systems of symbols, but they were not thought as comprising the deeper structure of the world or of the human psyche. On his part, Lacan would most probably be critical about Heidegger's research for the same reasons that impelled him to criticise the whole of philosophy. Building on Freud's discovery, and in contrast to Heidegger, Lacan focused on the origins of signifierness, i.e. on the fact that there are signifiers, and on the fact that these signifiers are interconnected in a network. Indeed, one can read Lacan's whole theoretical work as an attempt to reach beyond meaning, beyond language, even beyond speaking and speech, and explain the emergence of signifierness. In a sense, he was trying to run *counter* to meaning—and he said as much.[1] In Lacan's view, philosophers and metaphysicians are confusing themselves when discussing the question of being because they fail to see it as a corollary of signifierness. One could imagine then that, even if he did not say it explicitly, Lacan saw Heidegger as just another confused philosopher and thought of his fundamental ontology as trapped on the imaginary axis and therefore narrow.

Moreover, Heidegger's deontic worries and focus were far removed from Lacan's concerns. Heidegger bemoaned the prevalence of the modern, scientific world view. Lacan, in contrast, could not but welcome its emergence since it was the advent of the Cartesian subject—the subject of science—that made psychoanalysis possible. Crucially, Lacan was not a moralist; he was not interested in discussing human experience in a deontic framework and was rather sceptical about attempts to rebel against the "regime", seeing it as an attempt to exchange a master with another master (within the same master's discourse).[2] In many respects, Lacan was a pessimist with diminishing interest in politics or current

---

[1] See Jacques Lacan, *The Seminar of Jacques Lacan, Book XX: Encore, On Feminine Sexuality, the Limits of Love and Knowledge* [1972–73], ed. Jacques-Allain Miller (New York: W. W. Norton & Company, 1998), p. 93.

[2] See, for example, 'Impromptu at Vincennes' [1969], in Joan Copjec (ed.), *Television* (New York: W. W. Norton & Company, 1990), 117–128.

affairs. He was only interested in showing in his mathemes the phenomena in the very way in which the phenomena show themselves from themselves.[3] His teaching was a work in progress—a work that was destined to remain largely unfinished, as he himself was acutely aware.

## From Heidegger Through Lacan

It is not easy to read Heidegger together with Lacan, not only because of the enormous differences in their respective terminologies and lines of work, but also because of the apparent disinclination of either of the two to lay the foundations for—or, conform to the requirements of—such a task. Notwithstanding this, a first obviously connecting element is the importance they accord to language. They both talk about the constitution of a world through language—and have the same starting point, that of the individual human being who is *thrown* into the world and *encounters* language. They also coincide in their abandonment of the tools of tradition—that is, in their belief in the sheer inadequacy of traditional ontology and metaphysics. They differ radically, however, in how they see language. For Heidegger, language is a special kind of equipment, both ontic and ontological, which discloses the world to Dasein. This world is a meaningful world, in which Dasein dwells in its concernful comportment towards the beings it encounters. The source of its intelligibility, i.e. being, and the historicity of being is what interests Heidegger most. For Lacan, language qua symbolic order is that what provides a scaffolding for the subject who is represented in the chain formed by signifiers. This divided subject is tortured by language, endlessly tormented in the course of its striving to assume the alienating identity forged for it by the Other.

However, we might be faced with a difficulty here. Lacan's concepts appear to lack a proper foundation and it is necessary to clarify whether or not this is in fact the case. Lacan's insistence on the primacy of

---

[3]By writing that in this way, I am of course alluding to Heidegger's understanding of phenomenology. See above, p. 24.

signifier, his insight regarding signifierness, and, accordingly, his unconcern for the signified are but conclusions, theoretical results and corollaries. They are related to the phenomenon under study, but they are *not* it, that is, they are *not* primary data. The same can be said about metaphor and metonymy, the three registers, the theory of discourse or the Borromean clinic: all these hypotheses and theoretical models do not form part of, nor are they identical with, the phenomena as such. William Richardson has argued that Lacan's interpretation of the Freudian discovery "desperately needs a philosophical base that mathematical formalism and all the topology in the world cannot give him".[4] In Richardson's view, without a solid philosophical grounding Lacan's theoretical constructions are magnificent but arbitrary structures simply hanging in the air, just like some of the great philosophical systems of the past. Lacanian theory runs the risk of being eventually left behind as nothing more than a failed or incomplete metaphysics.

Lacan's thinking is not axiomatic. He did not start by postulating general statements and did not deduce the rest of his theory by logical reasoning. For all its abstraction and complexity, the Lacanian project is a project of experimental research, with all the delays and false starts that a research project entails.[5] Considered thus, then, Richardson's requirement for a solid philosophical base appears unnecessarily restrictive and somewhat problematic—as problematic as it would be to interrupt Heidegger's project because of an alleged failure to recognise the essential circularity of Dasein's comportment towards being. Lacan's project also involves an essential circularity. Unavoidably so.

Still, Lacan's justification for using mathematics and topology would perhaps need to be rethought vis-à-vis a Heideggerian conceptual framework. Heidegger's philosophy represents a cut with the world of

---

[4]William J. Richardson, 'The Word of Silence', in Sonu Shamdasani and Michael Münchow (eds.), *Speculations After Freud: Psychoanalysis, Philosophy and Culture* (London: Routledge, 1994), 167–184, p. 182.

[5]Cf. at this point Lacan's frustration at the slow progress of his work, and his complaint as late as during his *Seminar XXIII*, that he seems to have started going around in circles and that it is tougher for him to clear his path. See Jacques Lacan, *The Seminar of Jacques Lacan, Book XXIII: The Sinthome* [1975–76], ed. Jacques-Allain Miller (Cambridge: Polity Press, 2016), p. 74.

modernity and paves the way for the emergence of the post-Cartesian subject. Lacanian metapsychology would not be possible were it not for the preparatory work that Heidegger has done with his questioning regarding the meaning of being. Heidegger's discussion of time and temporality cannot but be at the foundations of such a task. Being requires time, and without a primordial event of appropriation (or affirmation, as Freud had it), there can be neither presence nor absence, and, in the same vein, neither lack nor desire. Without time, there would be no signifiers, no signifying chain, no law of the signifier. The "time" that we are talking about here lies at a more basic level than Lacan's logical time, which remains at the level of the symbolic. Is Lacan's description of language as a corporeal game of imitations, and his conceptualisation of a discourse enough to sidestep this limitation?

What all this brings us to is this: if this discussion is to be taken as something broader than a derivative regional ontology, it does indeed need to be secured on a robust base. One would first need to establish how a world is opened to the human being through language and what the source of world's meaningful presence is; it is only then that it can become possible to see that the speaking being is in fact a decentred subject, a semblance, a product of recursive and retroactive overlapping identifications, a made-up being. The first part of this task is accomplished by Heidegger. But Heidegger doesn't go as far as to provide a full account of the relation of language to the body. For this, we will need to turn to Lacan. To use Wittgenstein's analogy, Heidegger provides a "ladder" that allows Lacan to climb up and see that the history of ideas has been a history of idiocy.

I am envisaging here a conceptual bridging between Heidegger and Lacan, whereby some aspects of Heidegger's *analytic* can be used to inform and support Lacan's post-Freudian metapsychology. It would represent much more than the sum of its parts and, strictly speaking, would be neither Heideggerian nor Lacanian. On the basis of what has been discussed so far, I would see it as informed by the terminology, insights, concepts, hypotheses and conclusions of both Heidegger and Lacan, and involving a discussion about the human being as a being which is being *there* in language; about the world into which the human being finds itself thrown and about the ways of its comportment towards this world; about the attainment of an identity as a sexed being, and the suffering that this alienation entails; and about the structure of the subject's engagement with the Other. In short, it would be an attempt to outline an ontology that emerges from discourse.

This is what I suggest it be called: *discourse ontology*.

# The Case for an Ontology

Retaining the term ontology, with all its long and convoluted history, is perhaps unexpected in the context of our discussions so far. What is the justification of using it if Heidegger had dropped the term altogether and if Lacan would count it among, the fruits of collective idiocy in the history of ideas?

As a term, "ontology" comprises two other terms that have been of major importance in our discussions, the term "on" (gen: onto-), in the sense of *being, entity, thing*; and "logos", in the sense that Heidegger emphasises, of *collection* or *gathering* (of beings). When we speak of an ontology, then, we refer to beings in their being, i.e. in the open space, or clearing, where a world presents itself intelligibly to the human being as logos. The source of this intelligibility is signifierness, i.e. the fact that entities can stand as signifiers for other entities. Signifiers form a signifying chain. As we saw above, however, the signifying chain is but an automaton, a lifeless network of signifierised jouissance—unless we also consider the subject and its engagement as a desiring being. The speaking being can only bring up a world in his or her engagement with the network of signifiers. But then, of course, we are referring to a discourse. In short, ontology is impossible unless there is a discourse.

The term discourse here includes Lacan's notion but only as a special case, so to speak. As I employ it, a discourse can basically be just a chit-chat. Discourse (as chit-chat) brings up time (as that what is revealed in the very act of chit-chat). By designating a field of study as a discourse ontology, I indicate that I refer to being-and-time, seen as a composite concept, and in reference to the speaking being. In this way, I emphasise and acknowledge the circularity involved: there is no way one can formulate an ontology that can ex-sist alongside the phenomena, as if at a "meta" level, unless one sees it as a product of a discursive activity. To paraphrase Lacan, just as there is no metalanguage, there can be no ontology either if not as "a fact of what is said".[6] To broach discourse ontology, therefore, represents but an attempt to outline the basic structure that makes the human world—as a domain of recursive consensual coordinations of actions, distinctions and references—possible.

This discussion unavoidably involves (and perhaps calls for) some repetition and overlapping. I do not intend to provide the full layout of a completed system. I think that we need to be able to see the pathways opened to us before we decide to explore them systematically and in detail. In other words, we need to see what follows as the first iteration of a circle of understanding.

First, let us try to clarify a number of key concepts, such as *signifier*, *beings* and *being*, *time* and *unconscious*. A presentation of what I consider to be the central five themes of a discourse ontology will follow.

# Preliminary Considerations

## What Is a Signifier?

Signifiers are misleadingly straightforward entities. By definition, "signifier" is an entity—*any* entity: a thing, a sound, a gesture, a figure etc.—that bears a signification, that signifies. Signifiers are founded upon a conception of identity: in order for something to be a signifier, it has to have specific features that remain stable for as long as it is needed for it to participate in a signifying process. The fundamental characteristic of a signifier is its distinguishability. You need to be able to identify a signifier; you need to be able to differentiate it from other entities in its neighbourhood. Depending on the domain of reference, the exact requirements of identity and stability can vary. When considering linguistic signifiers in particular, the identity is decided on the level of the word. When considering the signifiers comprising a signifying chain, then, the identity becomes much more difficult to define

---

[6] *Seminar XX*, p. 118.

or establish. What we can easily see, then, is that the signifying elements we are talking about cannot be rigorously defined. A signifier is a signifier only by virtue of its potentiality to serve as a signifier. Moreover, talking about potentiality involves a decision. Whether something will be a signifier or not is a question of a decision.

This conceptualisation of the signifier seems to be at odds with what we described earlier as a recursive process of increasing complexity, whereby signifiers are recreated, transformed, retroactively assigned etc. If we consider the set of signifiers from a set-theoretical point of view, as Lacan's models necessitate, we only have a virtual or potential set, because the members of this set are also virtual or potential. Signifiers belong to the symbolic, which by definition is discontinuous. But such conceptualisation of the symbolic seems to run counter to the premise regarding the continuity of the matter out of which the symbolic is formed (i.e. jouissance and the real). How does this happen? How do we pass from something that is continuous to something that is discontinuous? How do we understand the discontinuity of the symbolic when we consider it in terms of the continuous Borromean triad?[7] The real question here is whether set theory is appropriately equipped to deal with such virtual members. The answer is far from straightforward. Any virtual signifier is itself a set of other virtual signifiers. The details of this double nature of the signifier need to be worked out. The issue I am identifying here is that there seems to be no clear set-theoretical way to discuss signifiers. Even if we decide to restrict our discussion to elements that *are* linguistic—that is, comprising phonemes that can be pronounced by humans—it's never clear what the cardinality (i.e. the number of elements) of a set of signifiers is.[8] It might be the case that

---

[7]In the words of psychoanalyst D. Lécuru and mathematician D. Barataud, "it is in the very *nature* of the sign to exist only through discontinuity, that is, through *distinctive opposition*: you do not go from one symbol to the other by means of an infinitesimal transition". (Quoted in François Roustang, *The Lacanian Delusion* (New York: Oxford University Press, 1990), p. 99.) Lécuru and Barataud consider this difficulty to be a major problem of Lacan's Borromean clinic. See also above, pp. 166–167.

[8]Let us look again at Freud's Signorelli incident and take once more the example of the name "Botticelli". On its own, "Botticelli" is a signifier, the name of a painter of Early Renaissance. The first syllable of this name, "Bo" is also a signifier, a connecting pathway between Botticelli and

the concept of a "signifier" is not well defined at all—at least not in a way that a mathematician would want in order to justify discussing it with mathematical tools.[9]

This indefinability of signifiers—as I call it now—is connected to a further question regarding the nature of a thing. This too is a far from trivial question. The conception of a "thing" rests upon two assumptions: identity and constancy. Any discussion of a thing involves a definition and a criterion of demarcation. When we consider a thing, we usually need to know what we are talking about and have a means to distinguish it from other things. Most of the time, however, our definition is approximate: an object is an object only in reference to a framework of human understanding. As a concept, "thing" is parallel to "signifier", since both thing and signifier depend on the possibility of a distinction. Strictly speaking, the world does not comprise things. The world is a manifold of overlapping *continua* that may be distinguished as identities with no restriction pertaining to the properties of these continua. The "mechanics" of a distinction is not what is important here. A distinction might be possible in terms of some feature such as temporal patterning; shape; colour; size; predominant material; and so on. There is nothing that will indicate beforehand what the chosen distinctive feature would be.[10] However, as soon as a distinctive feature is available and a distinction possible, a thing becomes possible too.

---

Boltraffio, and also between Botticelli and Bosnia. The ending, "-elli" is also a signifier, a third one, connecting Botticelli with Signorelli. So, the signifying set "Botticelli" comprises at least 3 signifiers. Does it end here? In Freud's case, it apparently does—or at least that much is what he chooses to share with us. But there is no reason to assume that it would necessarily stop there. It could comprise four or five or more signifiers. There is no way this can be known beforehand, and there is no reason to assume that it would remain constant.

[9]It's interesting to compare, in this connection, B. Fink's discussion of the set of all signifiers which can "never" be complete as per Russell's paradox. (See Bruce Fink, *The Lacanian Subject: Between Language and Jouissance* (Princeton, NJ: Princeton University Press, 1997), pp. 29–30). The difference here is that Fink is pointing out the paradoxical features of sets of signifiers, while what I am claiming is that signifiers appear to be not well defined, *as such*.

[10]As an example, one can take music. While music can be seen as a semantic system comprising signifiers of a specific type (musical signifiers), it is difficult—if not impossible—to define beforehand what the distinctive features of such signifiers are. Moreover, any attribution to "meaning" to a piece of music depends on a recursively retroactive process of deciding what music element of feature will be taken as a signifier and what not. In contrast to language, however, the

The thing is a product but also a prerequisite of the signifier. This process seems to be re-iterative and involves "choosing" some out of a manifold of continua, in a way that looks like putting them in pigeon-boxes and is reminiscent of what Husserl described as "eidetic intuition". It's only then that a thing can be recognised as a thing. In other words, a thing becomes a thing only within a discursive domain. It is within such a domain that a world is opened up as a possibility—or a choice.[11]

## Beings, Being, and History

According to Heidegger, reflecting on Dasein's concernful comportment towards the entities it encounters is tantamount to acknowledging the question of being and reflecting on its meaning. It is a question that refers to the foundations of the (human) world: being cannot be thematised except through language. "Language is the house of being". But the thematisation of being, and language itself, are both historical; likewise, the question regarding the meaning of being is also historical. Heidegger wants to bring up the historicity of the ways in which Dasein comports towards being. This installs immediately a hierarchy of sorts, a moral hierarchy even, according to which certain manners of comportment towards beings are more complete, more rich, or just plain better than others. It is on this basis that Heidegger considers the adoption of the modern scientific world view as an impoverishment. He argues that it comes with a number of unexamined presuppositions which narrows the ways Dasein is opened to being and encounters other beings in the world.

---

attribution of meaning to music is not consensual in any straightforward way. For a discussion see Spyros Tombras, *Μουσική και Σημειολογία: Μια Μέθοδος Ερμηνευτικής Προσπέλασης του Μουσικού Έργου* [*Music and Semiology: A Method of Interpretative Access to Musical Work*] (Athens: Gkovostis Ekdotiki, 1998), pp. 218–222.

[11]It might be the case that Badiou is on to something when he argues about the monumental importance of Paul Cohen's "axiom of choice". The whole question seems to be connected to what Badiou attempts to address with his definition of a number as "the conjoint givenness of an ordinal and a part of that ordinal". (Alain Badiou, *Number and Numbers* [1990] (Cambridge: Polity Press, 2008), p. 102).

Heidegger's criticism reflects, as we said above, the *deontic* aspect of his thinking.[12] This aspect is ontologically immaterial, especially when one considers these questions from a Lacanian point of view. For Lacan, the question is not whether one type of comportment is preferable to another. In fact, he claims that there is no question of being as such. For Lacan, being is nothing more than a designation for a discursive domain which is opened up just by the very fact of speaking; and so, he is much more agnostic with regard to the meaning accorded to being by any given epoch and not concerned about its particulars. Meaning is something circumstantial—a malleable, unstable, and always retroactively renegotiable layer made to conform to the network of signifiers of a given speaking being. To be a subject of language always involves a specific discourse in which the speaking being is engaged. Lacan's theory of the four discourses and his later theoretical constructions, such as topology or the theory of knots, are *non-factical* and ahistorical—i.e. ontological—attempts to view clearly the phenomena at hand. They are independent of specific discourse configurations and structures.

Still, at any given moment, every speaking being is engaged in a number of discourses. But one of these discourses predominates, providing a common backdrop, something like a zeitgeist, which can be called a *historical epoch*. The distinction between the ancient and the modern world view reflects an underlying periodisation of discourses. For example, the emergence of the modern world can be understood better if we think that there was a change in the way the predominant discourse thematises truth and knowledge. For Lacan, however, there is no temporal or other hierarchy between the discourses. Each discourse represents a formulation of what is at stake for the speaking being and the general outline of how this happens. Lacan refrains from any value judgement about our current, or any other, epoch. What is important

---

[12]It has been argued that Heidegger's deontic criticisms are unmistakable clues of his covert endorsement of Nazism—covert in so far as his major texts are concerned. See, for example, Peter Trawny, *Freedom to Fail: Heidegger's Anarchy* (Cambridge: Polity Press, 2015). This might well be the case; but as I have argued earlier (see above, p. 11), such ontic—and *deontic*, for that matter—aspects of Heidegger's thought are not affecting the core tenets of his philosophy, at least as far as the present research is concerned.

for him is the structure of a subject's engagement with networks of signifiers—which he considers to be homeomorphic with structures of topology or knot theory.

## Four Aspects of Time

Heidegger thinks of time as the horizon of being and explains that being and time determine each other reciprocally. They are revealed together as an *event of appropriation*. The ontic presence of beings before Dasein implies and *requires* temporality, i.e. that what can allow them to "step outside" themselves, to ex-sist. Dasein is fundamentally oriented in time as a *being-towards-death*. Death, as the absolute possibility of the impossibility of ex-sistence, provides Dasein with a trajectory and an end. Historicity is only possible because of the world and death. It is what allows Dasein's possibilities to be thematised. For every human being, history and trajectory are one's own. The present, however, is always shared.

Lacan sees objective time as a product of the function of the signifying chain. But time itself is also a prerequisite for the differentiation between presence and absence, which, in itself, is the necessary step required for the establishment of signifiers. So, time, in Lacan, is both a presupposition and a construct (qua temporality). In regard to its being a construct, Lacan stresses the discursive aspect of time seen in terms of a series of steps whose order is not arbitrary. It is this "logical" time that creates what humans perceive as the arrow of time, with the help of which they situate themselves and formulate their history.

We can distinguish, therefore, at least four aspects of time.

First is a *primordial* sense of time that is necessary as a backdrop, so to speak, on which all other kinds of time can be thematised. This is time as a horizon of being. Presence, absence and repetition cannot be thematised without it. All further discussion is impossible unless this aspect of time is seen.

Then comes time as *flow*. This is the minimum required to conceptualise living as such. All living happens in a configurational frame of relations which we can, perhaps usefully, call "now" or the "instant".

We need to remember however that what we designate as "now" or "instant" is ek-static, rather than (in)static—linked as it is to other adjacent configurational frames of relations. The concept of duration derives from the concept of flow.

Time as *temporality* follows. This is the aspect of time that allows the thematisation of present, past and future. Temporality might refer to minimal temporal differences such as the ones that we could describe, for example, with the words "now", "earlier" and "in a bit"; or to longer differences—for example, "these days", "when I was young" or "after the summer".

And finally, we come to time as *historicity*. This refers to the characteristically human quality of having an awareness of coming *from* somewhere (the past), and going *towards* somewhere (the future), with an end point that is unavoidable, but just not here yet, namely *death*.

These aspects of time are connected to each other—in the sense that each is founded on the previous. There is a progression, of sorts, but it is important to recognise that this progression is not necessary nor unavoidable. It only becomes possible because of signifierness.

## The Position of the Unconscious

Human beings qua subjects of language are under the sway of something that only makes itself seen through the disruptions it creates: the *unconscious*. Recognising that the human being is not the master in his or her own (psychic) house, Freud postulates the unconscious as an agency which can help establish a causal continuity, not constrained by the fragmented nature of the immediate data of consciousness; and Heidegger criticises Freud for being trapped in a naïve Cartesian subject–object framework.

Heidegger called for an entirely different understanding that would involve the recognition that the unconscious, and also consciousness, are problematic notions.

In a similar vein, for Lacan the reflective subjectivity of human being—the so-called ego—is an imaginary construction, a product of identification processes related to what he called the mirror stage.

The Lacanian subject—a subject of language—is not identical with the subject as conceived by Freud or by Descartes: it is not an observing consciousness vis-à-vis the world. Accordingly, designating something as "unconscious" is tantamount to assigning a name to an observed phenomenon: *Unconscious* is a description of a psychic function. Lacan considered conscious thinking as belonging in the realm of the law of signifier, of the Aristotelean *automaton*. In it, jouissance is deadened—in the sense that it has become fixed and presents no further surprises. The speaking being, qua divided subject, is only heard when there is a disruption of the chain of signifiers, where there is a gap. The gap reveals desire and can surprise the speaking being, makes it *stop and think*, as it were, or change attitude. The disruption is brought about by desire or lack—i.e. ultimately, by what is still beyond the immediate reach of the symbolic. This is where the unconscious is to be found. Its status is ethical: after Descartes, we cannot avoid referring to it as that which breaks down the law of the signifier; we cannot avoid being taken aback by desire.

Desire can never be fully articulated as such. It can only be seen as the drive behind the functions that govern the interconnections between signifiers, such as metaphor and metonymy. Freud's discovery allowed the psychic suffering of the human being to be properly thematised as a suffering dictated by language. Lacan's reading of Freud enabled him to see that there is no foundation of truth other than that of what he called the real and jouissance, and that the world is created and inhabited by beings "tortured by language". He acknowledges that the emergence of what he called the subject of science was made possible by the modern, Cartesian world view; it is because of this that psychoanalysis itself is made possible.

Nevertheless, there is no intrinsic reason for this state of affairs to persist. To speak of consciousness, or of an unconscious, only becomes possible within the frame of a specific discourse; it can only make sense to participants in a specific discourse, namely the discourse of the hysteric and the discourse of the analyst, respectively—the discourse of the hysteric being the discourse of the subject of science, and the discourse of the analyst being the one that allows the cause of desire to be thematised.[13] For as long as human beings are surprised by this fact, and feel the need to reflect on their surprise, articulating it as something that concerns them, psychoanalysis will continue to exist. In other words, the future of psychoanalysis is not guaranteed by some truth that was revealed and should now be remembered and protected; it is only dependent on those speaking beings who will desire to keep it going.

# Five Themes of a Discourse Ontology

As I envisage it, the major themes of *discourse ontology* are *speaking being*; *truth*; *time*; *body*; and *world*. Each is distinct, and yet all overlap with each other.

## Speaking Being and the Emergence of Signifierness

We begin with the *human being* in its being human. What Heidegger called *Dasein*—i.e. the human being considered ontically, in its factical existence, and ontologically in its concernful comportment towards being and the world being reveals—is very close to, but not identical to, Lacan's speaking being (*parlêtre*). By choosing to use the term "Dasein", Heidegger drew on a linguistic tradition that took the term as synonymous with "human being", drawing a measure of attention to the spatial aspect of being human. For Heidegger Dasein is (ontically) a localised being, a being that *is (t)here*: Da-sein. Lacan's term, *parlêtre*, draws attention to the fact that the human being is a being that speaks and has a world *inasmuch as* it speaks. For Lacan, speaking is corporeal, and characteristically, but not exclusively, human. Speaking is a specific type of intentional coordinated bodily activity, the "prototype" of which can be found in the intentional consensual interaction

---

[13]This would perhaps allow us to understand why there are cultures less favourably disposed towards psychoanalysis: they might be conforming to a different kind of predominant discourse. See also above, pp. 151–156.

between two or more speaking beings. This consensual interaction creates a discursive domain where further consensual interaction (speaking, talking, doing) is possible. Every speech act can be taken as such only within the domain in which it can be taken as such. This appears to be tautological, but the fact is that outside such a domain there is nothing to differentiate between, say, a word that was intentionally uttered and a random sequence of voiced phonemes. It is the domain that gives a *sense* to the speech—the term "sense" being understood here both as *meaning* and as *direction*—and provides the backdrop for the emergence of meaning. Contrary to what might seem to be the case, a discursive domain is not founded on meaning; in fact, meaning is irrelevant. "Meaning" is but the name we give to the consensual retroactive attribution of relations of inter-correspondence between chunks of speech qua lalangue: that way, any given chunk of spoken sounds may become a signifier, i.e. may become a word, or form a part of a word, etc. So, what is unique for the human being qua speaking being is that speaking involves a domain of recursive consensual coordination of distinctions, actions, or interactions with other human beings—i.e. a big Other or a discourse.

By stating that the attribution of meaning is recursively retroactive and consensual, I am simply stressing the fact that the meaning of an utterance is implicitly reaffirmed every time it brings about consistent—i.e. not random—results. A stream of spoken sounds (i.e. lalangue) is retroactively being cut into identifiable speech elements called words, which are thought as signifiers and are consensually made to correspond or refer to other identifiable speech elements as their "definitions", "descriptions", etc. Establishing a correspondence is equivalent to saying that a signifier obtains a referent and a domain where a meaning is possible; it is thus that a linguistic sign is created.

To generalise a bit, this is both how language seems to have been created and how it is acquired by the new-born human infant—namely by establishing inter-correspondences between chunks of spoken sounds, i.e. by rendering them into signifiers. And it is in this where Heideggerian being is to be found. Speaking qua coordinated interaction between human beings opens a space, or clearing, where the emergence of significations—i.e. meaning—or rather signifierness is possible. In other words, language—more precisely: speaking—brings up being by providing a (linguistic) domain where being can be presumed. If there were no speaking, there would be nothing to comport concernfully towards, i.e. there would be no being. This process is transparent and spontaneous, and readily recedes into the background. We, as participating human beings, lose sight of it. It is in this sense that Heidegger speaks of a "forgetfulness of being".

Signifierness involves desire, and desire is founded on lack. Signifiers are chunks of jouissance that stand as pointers to other signifiers, and eventually, to a lack. In the process of signifierisation, jouissance is taken out of circulation: it is crystallised and rendered lifeless in the form of a signifier. In their dealings with the world, human beings recursively create increasingly complex networks of interconnected signifierised jouissance, with multiple levels of overdetermination. These networks are unique to each human being in such a way that we can say that the individual speaking being is represented in the interconnections between signifiers. In short, the subject, as well as its world, is an effect of the signifierisation process.

Our starting point, then, is the being that speaks and ex-sists in a world constituted through its speaking. It is an alienated, divided being, constructed recursively around a lack it pretends, and desires, that it didn't exist.

## Truth as a Rule-Governed Activity

Truth can be understood in two related but fundamentally different ways. The first, truth as *a-letheia*, can be seen as that which is given or accepted as given. It is an ontological concept and should not be confused with *ontic* truth—for example, when we speak about the truth value, or veracity, of a statement. Ontological truth is correlative to signifierness; it always involves the field of discursive consensual interactions between speaking beings and always reflects the "sense" that something is "at stake"; it doesn't have much to do with the veracity of statements or veracity as such. It is not a question of a correspondence of a statement with a state of affairs.

For both Heidegger and Lacan, ontological truth is not seen as the product of a judgement but rather as an acceptance, which, for Heidegger, constitutes what he calls an event of appropriation, while, for Lacan, has the form of what Freud had in mind when he referred to a primordial affirmation. Their respective conceptualisations are not identical. The main difference seems to be related to the function giving rise to truth: for Heidegger, truth qua a-letheia is related to being and its opening up to Dasein. For Lacan, however, truth is related to speaking as such.

As soon as I speak, I speak the truth (or, perhaps, truth is spoken through me). Truth, then, means that I accept that I am the subject of language. Speaking represents an indirect affirmation that the speaking being is engaged in a discursive social bond. In order to see this process with more clarity, we can draw on the work of the Finnish logician Jaakko Hintikka. Hintikka wanted to free logic and mathematics from the severe limitations of Tarski's understanding of truth.[14] He developed a first-order logic in which truth is defined and expressed with no need to refer to a metalanguage. As he explains,

> to speak of truth is not to speak of any independently existing correspondence between language and the world. There are no such relations. Or, as Wittgenstein once put it, the correspondence between language and the world is established only by the use of our language. … Truth is literally constituted by certain human rule-governed activities.[15]

Hintikka manages this by help of what he calls semantic or language games (a reference to Wittgenstein's own language games). As he writes, "the idea of language games can be made a cornerstone of an extremely interesting logico-semantical theory. … The involvement of humanly playable language games does not make a concept of truth any less objective or realistic".[16] The challenge, then, is to establish an analogy

---

[14]See above, p. 145n31.
[15]Jaakko Hintikka, *The Principles of Mathematics Revisited* (Cambridge: Cambridge University Press, 1996), p. 44.
[16]*Principles*, p. 23.

between a winning strategy to this language game and the notion of truth. For Hintikka, "this kind of truth definition is not restricted to formal ... first-order languages but ... can also be extended to natural languages".[17]

As I see it, Hintikka's work bears important similarities with Lacan's. Both Lacan and Hintikka were faced with a metalanguage-related problem. Lacan understood that there is no metalanguage and needed a different way to secure the foundations of psychoanalysis. Both Lacan and Hintikka chose to see their respective problems in terms of a language, or a semantic game, or, more generally, in terms of a discourse. Ontological truth is constituted as a language game or, rather, as a rule-governed activity within a discursive domain constituted by speaking. In other words, truth is always involved in any structure of discursive relation and can be thought of as its backdrop (or point of reference). In their interactions, speaking beings always have recourse to this truth and refer to a lack in order to create a symbolic system that provides the framework for a social bond. *Ontic* truth becomes an issue when speaking beings are involved in the same "type" of discourse and have to agree, so to speak, to be bound by the terms or rules of a "game". A statement is validated or accepted as (ontically) true when a "round" of the game can be won. States of affairs are aspects of being and as such cannot be thematised unrelatedly to language. Both a statement and a state of affairs are on the same level. In other words, ontic truth, or veracity, is defined and established within the boundaries of a discursive domain, without any necessity to resort to a metalanguage.

From this simple conception of ontological truth as acceptance, and of ontic truth as the outcome ("win" or "lose") of a *game* within a given discourse, we can preliminarily describe knowledge as that set of ontic narratives that are, or can be, accepted, believed, confirmed or debated on a field of exchanges by speaking beings. Knowledge, in other words, can be thought as a set of articulated narratives that refer in various different ways (acceptance, belief, verification, etc.) to states of affairs.

---

[17] *Principles*, p. 28.

On the level of the individual speaking being, knowledge is a recursive construction—a kind of systematic and articulated lalangue, one might say—that involves a recursive self-referential network of signifiers and some of their interconnections.

## Discursive Constitution of Time

When human beings speak, they address someone or something directly or indirectly; they intend to convey something. Speaking is guaranteed, so to speak, by language as such: language is the consensual backdrop of the discursive domain shared by speaking beings. Use of language constitutes a domain into which all human beings are *thrown*. Language, itself, is a formal system of interconnected signs of a specific nature. In the case of natural, human language, the signs are *linguistic* and defined (by F. de Saussure) as comprising a signifier and a signified. The meaning of the signifier—i.e. its signified—is unstable, unclear, movable and flowing. A signifier can be seen as an ontic as well as an ontological concept. Ontologically, it brings up *signifierness*—i.e. the possibility of establishing consensual inter-correspondence s between words (as signifiers) and other words (as signifieds).

Speaking is corporeal. It involves jouissance. The emergence of signifierness imposes a structure on jouissance by establishing a distinction between signifierised and not-yet-signifierised jouissance. When we consider the emergence of signifierness, we need to remember that jouissance is in the domain of the real. Signifierness brings with it the imaginary and the symbolic register. The possibility of a signifier and the emergence of the imaginary and the symbolic are equiprimordial. It is not the case that the one brings the other. Also, speaking happens in time—the term used here in the most basic sense of time as a backdrop and flow. Speaking can be seen as having a beginning, a duration and an end. The emergence of signifierness makes this temporal aspect of speaking visible in that the speaking being needs to *wait* until the "end" of a clause of speech in order to get to what is intended by it, i.e. to its meaning.

Signifierness presupposes time and involves it ontically in the sense just mentioned—namely that of time as duration—as well as ontologically: signifierness allows the freeing from the *now*. Via signifierness the things and a world are brought into ex-sistence. Heidegger understood being as the opening, or clearing, where entities are meaningfully encountered; and time as *presence*. What Lacan brings to this is an understanding of how presence can be thematised vis-à-vis *absence*. In fact, to say that presence can be thematised is equivalent to saying that world ex-sists, or, by the same token, that signifierness is possible. If presence can be thematised, then time—as well as being—can also be thematised. Signifierness and retroaction give direction to time and allow the present, the past, and, by implication, the future to be thematised. To paraphrase Lacan, not only being, but time too, is "but a fact of what is said". The horizon of time *is* discourse.

## Body, Jouissance and Sexuation

For Lacan, the body is the locus where all happens. There is a specific aspect of Lacan's discussion of the body's engagement with the world that in Heidegger is not at all considered. It pertains to what Lacan presents under the rubric of jouissance. Jouissance is an effect, so to speak, of the body's structural coupling in the world. As a concept, jouissance is both ontic and ontological: it is ontic in the obvious sense of the circumstantial details of the specifics of this or that event of the body that gave rise to it, but also ontological in the sense that it gives rise to signifierness. Jouissance is a correlative to Dasein's being-in-the-world: the human being qua Dasein cannot but be-in-the-world. And *being-in-the-world* cannot but mean that *there is* jouissance. It is precisely *because* there is jouissance that the human being is opened up to signifierness. Signifierness is that which opens the clearing for a signifier to be installed, and a signifier is what allows jouissance to be thematised. It appears, then, that for Lacan, the conceptualisation of jouissance makes possible the discussion of the primordial revelation of being that Heidegger envisages, without recourse to a meaning that, for Heidegger, being entails.

The material body qua biological organism is not identical to the body as lived by the speaking being. Jouissance populates the register of the real. By submitting to language, the human being obtains an image of the body and a schema, or identity, with which the speaking being occupies the body or inhabits it. In the process, some of the body's jouissance crystallises, populating the imaginary and symbolic registers. It becomes signifierised. The remainder jouissance becomes a cause for the emergence of desire. In becoming a *subject* of language, the speaking being remains tormented by a tension between the body as an *ontic* entity (i.e. a thing) and the body as an imaginary entity that the speaking being inhabits.

This tension can also be understood in terms of Heidegger's insistence that the body is far away from Dasein *despite* appearing to be very near to it. For Heidegger, the question of the body is extremely important but latent. From his point of view, his ontological project would be incompatible with a discussion of the question of the body, and spatial bodiliness, as such, which verges on the ontic. Heidegger sees space as something that is disclosed to Dasein through its bodiliness and points out that even though the actual (ontic) body is a corporeal thing with specific dimensions, Dasein is not confined in it; rather, Dasein is beyond the limits of the corporeal thing. Heidegger says little about the ontic aspects of the body (especially sex), struggling, one could say, with how to approach it *without* falling in the trap of the Cartesian mind/ body distinction. He does not seem at all interested in the ontic role sex or gender plays in shaping Dasein's concernful comportment to the world. Dasein is conceived as ontologically neutral; its neutrality is, of course, broken as soon as we consider Dasein in its factical concretion, but ontologically Dasein is neither masculine nor feminine. This is Heidegger's premise, and his analysis proceeds from there.

This, clearly, is very different from Lacan's view. For Lacan, the question of sexuation is crucial *ontologically*. The two positions, feminine and masculine, are shown to be fundamentally different. Granted, jouissance is asexual, at least in the beginning, but as soon as some of it is signifierised, it becomes differentiated as *phallic* jouissance and *other* jouissance. The difference between the feminine and the masculine positions represents a difference in the manner of a subject's alienation in language, and its submission to the phallic function. It is *not* reflecting a biological reality.[18]

The human being obtains a language body through its introduction to language, and this language body is very distinct from the biological—in a way, it is the only body that ex-sists. The major challenge here is to build a model of human bodiliness which would take into account the fact that speaking beings are forced to occupy a body which they have obtained from language, and which does not correspond in any systematic way to their actual biological body. This is a paradoxical situation that again involves a circularity: you can only obtain language because you have a body, and this body is the locus of jouissance, but you can only obtain a language body when already in language. There is a tension between the language and the biological body that cannot be easily reconciled. The speaking being, then, is a sexed being that engages in a world constituted discursively around a lack which represents a challenge depended on the position occupied.

The human being qua divided subject becomes alienated from the biological body it occupies as evidenced by many clinical manifestations of issues related to body image, body dysmorphia, sexuality and gender dysphoria.

## Constructing and Sharing a World

The speaking being is concerned about being, in the sense that Heidegger gives to this term. Being can only be an issue when signifierness has emerged, a process that, for the speaking being, reveals *world*. World is revealed via the possibility of meaning and is not dependent on a specific meaning as such. Of course, these are phenomena that take place equiprimordially: the world emerges together with signifierness and is revealed together with being.

---

[18]The term "biological" needs to be read here in contradistinction to "language" and not as referring to biology as a scientific discipline.

The world is not an empty container that the speaking being occupies. The speaking being is fundamentally *in* the world, as denoted by the compound expression *being-in-the-world*, in the sense that there is no ontological (or ontic, for that matter) way to separate one from the other. In fact, the human being is essentially a world-forming being; objects, such as a stone or a chair, do not have a world (they are "worldless"); animals are "poor in world"; and human beings are "world-forming", and their world is a shared world.[19]

The world that the subjects of language share is a discursive domain revealed and guaranteed by the symbolic order and the signifier. The world is a discursive domain where signifierness is possible. Its emergence is an event that becomes invisible and forgotten. It is an ontic world of signifierised jouissance and has little to do with meaning: its meaning is established retroactively, in a sort of a secondary revision,[20] whereby the network of the signifiers is being interconnected with the network of signifieds via quilting points. The world is *shared*, in the sense that each and every one of us is subject to a symbolic order that was established beforehand, but also *private* in the sense that every subject has added his or her own signifiers and has created his or her own network of meanings (signifieds). This distinction between private and public has some limited usefulness when we consider the structure of our engagement with the world from some distance but becomes irrelevant when we look closer to the phenomena. Our own private world is never completely private and our own (or authentic as Heidegger would have it), but also never completely shared and public.

## Recasting the Mind/Body Split

Heidegger had employed the concepts Dasein and being-in-the-world in an attempt to eliminate the problematic object–subject distinction. Accepting this distinction would reflect the uncritical adoption of the

---

[19]See also above, pp. 30–33.
[20]See above, p. 95.

modern scientific, or Cartesian, world view, whereby the human being was seen as an objective observer in a world that can contain measurable entities. This was the world of material entities which were extended in space, or *res extensae*, and Descartes differentiated it from the world of non-material entities, or *res cogitantes*, in order to account for the "obvious" differences between the material and the spiritual world—especially in connection to the possibility of scientific knowledge and truth. From the differentiation between body, or soma, and mind, or psyche, it followed that spiritual entities cannot be scientifically studied (since they are not measurable). The repercussions in the conceptualisation of causality, especially in regard to the relation between causality and space, were enormous—one can still discern their echoes, for example, in Freud's attempts to reconcile the material spatiality of the human being—e.g. the dimensions of the brain—with the spatiality of the mental apparatus.[21]

For both Heidegger and Lacan, the relation of the human body to space is not a manifest one. For Heidegger, space is thematised by Dasein via the body. The body is in space in an ontological sense: space is opened, or disclosed, to Dasein through Dasein's bodiliness and not the other way around. This involves the human being in its localised sense (the "Da" or "here" of Dasein) as well as its reach beyond corporeal limits, via the gaze and also via sound. Heidegger criticises the impoverished conceptualisation of being-in-the-world in terms of a distinction between a bodily/psychic interior (i.e. subjectivity) and an exterior (i.e. objectivity), and stresses the "ek-static" aspect of bodiliness. And there he remains: he does not seem willing (or prepared) to look into this phenomenon more closely.

Similarly, Lacan too does not seem willing (or prepared) to recast his own research in terms of a systematic and comprehensive phenomenological exposition. For example, a proper post-Cartesian phenomenology of the speaking being's spatiality as a being-in-the-world, would need to focus on aspects of the speaking being qua body, such as the use of the bodily functions (eating, breathing, defecating, urinating),

---

[21]See also above, p. 91n9.

orifices (oral, anal, genital), or organs (eye, ear, nose, skin). Lacan did not proceed systematically along this path. He employs his mathematical objects and insights as partial suggestive illustrations, and, after the introduction of his Borromean models, his teaching becomes more and more abstract. The distinct feeling of a project left unfinished is unavoidable.

The question regarding spatiality and the human being remains crucial. Space can only be opened when objects become an issue, i.e. when signifierness is installed. An object can only be thematised in contrast to its absence. When an object is not there anymore, what is emptied is the place that the object had previously occupied. Indirectly, what becomes manifest is space itself.

Heidegger attempted to derive spatiality from temporality—temporality being the frame within which objects can be thematised. Later he admitted that this was untenable. He turned to dwelling and building. Dwelling and building involve claiming a space and delineating its boundaries, i.e. the limits of places where objects can be placed. In this way, building (a place) becomes connected with presence vs. absence, i.e. with temporality.

Lacan focused on the question of limits in connection to the human body. The rims around holes on the body's surface were thought as loci where jouissance "flows" faster, so to speak. To picture this, Lacan used a small parable in which he referred to the human being as a smooth-surfaced egg that breaks because of language, making a *hommelette* (or *manlet* in B. Fink's translation).[22] He described jouissance as enveloping the biological body like a lamella (i.e. a thin plate or layer), flowing incessantly and speeding around rims or holes.[23] This was a myth, of course, a metaphor employed by Lacan at that particular point in his teaching, in order to make more visible the distinction between the biological and language bodies, a distinction that he never stopped stressing.

---

[22]See Jacques Lacan, 'Position of the Unconscious' [1960], in *Écrits* (New York: W. W. Norton & Company, 2006), 703–721, p. 717.

[23]Lacan went so far as to comment that the flow of jouissance around the rims and holes of the body could be described by Stokes' theorem of fluid dynamics in lamellar vector fields. ('Position of the Unconscious', *Écrits*, p. 718).

Here, we have a paradox: the biological body is in space and is the locus of the speaking being qua parlêtre. This speaking being inhabits a language body. The two do not coincide; in fact, they constitute two entirely different domains. It looks as if Lacan's conceptualisation re-introduces the mind–body split—via the back door, as it were. Žižek reads this as evidence that Lacan moves away from Heidegger and makes a "totally unexpected move ... back to Descartes, to the Cartesian *cogito*. ... The *cogito is* the subject of the unconscious—the gap/cut in the order of being in which the real of *jouissance* breaks through".[24]

For Lacan this split is an imaginary rather than a proper split—a semblance of a split, so to speak, which is only reflecting the differentiation between bodily jouissance and the signifier. Lacan's move to Descartes is not a proper return. The "mind" present in this newly found mind-body split is not a self-contained, reflective *res cogitans*. It is not the case of a mind meeting body (as res extensa); it is, rather, a fleeting product of the body as a being-in-the-real, something like the famous incorporeal of the Stoics.[25] The most important, but indirect, result of Lacan's re-introducing—or rather, recasting—the mind–body split is that the human being is brought back into focus as an intentional agent. For Descartes, a devout Catholic, the question of human agency belonged to the realm of res cogitantes, and, as such, was beyond the reach of science. Predictably, when scientists attempted to speak scientifically about the human being, they thought that the best approach would be to remove agency from the picture as irrelevant: in the name of objectivity, concepts such as free will and intentional behaviour were discarded as illusions.[26] This hasn't changed. Time and again, it is being declared that science will "soon" be able to have a complete

---

[24]Slavoj Žižek, 'Why Lacan Is Not a Heideggerian', in *The Ticklish Subject: The Absent Centre of Political Ontology* (London: Verso, 2008), vii–xxi, p. xx.

[25]See above, p. 141.

[26]An example of this approach is the scientific determinism of P. S. Laplace, according to which we ought to consider "the present state of the universe as the effect of its previous state and as the cause of that which is to follow". (Pierre-Simon Laplace, *Philosophical Essay on Probabilities* [1825] (New York: Springer, 1994), p. 2). There is no space for human agency in this picture of the world.

understanding of human behaviour and the mechanisms involved in it. Human beings will "soon" be shown to be no more (and no less) than rational, information processing beings. In a similar vein, it is announced that our understanding of human societies will soon reach such a level of sophistication that their study would be qualitatively similar to the study of termite colonies, while computers or networks of computers will soon develop levels of (artificial) intelligence that will prevail over their human "prototypes" and render obsolete all discussions regarding free will, agency or authenticity.

Notwithstanding his sharing a similar scientific world view, Freud shattered this programme by showing that the human being is not the master in his or her own house. A fully rational understanding of our mental behaviour will not be possible unless we take into account factors such as the drives, the id, libido, or the unconscious. And while Heidegger would still argue that Freud dreamt of a total scientific understanding of the human being, an approach just as problematic as that of the nineteenth-century scientists, Lacan comes into demonstrate the actual import of Freud's discovery. There is indeed a place where the speaking being shows agency; it is there where the automaton of the signifying network breaks. But this agency is not of the same order as before. The speaking being is not the rational Cartesian being who stands objectively vis-à-vis the world and establishes certainty in the rational products of its observing intellect. It is a divided being, alienated by language, forced to inhabit a semblance of identity, and constructed recursively around a lack.

## The Position of Consciousness

Freud wanted to write about consciousness in the context of his metapsychology papers but something made him abandon the attempt and leave the project unfinished. Out of the 12 papers he had in mind to write only 5 were eventually published, while the drafts of the others were destroyed. It is something of a paradox to realise that Freud found writing about consciousness somehow more problematic than writing about the unconscious, and we might never know what were the unforeseen obstacles we presume he encountered.[27] It is tempting, however, to imagine that Freud was met with similar difficulties as the ones encountered by those trying to solve what has become known as the "hard problem of consciousness".

I am referring here to a term introduced by David Chalmers in the 1990s. As Chalmers explained,

> the really hard problem of consciousness is the problem of *experience*. When we think and perceive, there is a whir of information processing, but there is also a subjective aspect. ... It is widely agreed that experience arises from a physical basis, but we have no good explanation of why and how it arises. Why should psychical processing give rise to a rich inner life at all? It seems objectively unreasonable that is should, and yet it does. If any problem qualifies as *the* problem of consciousness, it is this one.[28]

The main difficulty in approaching what Chalmers calls a hard problem can be located in our failure to examine properly the terms we use and the questions we formulate using these terms. It is, in other words, a question of a problematic regional ontology, one that obscures the phenomena instead of illuminating them. To begin with, it is easy to see that Chalmers's overall conceptual framework is Cartesian. He presents his question in terms of a "subjective experience" in need of an "objective explanation"; he takes for granted, that is, a picture of the human being as an observing agent that collects and processes information from the world around. In this way, Chalmers fails to grasp the totality of being-in-the-world as a phenomenon, and unavoidably, distorts it. There is indeed a hard problem here, but it is not the problem of consciousness; rather, it is a problem of recognising the limits of one's conceptual tools.[29] We can only think consciously of conscious thinking

---

[27]See also above, p. 93n15.

[28]David J. Chalmers, *The Character of Consciousness* (Oxford: Oxford University Press, 2010), p. 4.

[29]It is interesting to note, in this connection, that the real nature of the problem escapes even from Chalmers's critics. Daniel Dennett, for example, finds enough to assert that "the tempting idea that there is a Hard Problem is simply a mistake", admitting, however, that he cannot prove this, because people who believe it will not be convinced. "So I won't make the tactical error of trying to dislodge with rational argument a conviction that is beyond reason. That would

because we already operate in language, i.e. in a field where consensual linguistic interaction is possible. Conscious thinking is *public* despite the fact that it takes place in private. It follows from this that attempts to study it in vitro, as it were, i.e. with no reference to the public field where it becomes possible, are unavoidably incomplete and destined to fail.

The first step around the problem here would to recognise that what we call "consciousness" or "experience" is not the primary phenomena. We can speak of consciousness only after we have spoken of a subject that is able to conceive their own "subjectivity" as an object. This tacitly implies that we have already adopted of a subject–object point of view, and that the subject of science has emerged; we are, in other words, in the modern, Cartesian era. To put it differently, "consciousness" is an entity that we are in a position to postulate only when we have already uncritically accepted an understanding of our concernful comportment towards being in terms of an observing intellect vis-à-vis a "world" out there. This picture, however, is already an interpretation and not the phenomenon itself.[30] Taking our lead from Heidegger we can assert here that it is misleading to describe human beings, qua Dasein, in terms of experiences that arise from information processing. Dasein is-in-the-world and cannot but be. What Chalmers describes as experience or a rich inner life are aspects of being-in-the-world. By attempting to present what this entails in terms of data processing, we demonstrate

---

be wasting everybody's time, apparently". (Daniel Dennett, *Sweet Dreams: Philosophical Obstacles to a Science of Consciousness* (Cambridge, MA: The MIT Press, 2005), p. 72). The weakness in Dennett's argument is not his unwillingness to waste time, but his failure to see that the terms used in approaching and discussing the problem are not well defined.

[30]A similar argument was put forward in the 70s by psychologist Julian Jaynes. As he wrote, "Consciousness is an operation rather than a thing, a repository, or a function. It operates by way of analogy, by way of constructing an analog space with an analog 'I' that can observe that space, and move metaphorically in it. It operates on any reactivity, excerpts relevant aspects, narratizes and conciliates them together in a metaphorical space where such meanings can be manipulated like things in space. Conscious mind is a spatial analog of the world and mental acts are analogs of bodily acts. Consciousness operates only on objectively observable things". (Julian Jaynes, *The Origin of Consciousness in the Breakdown of the Bicameral Mind* [1976] (Boston: Mariner Books, 2000), pp. 65–66). In Jaynes's view, it only became possible to conceive consciousness after the breakdown of the previous metaphor, which he described as the bicameral mind.

that we are trapped in a Cartesian framework of understanding that is uncritically accepted. It is an approach that is doomed to fail.[31]

Speaking more generally, phenomena such as consciousness, experience, intelligence, emotion, free will, rationality and the like, cannot be considered outside the framework established by the meaning that has been retroactively attributed to them: one could more accurately describe them as second-order phenomena, underlying which one or more other, first-order phenomena can be observed, postulated or hypothesised. What this means, in practical terms, is that a complex second-order phenomenon (such as speaking) cannot be adequately understood unless thought of in terms of a number of more elementary first-order phenomena (such as hearing, breathing, articulating), which are intertwined and interconnected. This, of course, is meant to be just an indication of the approach to be followed, and not a complete inventory of the steps involved, which would remain within the remit of an appropriate regional ontology. In any case, it is necessary to see that these phenomena and the underlying first-order phenomena stand in a type of relation similar to the one that linguists designate as *duality of patterning*.[32] It is only after establishing that second-order phenomena are exactly that—namely second-order and not first-order—that we can begin to account for the role played in them by retroaction and thus avoid conceptual pitfalls. This relation, or rather the distinction it implies, needs to be read in connection to Heidegger's ontological difference.

As an example, we could focus on our current difficulties in properly understanding the impact of gradual mental impairment or dementia

---

[31]For similar reasons we can see that concerns about the imminent development of sentient machines endowed with artificial intelligence that will use their information processing superiority to take over our world—in a sort of a "Matrix"-type nightmare (the reference here is to the 1999 science fiction film)—are wildly overstated, stemming as they are from an impoverished Cartesian understanding that sees the human being in terms of information processing. As we have discussed, however, the speaking being is not driven by information processing or intelligence, but rather by signifierness, i.e. by anxiety and desire. It is there where the source of their agency can be found. Artificial intelligence systems have no agency. They can be a threat to human beings only to the extent that they will be so used by other human beings—not on their own behalf (That's hardly reassuring, though).

[32]See above, p. 142n26.

on intelligence, personality, sense of identity and "character". Rather than regarding the variety of clinical manifestations of mental deficiency as the more or less direct behavioural result of pathological processes involving one, two or several hypothetical brain subsystems, one could see them as the result of the individual's attempt to retroactively undo the gaps that appear in their thinking because of their illness, in much the same way that people attempt to smooth out the gaps they observe when they reflect on one of their dreams (i.e. what Freud called secondary revision). It is conceivable that many phenomena of cognitive or affective decline—phenomena that are known to result from organic damage traceable to illnesses such as, say, vascular atrophy or Alzheimer's disease—could be better understood if studied in the same way as those psychopathological phenomena that Freud focused on: namely as increasingly failing attempts by the suffering speaking being to recursively establish a second-order discursive coherency in an ever more fragmented psychic space.

We are approaching the phenomena with the help of conceptual tools such as information, communication, perception, cognition, attention, learning, memory and intelligence. This conceptual arsenal has offered a good starting point to observe properly and study the phenomena, but it is now increasingly evident that it is restricted and misleading. We would need, now, a complete reconsideration of our understanding and terminology, i.e. a new regional ontology—or a paradigm shift—that would take into consideration the discursive constitution of truth and the malleability of meaning. We need to be able to formulate properly what we have in mind when we speak of truth and evidence.

## Truth in the Era of Alternative Facts

Let us return to the question of truth then. Having followed Lacan's argument so far, one might be tempted to think that the absence of metalanguage, i.e. the absence of a solid external foundation of truth, opens the door to relativism. However, this is not the case. Even if there is no Other of the Other, as Lacan claims, this doesn't mean that "everything goes". In this era of alternative facts and post-truth, such a position would be slippery, to say the least, if not outright danger-ous. However, conceptualising ontic truth or veracity in terms of a dis-cursive "game", we have a very solid foundation from which to prove things, albeit differently from before. A proof is a logical outcome of an interconnected series of statements. The only requirement is that the participants of the game have agreed on the rules that show how such statements are formed.

On the other hand, considering the issue more carefully, we can see that truth and knowledge have always been "vulnerable" concepts. Even when truth is thought in the most certain and solid terms, there is noth-ing as such that can force us to accept it.

There are two modes of exception to truth, a weak and a strong one. The weak refers to what in the recent years has been called post-truth. The term came to prominence in 2016, when the Oxford Dictionaries announced it as their "word of the year", but in reality, it is not really anything new. It regards the observation that one may fail (or even refuse) to be bound by the winning strategy for any reasons. This is an ontic weakness and is related to phenomena of irrational thinking, for example, when someone holds tight onto ideas that are manifestly wrong, unsubstantiated, or even contradictory. As Oxford Dictionary has it, in the era of post-truth, objective facts are less influential than appeals to emotion and personal beliefs. One could even say that the era of post-truth is a post-rational era—which I take to mean: an era immune to rational criticism and debate.[33] There is not much more one can do here. Lacan's theory of discourse might be helpful in giv-ing us some understanding of the structures the subject is engaged with, but that's about all one can do here. There is nothing binding in the conclusions.

---

[33]This is exactly the sense with which it was claimed that the White House calculations regard-ing the numbers of people attending the 2017 presidential inauguration ceremony were based on "alternative facts". This was a claim that would be impossible to debate, since the representative of the White House had made it clear that there was no common ground on which an argument could be based. Any set of facts offered by one side would be countered by other alternative facts from the other side.

The other state of exception to truth, the strong one, is related to phenomena such as the ones described in psychopathology. A person suffering by paranoid ideations, for example, will not be willing to accept any argument regarding the baselessness of their delusional systems, whatever the strength of the argument. Again, it would be difficult to see any room for rational debate here. A belief in a delusional idea cannot (and will not) be shaken by any argument.

In fact, these two exceptions to truth make manifest that conventional theories of rationality, reasoning and truth do not appear adequately equipped to comprehend these phenomena. Granted, whenever we encounter someone who is willing to believe the newest conspiracy theory, or to accept the most dubious "alternative" fact despite the abundance of contradicting evidence, we might feel inclined to consider is as a failure of thinking, and attribute it to a defect in reasoning, or to take it as an example of an appeal to emotion than rational thinking (like the Oxford Dictionaries which brought the term in the spot-light). Indeed, many of those who condemn our post-truth era subscribe to ideas such as this. This understanding, however, is doubly problematic. For one, it distorts the phenomena. There is no such thing as a tension between the rational and the emotional mind or whatever else we might choose to call it. The conceptualisation of the human mind as a rational apparatus processing information and data is a mistaken one, and willingness to accept alternative facts and conspiracy theories does not come about as a failure of rationality.[34] Instead, phenomena of post-truth would need to be understood in terms of a discursive game where the rules are not consensual anymore. Whether it is because of anxiety, emotional uncertainty, identification with some personality or cause, what we are faced with is the realisation that truth cannot be established in terms of a …big enough big Other. As Lacan says, there is no Other of the Other.

And it is thus that Lacan's programme of anti-philosophy obtains its full import: "It is not the history of ideas, sad as it is, that will be able to

---

[34]To be sure, a failure of rationality can indeed be observed, but it is not *causing* the phenomenon. It can only serve as a description.

face up to the challenge. A patient collection of all the idiocy that characterizes it will, I hope, allow to highlight it in its indestructible root, in its eternal dream. Of which there is no other awakening if not one's own".[35] The eternal dream of all efforts at gaining knowledge is that there be a solid meta-foundation for truth.

It is exactly that: a dream.

And the challenge we are faced with is to come in terms with this, take responsibility, and wake up.

❖     ❖     ❖

# Bibliography

BADIOU, ALAIN, *Number and Numbers* [1990], trans. Robin Mackay (Cambridge: Polity Press, 2008).

CHALMERS, DAVID J., *The Character of Consciousness* (Oxford: Oxford University Press, 2010).

DENNETT, DANIEL, *Sweet Dreams: Philosophical Obstacles to a Science of Consciousness* (Cambridge, MA: The MIT Press, 2005).

FINK, BRUCE, *The Lacanian Subject: Between Language and Jouissance* (Princeton, NJ: Princeton University Press, 1997).

HINTIKKA, JAAKKO, *The Principles of Mathematics Revisited* (Cambridge: Cambridge University Press, 1996).

JAYNES, JULIAN, *The Origin of Consciousness in the Breakdown of the Bicameral Mind* [1976] (Boston: Mariner Books, 2000).

LACAN, JACQUES, 'Impromptu at Vincennes' [1969], trans. Denis Hollier, Rosalind Krauss, and Annette Michelson, in Joan Copjec (ed.), *Television* (New York: W. W. Norton & Company, 1990), 117–128.

———, 'Peut-être à Vincennes...' [1975] in J.-A. Miller (ed.), *Autres Écrits* (Paris: Éditions du Seuil, 2001), 313–315.

———, 'Position of the Unconscious' [1960], trans. Bruce Fink, Héloïse Fink, and Russell Grigg, in *Écrits* (New York: W. W. Norton & Company, 2006), 703–721.

---

[35]Jacques Lacan, 'Peut-être à Vincennes...' [1975], in J.-A. Miller (ed.), *Autres Écrits* (Paris: Éditions du Seuil, 2001), 313–315, pp. 314–315 (my translation). See also above, pp. 175–177.

————, *The Seminar of Jacques Lacan, Book XX: Encore, On Feminine Sexuality, the Limits of Love and Knowledge* [1972–73], ed. Jacques-Allain Miller, trans. Bruce Fink (New York: W. W. Norton & Company, 1998).

————, *The Seminar of Jacques Lacan, Book XXIII: The Sinthome* [1975–76], ed. Jacques-Allain Miller, trans. A. R. Price (Cambridge: Polity Press, 2016).

LAPLACE, PIERRE-SIMON, *Philosophical Essay on Probabilities* [1825], trans. Andrew I. Dale (New York: Springer, 1994).

RICHARDSON, WILLIAM J., 'The Word of Silence' in Sonu Shamdasani and Michael Münchow (eds.), *Speculations After Freud: Psychoanalysis, Philosophy and Culture* (London: Routledge, 1994), 167–184.

ROUSTANG, FRANÇOIS, *The Lacanian Delusion*, trans. Greg Sims (New York: Oxford University Press, 1990).

TOMBRAS, SPYROS, *Μουσική και Σημειολογία: Μια Μέθοδος Ερμηνευτικής Προσπέλασης του Μουσικού Έργου [Music and Semiology: A Method of Interpretative Access to Musical Work]* (Athens: Gkovostis Ekdotiki, 1998).

TRAWNY, PETER, *Freedom to Fail: Heidegger's Anarchy*, trans. Ian Alexander Moore and Christopher Turner (Cambridge: Polity Press, 2015).

ŽIŽEK, SLAVOJ, 'Why Lacan Is Not a Heideggerian' in *The Ticklish Subject: The Absent Centre of Political Ontology* (London: Verso, 2008), vii–xxi.

# 7

# Conclusion: Psychoanalysis as a Cause

We start in the seventeenth century, with Descartes. A pious man, he is concerned about his faith. He is worried that it has no solid grounding. What if the representatives of the Church are liars? What if the ultimate guarantor of truth, God, is trying to deceive us? What if our senses have been taken over by a malevolent demon who tries to trick us into thinking what it wants us to think? What if all that we can see and feel is not to be believed? Descartes is overcome by doubt. There can be no foundation of certainty. Everything is up in the air.

Everything apart from one thing. Descartes can doubt about all, and yet of one thing he can be certain: he is there, he doubts. That is, he thinks. And by virtue of this, he can assert: I think, I exist. *Cogito*, sum. With this simple step, Descartes inaugurates the era of modernity. Truth is emancipated from God and the Church; it becomes within the reach of the thinking, rational human being who stands vis-à-vis reality and a world laid out for him *objectively*.

◈　　◈　　◈

Freud, a medical doctor by training, envisaged psychoanalysis as being a proper science. Freud was a Cartesian. Like Descartes, he too sought certainty. His premise was that science only has the methodologies and

© The Author(s) 2019
C. Tombras, *Discourse Ontology*, The Palgrave Lacan Series,
https://doi.org/10.1007/978-3-030-13662-8_7

tools necessary to study, comprehend and explain the human psyche in an objective way. His whole working life was dedicated to building this science for the psyche.

Lacan, also a medical doctor, had trained as a psychiatrist. Influenced by the intellectual climate of the early twentieth century, he turned to Freud in an attempt to further his understanding of what we could vaguely call mental illness or suffering. Widely read in philosophy, the sciences, literature and other fields, Lacan remained until the end of his life dedicated to issues pertaining to psychic life and suffering.

Heidegger was planning to become a priest, but, after changing his mind, went on to study mathematics and then turned to philosophy. He remained dedicated to philosophy until the end of his life. Heidegger was very sceptical of the course that metaphysics had taken since the time of the ancient Greeks and, with a view to challenging tradition and deconstructing Western philosophy, sought to bring back some of the originality and incisiveness of their thinking. A pupil of Husserl, he took the promise of phenomenology seriously. He rejected the naïve Cartesian view of the human being as a subject standing vis-à-vis the world as object, recognising that acts of observation are never unmediated. He presented the human being, Dasein, as the clearing in which a world is opened as truth and shared: in its concernful comportment towards beings, Dasein allows being to be opened up and shared.

Heidegger criticised Freud on the basis of what he took to be Freud's uncritical adoption of a naïve scientism, directly inherited from the nineteenth-century scientific world view. For Heidegger, the belief that science progresses by collecting data, formulating hypotheses and creating testable theories, has limited scope and fails to question the presuppositions, foundations and historicity of scientific conceptual framework and methods. What is missing from the nineteenth-century view is, according to Heidegger, a careful reconsideration of the ways in which the world is opened up as intelligible to human beings (to Dasein). Reflecting on this "question of being", as he called it, can reveal science as a historical enterprise and expose its limitations in connection to the applicability of its methods to the study of the human being as such. Modern scientific reasoning involves representing entities by way of their quantifiable features, i.e. by data, and processing of data with the help of elaborate mathematical formulas, tools and models. If this is science, then science is not adequately equipped to speak about the human being as a being-in-the-world.

For Freud, psychic life was in principle understandable, and psychical phenomena in principle deterministic, i.e. not arbitrary. For Heidegger, this very principle is problematic as it involves the uncritical adoption of an inapplicable research programme, namely the intention to study the psyche, as if it were an independently existing and observable object, with the help of inapplicable hypotheses founded on unexamined premises. For Heidegger, the whole theoretical structure of psychoanalysis was built on unsound premises.

Lacan took Heidegger's critique very seriously. A student of Koyré, he shared with Heidegger a theoretical understanding of the historical nature of science. He recognised that Freud's research programme would not have been possible prior to the advent of what he (Lacan) called the "subject of science". Contrary to how it would appear at first sight, however, for Lacan a *subject of science* is neither a subject that adopts scientific methods—i.e. a scientist—nor the human being as a subject of scientific research. It is, rather, the subject that is surprised by the products of his or her own psyche, which he or she then considers as concerning him or herself. The subject of science is the doubtful Cartesian subject who is perplexed—and sometimes disturbed—by his or her own desire, but knows that there is a choice whether to do something about it or not.

Lacan too rejected the Cartesian view of the human being as an observing subject, vis-à-vis, the world as object, on the basis that the observing thinking subject (the subject that declares "I think", or *cogito*), is an alienated, divided subject. He showed that the speaking being is not a mythical Cartesian subject that can find certainty and truth. As a subject of language, the human being is a decentred subject, a semblance, a product of recursive retroactive overlapping identifications, a made-up being that goes around pretending to be what it is not.

In Lacan's understanding, Freud did not uncover for us the workings of a fully deterministic "mental" apparatus that had previously remained hidden: what he discovered was the human psyche as subjected to the law of the signifier. The importance of this law, however, does not lie in its determinism. On the contrary, it becomes important at the gaps where it breaks down—namely the unconscious.

◈     ◈     ◈

Both thinkers, Heidegger and Lacan, represent a break with the past. In repositing the ontological question and demonstrating its historicity, Heidegger revealed the limitations and impasses of modernity and presented Dasein as the clearing in which truth, knowledge and science can be thought of and thematised anew.

In outlining the discursive structures in which the speaking being partakes and deconstructing the foundations of subjectivity, Lacan broke with traditional philosophy. Ontology and metaphysics are not feasible. Truth, traditionally, conceived as correspondence or adequation is a myth, a result of a negotiation or a compromise—a language, or discursive, game.

This leaves us with Freud's invention, psychoanalysis. It allows us to see that there is no foundation of truth other than that of the real and jouissance. The world is created and inhabited by human beings, captured and tortured by language.

Lacan drew on philosophy initially, and then on mathematics, in order to find the conceptual tools he felt he needed to develop his ideas further and bring them together in a coherent and robust conceptual structure. His theories always had the air of a work in progress. It was evident to anyone looking more carefully at the content of his teaching and the style of his delivery that he felt he did not have enough time to bring everything to a proper closure.

In contrast to Lacan, Heidegger moved in the opposite direction, gradually distancing himself from teaching and only writing and presenting increasingly short papers. In many respects, he showed himself to be a moralist, while Lacan appeared as an agnostic cynic.

◈     ◈     ◈

Freud had wanted his theory to be accepted and respected as a new science. Somewhat paradoxically, however, even though psychoanalysis is indeed a product of the modern world view, it is the one that allows us to break with the limitations of the discourse this world view

entails. Not burdened with Freud's need to assert the scientific character of psychoanalysis, Lacan approached the analytic field as a discursive
rather than a scientific one. Having a clearer view of the position of the
divided subject in its engagement within networks of signifiers, Lacan
was able to bring the question of cause back to the fore. In this way, he
allowed Aristotle to take his revenge on Galileo.

Lacanian thought can be seen as Aristotelian in so far as we can see
that the human being cannot be understood in terms of a distinction
between subject and object; the cause of psychoanalysis lies in the call
to recast the question in terms of a distinction between agency and
non-agency—or tuché and automaton. But this distinction cannot be
approached in terms of meaning: it is not a case of human imperfection
versus celestial perfection, as Aristotle believed; nor a case of a material
versus an immaterial world, as Descartes would want it. It's not even
about the question of being as such, as Heidegger insisted, unless we are
prepared to make one more step, following Lacan, and accept that being
is merely presumed in certain words—a fact of what is said.

In other words, the main challenge is to trace the passage from the
corporeal domain of the real and jouissance, to the incorporeal domain
of signifierness, the imaginary and the symbolic. It is this passage that
enables the discursive construction of the human and social reality, and
the world—that what I designated here as an ontology from discourse.

The basic themes of this discourse ontology touch on issues such
as the consensual emergence of signifierness; the opening to truth in
absence of a metalanguage; the constitution of time; our owning our
bodies and obtaining a sexual identity; and the question of constructing
and sharing a world. If we wanted to put labels to it, we could designate this approach as a materialist. Strictly speaking, however, this is not
accurate. The distinction between materialist versus non-materialist (or
by any other name, for example: transcendental, idealist, Platonist etc.)
is not appropriate because it leads to all kinds of false dilemmas, just as
the distinction between subject and object does. It is in this sense that
we can understand Lacanian anti-philosophy. Lacan urges us to wake
up from our eternal dream and look beyond the idiocy of the history
of ideas. If we decide to look away, that's fine. Psychoanalysis will be

remembered as one more in a long series of failed attempts to establish truth and certainty in terms of a "big" big Other. This would be a neat and, perhaps, convenient picture, but it is inaccurate. We know now that there is no "big" big Other. There is *no* Other of the Other *at all.*

In this era of post-truth and alternative facts, the challenge that psychoanalysis presents is more urgent than ever. The options are laid out in front of us, and the choice is ours. There is no other awakening apart from our own. We'll need to come into terms with this, and own the responsibility that comes with it.

This is the cause of psychoanalysis today.

❖    ❖    ❖

# Index

CPSIA information can be obtained
at www.ICGtesting.com
Printed in the USA
LVHW051801010419
612562LV00012B/368/P

9 783030 136611